THE NEW CHICAGO WAY

THE NEW CHICAGO WAY

Lessons from Other Big Cities

ED BACHRACH AND AUSTIN BERG

Southern Illinois University Press
Carbondale

Southern Illinois University Press
www.siupress.com

22 21 20 19   4 3 2 1

Cover illustration: cover photo by Joe Barnas;
cover design by Thea Baldwin

Library of Congress Cataloging-in-Publication Data
Names: Bachrach, Ed, [date] author. | Berg, Austin, [date] author.
Title: The new Chicago way : lessons from other
big cities / Ed Bachrach and Austin Berg.
Description: Carbondale : Southern Illinois University Press, [2019] |
Includes bibliographical references and index.
Identifiers: LCCN 2018053009 |
ISBN 9780809337514 (pbk.) |
ISBN 9780809337521 (e-book)
Subjects: LCSH: Economic development—Illinois—Chicago. |
Community development—Illinois—Chicago. |
Urban policy—Illinois—Chicago. | Municipal services—
Illinois—Chicago. | Municipal government—Illinois—Chicago.
Classification: LCC HC108.C4 B33 2019 |
DDC 320.609773/11—dc23 LC record available
at https://lccn.loc.gov/2018053009

To Henry and Betty Bachrach

To Jerry and Dr. Margaret Berg

~

*All of Mr. Bachrach's profits from this book will be
donated to the Kusanya Café in Chicago.*

*All of Mr. Berg's profits from this book will be donated to the
Young Center for Immigrant Children's Rights in Chicago.*

CONTENTS

List of Tables and Figures xi
Acknowledgments xiii

Preface: The Field 1

Introduction: The Cost of One-Man Rule 4
    The City and Its Problems 5
    What This Book Is About 6
    The Chicago Way 8

CHAPTER 1. Cutting the Mayor Down to Size 10
    A Bad Deal 10
    A Pattern, Not an Isolated Incident 18
    How the City Works: Strong Mayor, Weak City Council 20
        The Alderman and the Ward 20
        Too Many Aldermen 21
        Filling Vacancies 22
        Redistricting 23
        Hollow Committees and Committee Chairs 25
        Other Elected Offices 26
    What about Other Cities? 27
        New York 27
        Los Angeles 28
    Solving Problems: A Better Governance Structure for Chicago 29

CHAPTER 2: Discouraging Democracy 35
Chicago Municipal Elections 36
Other Major Cities 39
The Literature on Turnout 40
Partisan Elections 42
Encouraging Democracy in Chicago 44

CHAPTER 3. Governing the Schools and the City 46
Chicago's School Problems 48
The Immediacy and Imperative of Fiscal Improvement 52
Other Cities and the Largest School Districts 58
Scholarship on Mayoral Control of Public Schools 62
What Should Chicago Do? 65
Disruption 68
Disaggregation 72
The Urban School System of the Future 73
A Homework Assignment for Chicago Public Schools 76

CHAPTER 4. Chicago's Fiscal Ruin 79
Chicago's Fiscal Problems: Seen and Unseen 81
How City Finance Is Supposed to Work 86
How Chicago Has Worked 88
How Other Cities Work 91
Institutional Safeguards 92
Additional Measures 95
The Problem of Legacy Costs 97
Conclusion 99

CHAPTER 5. Pension Apocalypse Now, Not Later 102
The Holiday Habit 102
A Chicago Pension Snapshot 103
How Are These Pensions Supposed to Work? 106
How Have Pensions Worked in Chicago? 110
The Unfairness of Pension Debt 115
Solving the Pension Problem: Pain, Suffering, and Riddance 118
Freezing and Discontinuing the Plans 121

Alternative Pension Solutions   123
Apocalypse Now   125

CHAPTER 6. Overdue Oversight and the Reality of Corruption   126
Corruption Capital?   127
How Chicago Government Polices Itself   132
What Other Cities Do   134
New York City   135
Los Angeles   137
Houston   138
Philadelphia   139
Phoenix   140
Recommendations   140

CHAPTER 7. Public Support for Private Enterprise at the Metropolitan
Pier and Exposition Authority   143
The Black Box by the Lake   143
The Anatomy of the MPEA   144
McCormick Place   145
Navy Pier   150
Hotels   151
The Arena   153
The Mayor's Road   153
What Do Other Cities Do?   154
Orlando   154
Las Vegas   155
Atlanta   156
Commonality   157
What to Do   158

CHAPTER 8. Policing in Chicago   161
Crime, Public Safety, and Policing in Chicago   165
What about Other Cities?   172
New York   173
Los Angeles   174
Philadelphia   176

Houston 176
A Note on Dallas 177
Settlements 177
Chicago's Governance Structure and Public Safety 180

CHAPTER 9. Creations of the State 185
The Legal Foundation for City Law 187
City Charters 192
Two Choices for Illinois and Chicago 194
Entities Not Subject to Home Rule 196
Political Obstacles 197
The Possibility of Change 197

CHAPTER 10. The Audacity of Hope? 199
About This Book Again 199
About Chicago 202
About Government 206
About Change 208
The Audacity of Hope 213

Appendixes
    A. Proposed Governance Changes, Policies, and Actions 217
    B. Survey of Governance Characteristics of the Fifteen Largest US
       Cities by Population 221
    C. Survey of the Fiscal History and Characteristics of the Fifteen
       Largest US Cities, Excluding Chicago 229

Notes 235
Bibliography 257
Index 261

TABLES AND FIGURES

Tables

1.1. Selected Governance Attributes, Fifteen Most Populous US Cities 23

1.2. Manner of Selection and Accountability of City Controller and City Attorney 32

2.1. Chicago Voter Turnout by Election, Comparing Municipal Elections to Statewide and National Elections, 2000 to 2016 38

2.2. Terms and Timing of Elections for Mayor and City Council in the Fifteen Largest US Cities 40

3.1. Financial Data for Chicago Public Schools: Revenue, Expenditures, and Debt 49

3.2. Pension Data for Chicago Public Schools 50

3.3. Selected Chicago Public Schools Financial Information and Enrollment 53

3.4. Selected Data for Schools, Top Fifteen US Cities 59

3.5. Selected Data for the Top Twenty US School Districts, by Enrollment 60

4.1. Police and Fire Spending in Context, Chicago Versus Los Angeles 81

4.2. Comparison of Bonded and Pension Debt, Top Fifteen US Cities 83

4.3. Fiscal Control Features, Top Fifteen US Cities 92

5.1. Funding of Local Pension Plans in Chicago, 2017 104

5.2. Selected Beneficiary Data on Chicago Pension Plans 105

5.3. Pension Debt, Top Fifteen US Cities 106

5.4. Example of a Typical Employee's Earnings and Pension Benefits 108
5.5. Combined Required Annual Contributions and Unfunded Liability, Five Largest Pension Plans in Chicago, 2017 to 2055 113
5.6. Calculation of Payment Deficit, Policemen's Annuity and Benefit Fund of Chicago 117
6.1. Top Fifteen US Cities Ranked by Federal Public Corruption Convictions per 100,000 Population of Associated Federal Judicial District 129
6.2. Chicago City Officials Convicted of Corruption, 2007–2017 130
6.3. Top Oversight Official in Top Fifteen Cities 136
7.1. Ten Largest Convention Centers in the United States 146
7.2. McCormick Place Attendance and Authority Tax Collections 147
7.3. One-Year Snapshot of MPEA Tax Collections 148
7.4. Financial Comparison of the Four Largest Publicly Owned Convention Centers 155
8.1. Comparative Homicide Rates, Three Largest US Cities 165
8.2. FBI Violent Crime Statistics, Top Fifteen US Cities 166
8.3. FBI Nonviolent Crime Statistics, Top Fifteen US Cities 167
8.4. Police Officers and Homicides for the Top Fifteen US Cities in 2016 173
8.5. Average Payouts and Litigation Expenses, Top Fifteen US Cities 178
8.6. Chicago Police Department Lawsuit Payouts by Type, 2006 to 2012 179
10.1. American Responses to the Gap between Their Ideals and Their Institutions 210

Figures

1.1. Chicago's Second Ward 24
4.1. Moody's Institutional Rating Rubric 85
5.1. Forecast of Pension Debt and Contributions 112
5.2. Decrease in Unfunded Pension Liability with Level Pension Plan Contributions 120
8.1. Number of Homicides in Chicago, 2002 to 2017 168

ACKNOWLEDGMENTS

For decades hundreds of bright, committed, and tireless individuals across America have worked to modernize and reform municipal government. It is to them that the authors owe a debt of gratitude. They are the ones who have tried and erred and ended up with institutions and practices that Chicago can choose to adopt.

Some of those individuals reside in Chicago itself. This book builds on the lifelong scholarship of Dick Simpson at the University of Illinois Chicago. Likewise, the authors' work was inspired by the work and contribution of the late Paul Green and the late Melvin Holli. Today, scattered across the city are activists, journalists, and civic leaders who have been quoted or interviewed for this book. Where they allowed it, they are cited herein. Where they preferred anonymity, they have nevertheless given the authors invaluable guidance to relevant material.

The authors spoke with scores of leaders in all walks of life all across America who had meaningful contributions to our findings. Many current or former public officials were glad to speak on condition that they would not be quoted, but they too pointed us in the direction of valuable objective information, studies, and data. We acknowledge their accomplishments and willingness to speak with us.

In addition to municipal leaders are individuals without whom government would not function and this book would not have been possible. These are the administrative assistants, legislative liaisons, policy analysts, accountants, lawyers, and other rank-and-file professionals across the fifteen most populous cities examined in this book. Their interpretations of city statutes, access to difficult-to-find city data, and general insight—as well as the overall graciousness and politeness with which they assisted us strangers, calling out of the blue with pointed questions—was inspiring and invaluable.

There is a small group of individuals in New York and Los Angeles whose contribution to our thinking may not be obvious from our discussion in the text. One of us met with Dick Ravitch, the man who guided New York in its 1975 financial scrape and who headed the first Charter Commission in 1988. He was generous with his time, wisdom, and inspiration. He led us to Eric Lane, who was the executive director and counsel to both the 1988 and 1989 Charter Commissions. The effort Mr. Lane put into the exhaustive description of the 1989 charter revision is a gift to all major cities. Their counterpart in Los Angeles was Raphael Sonenshein, executive director of the Los Angeles 1999 Charter Commission. Mr. Sonenshein was generous with his time with us and in writing the story of that charter revision. Another Angelino who gave us patient guidance on policing was Richard Tefank, the Los Angeles Police Commission's executive director.

This book would not exist without the early support and encouragement of Sylvia Rodrigue of the SIU Press. The authors are especially grateful for the careful reading by Robert Ultimo and our great editor Siobhan Drummond.

Ed Bachrach and Austin Berg
Chicago, Illinois
September 15, 2018

THE NEW CHICAGO WAY

The Field

Men occasionally stumble over the truth, but most of them pick
themselves up and hurry off as if nothing had happened.
—WINSTON CHURCHILL

⮌

Mike Daffenberg awoke before sunrise.

It was the morning of March 31, 2003. Daffenberg was an air traffic control-ler. Each weekday he drove to Chicago from his home in suburban DeKalb, arriving before the start of his 6:00 a.m. shift. This day was no different, it seemed. What Daffenberg did not know was that before he had his morning coffee, before he put on his uniform, before he even got out of bed, a politician had ordered the bulldozing of his place of work under the cover of darkness.

Mayor Richard M. Daley had launched a clandestine attack on Meigs Field. Select city lawyers knew about the mayor's plan to capture the Northerly Island airfield, as did Daley's chief of staff and two city officials. Left unaware were, to name only a few, all fifty city aldermen, the governor of Illinois, the Fed-eral Aviation Administration, and the Department of Homeland Security—and Daffenberg, of course. He learned of Daley's decision while driving to work.

"I felt like I was laid off by the radio," he told the *Chicago Tribune.*

A lone camera, stationed just north of the Northerly Island airfield at the Adler Planetarium, would have captured a live feed of the Meigs assault. But a city fire truck trained a spotlight on the lens, blinding the public eye, at the very start of the operation. Backhoes carved six menacing "X-shaped" ditches into the runway. Sixteen planes sat stranded at the airport, which had seen 32,000 flights the year before.

Little Meigs was the most famous single-runway airport in the world. In early versions of the popular Microsoft video game Flight Simulator, Meigs Field was the pilot's default starting point. The views were iconic. But Meigs was not just a pretty place. Writing for the *Chicago Tribune*, John McCarron described it as an "economic jewel." Meigs filled a niche demand among business travelers looking for easy access to Chicago's central business district.

Daley justified the raid as a matter of national security. Meigs, he said, had become a potential launching pad for terrorist attacks. The nation's top domestic security official at the time did not echo Daley's concerns. When repeatedly questioned by reporters in April 2003 as to whether Daley's closure made Chicagoans safer, Homeland Security Secretary Tom Ridge refused to say yes. "I'm disappointed they closed it," Ridge said. He confirmed that Daley did not give him any advance notice of the closure. The Aircraft Owners and Pilots Association, which boasted nearly 400,000 members at the time, also dismissed the mayor's reasoning. "Aircraft utilizing Meigs Field pose no threat to the greater Chicagoland area, and certainly no greater threat than aircraft in transit to and from O'Hare and Midway," the association stated in a 2003 lawsuit challenging Daley's attack. The public wasn't buying it either. A June 2003 poll conducted by the *Chicago Tribune* revealed 65 percent of Chicagoland voters disapproved of Daley's raid on Meigs. A resounding 70 percent disagreed that the airfield, when operating, had heightened the likelihood of a terrorist attack. It appears that the first time Daley publicly voiced safety concerns regarding Meigs was after his raid. But over the course of his mayoral tenure, he frequently stated his desire that Northerly Island be transformed into a city park. Today, it is.

Neither the Daley administration nor the City of Chicago incurred any punishment for the actions at Meigs, save for a small fine levied by the Federal Aviation Administration for failure to give adequate notice of the closure. Members of the city council took no legislative action. The Park District, headed by a Daley appointee, complied with the mayor's orders. And city lawyers disposed of lawsuits against the administration in short order. Judges had lifted all potential legal barriers by the end of May, and demolition was under way by summer. Pacific Construction Services, which counted former

Daley aide and former Park District COO David Tkac in its ranks, won the $1.13 million contract to put Meigs out of its misery.

The mayor's decimation of the airfield is not difficult to criticize. After all, Meigs was a world-renowned landmark; it served a respected role in air transportation and brought jobs to Chicagoans. But none of these particulars should be the primary concern to a critical eye. Instead, the raid on Meigs is appalling for what it reveals about how Chicago government operates. A rubber-stamp city council, a lapdog board appointed by the mayor, hurried decisions, clout-heavy contracts, lack of fiscal considerations, secrecy, centralization, and destruction. These are hallmarks of Chicago governance. This is the Chicago Way, and it was on display at Meigs in 2003.

Much more than merely fodder for headlines, the Meigs raid represents a microcosm of the political culture that has brought Chicago to its knees. Discerning citizens now see its influence in the schools, in city ledger lines, in elections, in mini-fiefdoms controlled by local aldermen, and in the harrowing, grainy footage of young men gunned down by police. Meigs lays bare the perverted political process in Chicago, one fueled by dangerous decision making built on the will of a single person. Indeed, the Windy City is a modern metropolis of millions functioning with a government built for one-man rule. Deliberative democracy is dead here. Chicago is home, rather, to a form of government that resembles strongman authoritarian regimes that persist in far corners of the world. The mayor is the strongman; any perceived checks on mayoral power were proven illusory on that night in 2003. And they remain illusory. More than 2.6 million Chicagoans live under this broken structure of governance and the political pathologies that arise from it. It seems at times that the whole city is Meigs Field—a property upon which the mayor can impose his or her will at any time, for any reason, with little resistance. Chicagoans stumbled upon that truth in 2003.

The Cost of One-Man Rule

The simplest political system is that which depends on one individual. It is also the least stable. Tyrannies, Aristotle pointed out, are virtually all "quite short-lived." A political system with several different political institutions, on the other hand, is much more likely to adapt. The needs of one age may be met by one set of institutions; the needs of the next by a different set.
—SAMUEL HUNTINGTON

⁓

Although Chicago is not a tyranny, the mayor's power appears unlimited. The mayor of Chicago is the chief executive of the city and runs all city departments, including police, fire, streets and sanitation, and all other municipal workers. The mayor has the authority to appoint an alderman when a vacancy arises. Of the fifty current aldermen, twelve were initially seated by appointment and twenty-eight have been appointed by the mayor in the past twenty-eight years.[1] The mayor controls the Chicago Public Schools by appointing the school board, its president, and other top administrators. The mayor controls the Chicago Park District by appointing the park board. The mayor controls the Chicago Transit Authority by appointing four of the seven members of the board. The mayor controls the Metropolitan Pier and Exposition Authority, which manages the nation's largest convention center, by appointing nearly half the board. The mayor controls the Chicago Housing Authority by appointing its board. The mayor controls the two major airports through the Chicago Department of Aviation. And the mayor appoints the board for the City Colleges of Chicago.

Despite mayoral control of all these aspects of city government, composed of nearly 100,000 employees—almost 4 percent of the city's population—the city code spelling out the mayor's duties is minimal and perfunctory.[2] There is no mention of the mayor's role as it relates to crime, finances, pensions, taxes, or demographics. Likewise, there are no provisions for the mayor's duties and accountability regarding schools, parks, transportation, housing, aviation, or conventions. Indeed, the city operates without a written constitution. Nearly all public functions depend upon the favor of one single person, one fallible human being, the mayor.

This governance structure does not reflect the American political tradition of written constitutions, checks and balances, and distributed and decentralized power. The Chicago power structure does not serve the city's modern needs; it makes for consistently poor decision making and contributes to many of the city's problems. The results of this medieval political arrangement speak for themselves.

The City and Its Problems

Those who follow current affairs are well aware of the conspicuous problems that plague the city of Chicago today:

- The crime rate as measured by violent death is often the highest per capita of any major city in America.
- Chicago schools, described in 1988 as the worst in the nation, have made progress but are plagued by parent and teacher unrest and mistrust.
- The city has not balanced its budget in the last eleven years.
- The Chicago Public School District has not balanced its budget since 2001 and is now near bankruptcy.
- The pension funds of the five major employee groups (municipal workers, police, teachers, firefighters, and laborers) are underfunded by tens of billions of dollars. These prior service costs would require more than a 100 percent increase in property taxes to catch up funding in one generation.

These surface facts do not reflect the deeper hidden problems plaguing the city. The violent crime rate indicates that large portions of the city are lawless. These are places where people are not secure from rape, domestic violence, and sex trafficking and where property is unprotected from theft and vandalism. Poor schools mean the city is undesirable for young families; working-class immigrants, once the bedrock of Chicago's neighborhoods, now prefer to live in the suburbs; and poorly educated young adults cannot support sophisticated service industries. As a result, Chicago is left with a population of high-income professionals, low-income service workers, and the chronically unemployed. Despite the city government's fiscal problems, pension woes, and poor outcomes, Chicago residents bear a local tax burden that ranks among the highest of major American cities.[3]

These problems have taken their toll. The city's population has been falling for decades and is now no greater than it was one hundred years ago. It is down 25 percent from its peak and continues to decline. Both the Chicago metropolitan area and the state of Illinois are demographically stagnant. The large companies that once called Chicago home are no more: Continental Illinois National Bank, First Chicago, Sears, Montgomery Ward, Marshall Fields, Illinois Bell Telephone, International Harvester, and Borg Warner are just a few of the names that have disappeared. The new companies that locate their headquarters here often do so with skeleton staffs.[4]

The city government, the schools, and the convention center have failed either in their effectiveness or financially or both. Officials have not addressed problems head-on. They have resorted to short-term fixes of borrowing and selling off city assets; they have ignored the needs of the people, and they have not told city employees the truth about the fragile state of local pension systems.

Nonetheless, no one seriously doubts that the mayor of the city of Chicago calls all the shots.

What This Book Is About

Although we tell stories of poor decisions and their consequences, you will not find these pages to be a lament of the city's problems. There have been too many of these stories in books, magazines, and our daily newspapers. And although we are critical of specific mayoral decisions, this is not a personal screed against any individual. Our point is that anyone occupying the office of mayor under the current structure will, more often than not, make very poor decisions. Our objective in writing this book is not to apply some general principles or ideas to the city's problems in order to justify an ideology. Instead, we will be exploring practical nonpartisan solutions to municipal problems, many of which have been discussed for decades.

The stories collected here show how bad decisions have been made hastily and without deliberation, resulting in lasting problems for the citizens of Chicago. The discussion does not stop there but goes on to recommend specific solutions, or in some cases a choice of solutions, that would put in place structures to make it much harder to make poor decisions and much more likely to make better ones. We found these solutions by examining the policy choices of other major American cities through interviews with city officials, political scientists, and community leaders from around the country.

Over the past century, hundreds of civic leaders across America have worked hard, struggled with one another, tried and erred, and in the end created municipal institutions, structures, and practices that have overcome the same problems that plague Chicago. These efforts have resulted in more durable and sustainable change which has prepared these cities for a brighter future. By contrast, Chicago's civic leaders—its thought leaders, business heads, foundation boards, universities, labor organizations, and community activists—have failed to raise their heads, look around, and learn about the successes in other big cities. Only brief moments of outrage punctuate the insular adherence to the old Chicago Way.

The stories here will be familiar to many, but if not remembered, they will soon be forgotten. We retell the infamous story of the parking meter deal that harms the city to this day, and we make a case for strengthening the legislative capability of a new city council. Looking at the contentious 2015 mayoral race, we lay bare Chicago's rigged election system, which gives incumbents and other interested parties outsized sway in municipal elections. Most Chicagoans favor a more democratic school system; a look at a series of decisions starting with lengthening of the school day and ending with city budget hearings will illustrate their concern. We show that there are many ways to bring about a more accountable school system, which would be better not only for the schools but for city government.

Manufacturing has atrophied in the city, but a service economy led by tourism has emerged. Nevertheless, a policy that commits billions of taxpayer dollars to investments that benefit a few results in white elephants and large invisible burdens. It is time to reevaluate public support for McCormick Place, Navy Pier, and other tourism-related commitments. The city of Chicago has operating deficits and has run up debt for years. These bad habits have rubbed off on many entities under the control of a like-minded mayor, among them the schools, the parks, and public transit. Meanwhile, the mayor dreams up other ways to avail himself of money, from the Infrastructure Trust to the sale of municipal assets. We will look at how the power of city home rule has been abused and see how other cities keep a tighter rein on their finances. Within city fiscal mismanagement, the underfunded pension plans are a special case. Not only do they dwarf the bonded and bank indebtedness of the city and Chicago Public Schools, but they are passing on enormous burdens to future generations for services rendered years, even decades earlier. The desperately underfunded pensions will continue to dry up for decades to come. We show how this inadvertently got out of control, and how the only solution is to either pay up or settle.

Although poor decision making bred of autocratic governance accounts for much of the city's woes, we cannot ignore Chicago's reputation as the corruption capital of America. Like the weather, this topic has been talked and written about for decades. After telling the story of an ousted inspector general, we consider what structures could be put in place to check corruption's seemingly endless recurrence.

Chicago's home rule powers, along with its other municipal entities controlled by the mayor, are creations of the state of Illinois, so to make the changes we call for will require both legal and political action. What would these laws look like? And how would an advocate persuade the 80 percent of Illinois residents and legislators who do not live in Chicago to support them? An analysis that hopes to change the way Chicago is governed would be incomplete without answering these questions.

We conclude our study by looking at Chicago from the vantage point of the future. There is a race under way between visible and promising economic growth and the invisible growth of the city's problems. Will new institutions meet the needs of the next age or will the old institutions survive—leaving the city weaker and in decline? Nothing less is at stake.

The Chicago Way

The *Chicago Way* is one of those terms that has been adopted by many to serve their own point of view. It has been defined as the way you "get Capone."[5] For some it means unchecked corruption; for others it is the smashmouth politics of machine control over elections. It is sometimes the secrecy, silence, and impunity of inside deals; at other times it is the way the chosen prevail over the forsaken. Always, though, it revolves around power, one central power that is to be feared and obeyed.

When Chicago's leaders talk about government, they defend power concentrated in the mayor. They talk of the chaos that would inevitably result were enterprising officials to control their own fiefdoms. These independent fiefdoms, however, already exist. Those who defend mayoral control are fooled by the paradox of accountability and think that they can always hold the mayor accountable at the next election. But decisions of consequence are made every day, and the distant reckoning of the next election has little power to tame today's ambition. These defenders glamorize the reigns of historic Chicago mayors and fear the anarchy of the historic council wars. They analyze the power structure from a narrow point of view, informed only by their parochial experience in Chicago. It is breathtaking how little they know about how other big cities are governed. And most of all, they do not see that the troubles Chicago has are the result of their acquiescence.

It is time for a New Chicago Way, a Chicago where power and accountability are not concentrated or atomized but distributed rationally to those responsible for making the decisions vital to the running of a city. It is a Chicago whose leaders learn from their experience and seek the counsel of their peers. It is a Chicago that faces its legacy costs and prepares itself to face a future unburdened by them. It is time to define a New Chicago Way.

CHAPTER 1

Cutting the Mayor Down to Size

If men were angels, no government would be necessary. If angels were to govern men, neither external nor internal controls on government would be necessary. In framing a government which is to be administered by men over men, the great difficulty lies in this: you must first enable the government to control the governed; and in the next place oblige it to control itself.
—JAMES MADISON, *FEDERALIST PAPERS* NOS. 10 AND 51

⌐

A Bad Deal

Chicago residents and taxpayers have lost sight of what happened in 2008, when the parking meter deal went down. Perhaps they never even understood the impact of that fateful decision. It was not merely a bad deal; it was an egregious, hapless giveaway. In the immediate aftermath there was outrage and talk of challenging the deal. Now, more than ten years later, people have forgotten their outrage, they are delighted by new smartphone apps (making it easier to pay for parking at rates many times the quarters the old meters used), and wonder why the city is so broke.

It was a poor deal and poorly managed before and after. The simple story is that the city sold the concession rights to parking revenue for seventy-five years to Chicago Parking Meters LLC (CPM) for $1.156 billion, an amount that was later adjusted downward. Prior to the deal the city had been collecting around $20 million per year from parking meters. In 2013, the sixth year of the deal, CPM collected $135 million in parking meter revenue. It collected about the same amount in 2017. At current investment rates this stream of income, if it did not increase, would be worth $2.5 to $3 billion. As parking fees rise, the value of this deal increases by billions more, and parking fees in Chicago are now the highest in the country.[1] The public was told that the funds would be brought into the budget over the life of the concession so that the city finances would derive a net benefit for decades to come. Instead, the money was used to plug a deficit the very next two years.

To tell the political story of this deal there is no better source than an article published at the time in the *Chicago Reader* and written by Ben Joravsky and Mick Dumke. The following account is quoted directly from this article.[2]

The origins of the meter debacle actually date back to 2005, when Mayor Daley began selling off public property for up-front cash payments without much scrutiny from the City Council or the public. Then last year, when tax revenues plummeted, the mayor increased the pressure, directing his staff to be "creative" in attacking budget problems. But even as city officials celebrated privatization agreements for Midway Airport and the meters, both worth billions of dollars, they refused to release the most basic information about how they'd been reached—such as which firms had bid, how much they'd offered, and short- or long-term cost-benefit analyses. Both plans were hustled through the City Council in less than a week. As one alderman told the *Reader*, but not for attribution, during a hearing on Midway: "Somewhere in this deal we're getting screwed. I just can't figure out where yet."

Here's how it went down.

On October 17, 2007, *Sun-Times* columnist Michael Sneed reported that a source had told her that "a super secret deal is afoot at City Hall. . . . Sneed is told Mayor Daley's fiscal advisers are working on a deal to privatize the city's parking meters, which could potentially reap 1 BILLION bucks for the cash-strapped city."

January 24, 2005. Mayor Daley signs a deal to lease the Chicago Skyway for $1.83 billion to the Cintra-Macquarie Consortium, based in Spain and Australia, for 99 years. The dailies praise the deal—the *Tribune* calls it a "windfall"—and public officials around the country hail it as a model for privatizing public assets, indicating that it'd be a good way to manage the upkeep on toll roads and highways. Daley says he'll be looking into other lease agreements. And so it begins.

October 13, 2006. Daley announces plans to lease four parking garages under Millennium Park and Grant Park to a division of Morgan Stanley, the Wall Street investment bank, for $563 million. Daley calls the 99-year lease an "outstanding deal for the taxpayers of Chicago," which "allows for a massive shift of capital resources from downtown parking garages to neighborhood parks."

February 8, 2008. The city issues a request for qualifications (RFQ) inviting firms to present credentials for leasing the rights to the city's 36,000 parking meters. Collecting parking fees and fines is one thing the city seems to be pretty good at—with operating expenses of $4 million it hauled in almost $23 million in 2007. But chief financial officer Paul Volpe says a private company would do a better job managing the meters. The RFQ asks bidders to demonstrate their "financial capability" as well as outline plans to manage the system and provide service to meter users. Responses are due in March.

March 28, 2008. Ten groups have submitted packets detailing their "qualifications" for leasing the city's parking meters, including Morgan Stanley, JPMorgan Chase, Lehman Brothers, and partnerships led by Macquarie Capital Group and Cintra, the overseas firms that leased the Skyway. City officials keep the bids to themselves, declining to show them to the public and refusing a direct request from us. When we ask for details about the process, they say they'll spend the next few weeks determining whether the interested parties are qualified to continue with the bidding process.

August 14, 2008. The administration announces that its budget projections are a bit off—the city is $420 million in the hole. The figure grows to nearly $500 million in the following weeks as the housing market implodes and revenues from real estate transfer taxes dry up. Volpe rules out raising property taxes but admits, "We're going to have to make some tough choices." He declines to provide specifics, saying, "We're not here today to talk about solutions."

September 30, 2008. Two years after talks begin with federal and airline officials about privatizing Midway Airport, Mayor Daley announces the city has reached a $2.5 billion, 99-year deal with Midway Investment and Development Company. City officials say six firms went through the initial round of the bidding process, but they won't name them or reveal which ones submitted formal offers until the deal is closed. Daley staffers call aldermen downtown for closed-door briefings over the next couple days.

October 6, 2008. The Chicago City Council holds the first of two hearings to approve the proposed Midway lease. Many aldermen complain they haven't had enough time to study the details. Volpe says after paying off its debts the city should have about $900 million left to put toward pension obligations and $100 million for discretionary spending. He says aldermen will be consulted at a later date about where this money will go. Under questioning from 38th Ward alderman Tom Allen, Volpe reluctantly concedes the city will probably have to spend at least $1 billion on police and fire protection for Midway over the next 99 years, meaning the deal is essentially a money loser. Nevertheless, the council's finance committee approves it, which virtually assures its passage.

October 8, 2008. The full City Council approves the Midway lease deal by a vote of 49–0. One alderman who's been critical of the deal speaks frankly to us on the condition that we not identify him: he says he didn't really think the mayor would withhold services from his ward in retaliation for a nay vote but he voted yes anyway, figuring, "Why take a chance?"

October 15, 2008. Mayor Daley releases his 2009 budget, which he says will be balanced despite the city's "financial challenges." It hinges on hundreds of lay-offs, hiking various fees and fines, and an expected $150 million infusion from a parking meter lease. Many aldermen say this is the first they've heard that the city is close to such a deal.

November 19, 2008. The City Council approves Mayor Daley's budget by a vote of 49 to one. It projects a balance by firing workers, hiking various fees and fines, and leasing the parking meters. Daley and the aldermen congratulate themselves on working through a dire financial situation together. "Often the City Council is looked at as a body, that if we all vote one way or another, it's a rubber stamp," says 46th Ward alderman Helen Shiller. "But that doesn't fit the times." The lone dissenter, the 26th Ward's Billy Ocasio, has a different take: "Yes, these are hard times," he says. "But I think in this budget we haven't been that responsible."

November 21, 2008. Unbeknownst to the public or the City Council, the city receives two official bids for leasing the parking meters. According to the documents obtained by the *Reader* through the Freedom of Information Act request, the bids came from Morgan Stanley, for $1,008,500,000, and the Macquarie partnership, for $964,226,025.

Other records show that the city hired Chicago-based investment firm William Blair & Company as a consultant on the leasing process. On April 22, 2008, William Blair representatives presented city officials with a "Summary of Preliminary Valuation"—a sketch of what the meters might be worth on the market. But because any private investor would have to borrow big sums of money to finance a long-term deal, pay corporate taxes, and make capital investments, Blair concluded that the "estimated value of the Chicago On-Street Parking System is approximately $1 billion."

When pressed for details on how and why William Blair was hired, Daley turned to Volpe, who said the firm had specialized experience in municipal finance—as did the two other firms that had worked as financial consultants on the deal, Ramirez & Company and Gardner Rich. "There are very few firms that are qualified in this area," Volpe said.

Blair's Web site notes that the company was the principal player in an earlier privatization effort: the leasing of the city's downtown parking garages, which in 2006 were turned over for 99 years to a partnership led by Morgan Stanley in return for $563 million in cash up front." The company's site also explains that the firm was even more deeply involved in the meter deal. "William Blair & Company originated the idea for the transaction."

We later learned that both bidders—Morgan Stanley and a partnership led by Macquarie Capital Group, one of the investors that leased the Skyway in 2005—offered about $1 billion, right around what Blair had pegged as the "estimated value" of the meters.

December 1, 2008. Final bids on the parking meter lease are due. "We open the envelopes and the winning bidder is the highest bidder," Lisa Schrader, a spokesperson for the budget department, tells us later that day. In the last week Morgan Stanley has upped its bid to $1,156,500,000. The Macquarie group's final bid comes in at $1,019,022,803.

At 8:34 AM finance committee chair Ed Burke calls a special meeting for December 3 to discuss the deal; aldermen still have no information about who has bid or how much. At 3 PM, the mayor submits paperwork to the city clerk's office calling a full council meeting for December 4 "for the sole purpose" of approving the agreement.

December 2, 2008. Daley holds a press conference to announce that his administration has agreed to lease the meters for 75 years to Chicago Parking Meters LLC, a newly created entity led by Morgan Stanley, for nearly $1.2 billion.

Aldermen are invited to a briefing with city officials, who distribute an eight-page summary. It reads in part, "City Council retains the right to set rates, hours of operation and designate meter locations. However, reduction in meters, rates or hours that negatively impact the overall value of the meter system could result in a payment by the City to the Concessionaire." Due to the short notice some aldermen aren't able to attend.

December 3, 2008. An ordinance is required to finalize the lease deal, and the finance committee meets to consider it. Ten minutes into the meeting some aldermen point out that they still haven't seen it. After copies the ordinance have been provided, many remain confused. Where are the details of the agreement? What's the rush? Why haven't you kept us informed before now? And who in the heck is the company that will be managing the meters?

Volpe tells the aldermen it's critical to finish the deal quickly, since interest rates are at an all-time low and any upward movement will cost the city money. But he also assures them that the city will replace the $20 million it now clears annually from parking meters with 5 percent interest on the $400 million it intends to put in the bank.

Alderman Berny Stone praises Mayor Daley's fiduciary prowess by explaining that the lease will help avoid tax hikes: "You can't avoid death, but you can try to avoid taxes." Other aldermen pause to reflect on the deeper meaning of his remark.

Alderman Richard Mell points out that workers employed to write tickets and empty the meters won't be subject to the federal ban on patronage hiring. That means they could work the precincts or contribute to the campaigns of powerful politicians. The aldermen appear to consider the possibilities.

"We're rushing through this," says Alderman Robert Fioretti. "Why?"

"We've been working on this for the better part of a year, so we haven't been hasty," Volpe insists.

"You had a year, but you're giving us two days," says Alderman Ike Carothers.

To help aldermen understand some of the terms, Jim McDonald, a lawyer for the city, reads some legalese from the proposed agreement.

Ocasio bellows: "What does that all mean?"

City officials then pass out a corporate flow chart to offer some "clarity" on who exactly will be leasing the meters. At the top of the chart it says "Chicago Parking Meters LLC." It looks like the plan for a Rube Goldberg invention. Several aldermen turn the chart upside down to see if it makes more sense that way.

Alderman Burke warns that LLC stands for limited liability company, designed, as the name suggests, to help the owners avoid liability if they're sued. "It can be a shell," says Burke, who's recently delivered a series of populist speeches against the abuses of corporate America. "This is why we don't trust Wall Street. It's why they've brought us to the brink of financial disaster." Still, after a couple hours Burke and his colleagues conclude it's too good a deal to pass up, and the finance committee gives its stamp of approval.

December 4, 2008. The full council meets to consider the deal. Many aldermen privately concede they still don't understand it. Alderman Scott Waguespack unveils an analysis his staff has put together that shows the city would make far more money if it just held on to the meters—he estimates their value over 75 years is about $4 billion. "I argued that the city was not getting a good deal, and that at a minimum the Council should see the City's numbers," he later writes in an e-mail to constituents. "They instead argued our numbers were wrong (without having seen them). I was then told I could see some numbers, but not before the vote."

Others are less critical. Alderman Mell contends the council has had more than enough time to study the deal: "How many of us read the stuff we do get, OK? I try to. I try to. I try to. But being realistic, being realistic, it's like getting your insurance policy. It's small print, OK?" From the council floor Alderman Stone assures any citizens who are listening that "this money is not going to be spent like a drunken sailor."

The full council approves the deal 40–5, with the nays coming from Toni Preckwinkle, Leslie Hairston, Rey Colon, Waguespack, and Ocasio. Five aldermen—

Shiller, Carothers, George Cardenas, Ariel Reboyras, and Sandi Jackson—manage to miss the vote.

February 13, 2009. The city announces that it's finally finished all the final legal work and closed the deal with Chicago Parking Meters LLC and day-to-day management of the system will be turned over to LAZ Parking. Rates go up at some meters within days.

March 20, 2009. The *Tribune*'s Jon Hilkevitch reports that all hell is breaking loose on the parking meter front—the meters can't handle all the extra quarters required by the new rates. In some places the rates aren't posted clearly, and drivers are furious that they're getting ticketed as a result.

March 22, 2009. Sun-Times columnist Carol Marin describes an emerging parking meter boycott. She quotes the Parking Ticket Geek, the blogger behind theexpiredmeter.com, on his efforts to reach someone with LAZ Parking: "I called for a week straight. . . . I am friendly and nice and polite on the phone . . . and never ever get a call back."

March 25, 2009. The *Sun-Times* notes a surge in parking meter vandalism, and Marin suggests that the meter rate hikes and breakdowns could ignite a voter backlash similar to the one that drove Mayor Michael Bilandic from office back in 1979, after his response to a blizzard was perceived as inadequate.

March 26, 2009. Mayor Daley sends out city work crews to fix broken parking meters, even though Morgan Stanley and LAZ Parking are supposed to be responsible for maintenance now.

March 31, 2009. City officials stage the press conference with Chicago Parking Meters CEO Dennis Pedrelli. In addition to promising not to raise rates or write tickets till the system's been cleaned up, he announces plans to reimburse the city for the labor of its work crews.

March 31, 2009. The *Sun-Times* reports that the Midway privatization deal is on hold: Midway Investment and Development Company LLC is having trouble lining up the funds. City officials say they'll give Midway Investment up to six months to get the money together.

April 1, 2009. Mayor Daley holds a press conference in Douglas Park to assure the world that the city has a plan to pay for the 2016 Olympics that "protects taxpayers."

The parking meter and garage deals are still costing the city money. In the years after the transaction, the city was required to "true up" with CPM by paying it millions of dollars annually for parking spaces the city devotes for special purposes that otherwise would deprive CPM of revenue. Likewise, the city has paid the buyer of the parking garage concessions tens of millions for allowing other parking garages to be built within two miles of those conceded. The Midway Airport deal was never consummated.

To see this incident from an alderman's point of view, the authors interviewed Scott Waguespack, one of five who voted no. He had heard rumors that the parking meters were being studied and that the city might be hiring someone to manage them. His first exposure to the deal was a sketchy description he received on Friday, November 29, 2008, the day after Thanksgiving and the week before the city council was to vote. Despite holiday commitments he and two staffers spent the weekend making a rough estimate of the value of the deal. He wanted to be prepared. As he entered the hastily called Finance Committee meeting on December 3, he spotted Paul Volpe and approached him with questions. Volpe ignored him. The meeting lasted four hours, and throughout, he was raising his hand and waving the papers that contained his calculations and questions. Finally, after three hours and forty-five minutes and after most of the aldermen had drifted out of the meeting, the committee chairman (who like all committee chairmen was appointed by the mayor) called on him. Waguespack questioned the value of the deal and wondered why it had to extend seventy-five years. Later research by his staff showed that comparable deals worked out in France and Spain had terms of fifteen to twenty years. His questions were brushed off by Volpe and other loyal aldermen, and the measure was voted out of the committee. The next day the council approved it with five no votes. LAZ Parking's offices were located within Waguespack's ward, and a few months later his office got a call that there was trash blocking the alley behind its offices. Waguespack called Streets and Sanitation to clean it up but also went over to the site to see the mess. Littering the alley he found a treasure trove of documents from the deal, many that were dated before the council was made aware of it.

Another alderman who voted no is Billy Ocasio. Speaking from his office in the Puerto Rican Museum in Humboldt Park, he tells the same story of scant information provided at the last minute. Ocasio felt that increased parking fees were another expense with which the city was burdening lower-income residents. He, too, questioned the term of the concession and asked why the city could not just do a three-year deal and see how it turned out. That way, if the city made a mistake, it could correct it.

Alderman Robert Fioretti was one of the majority who voted yes. Discussing the vote years later, he cites the mood in the city and country in late

2008. What has come to be known as the Great Recession was only just beginning. The stock market had collapsed and home values were plunging
nationwide. The city of Chicago had been incurring fiscal deficits for years,
but the forecasts for the current and following year were dire. It was in this
light that Fioretti voted for the concession. His clear understanding at that
time was that the funds provided by the concession would be taken into the
city's general account a little bit at a time. Afterward, when he learned that
all of the proceeds were used to plug the budget gaps in just two years, he felt
betrayed. In retrospect, he says, if he were to vote today, he would oppose the
deal. He felt that it should have been a much shorter deal, perhaps thirty-five
years. He felt at the time and feels now that the concession should have called
for a smaller lump sum payment coupled with annual payments for the life of
the concession. Fioretti also blames the Transportation Department for not
modernizing the parking administration before selling off the concession. He
recalls Ocasio's dramatic dumping of quarters from a mason jar during de-
liberations to show how far behind the city's parking management had fallen.

A Pattern, Not an Isolated Incident

Dick Simpson, the eminent University of Illinois at Chicago political scientist,
has written extensively about the Chicago City Council. He should know;
he was elected alderman in 1971. In one analysis, he shows that the council's
baseline behavior is to rubber-stamp the mayor's decisions, only occasionally
deviating and descending into rancor and disorder. In recent years, with the
exception of the so-called council wars in Mayor Harold Washington's first
term, the council has not seriously challenged the mayor. The result for city
government has not been good, as can be illustrated with just a few of many
examples.

    The pattern of kowtowing to the police force led to lax oversight decades
ago, when Police Chief Jon Burge gained confessions from innocent citizens
by torture. Those acts have cost the city more than $100 million. What was
missing was the level of oversight that a truly independent city council could
provide.

    The same pattern can be seen in the way the city stonewalled requests to
release the video of the fateful Laquan McDonald shooting. McDonald was
shot sixteen times by a Chicago police officer in October 2014. Requests for
the city to release the video of the shooting were denied by the city attorney,

who is appointed by the mayor. Even though the city made a financial settlement with McDonald's family before the 2015 mayoral election, the video was still withheld from the public until November, when a court ordered it released. Could an independently elected city attorney have provided more transparency? Where was the city council in this matter? It must be noted that an elected state's attorney waited until after the court ruled on the video to charge the police officer with murder. She lost her bid for reelection.

On March 1, 2012, the mayor announced his intention to form the $7 billion Chicago Infrastructure Trust. On April 24, the city council voted to approve the creation of the trust, with no further details on the deal to be considered. Opponents rightfully asked why the council could not approve deals one at a time, but the mayor rejected such oversight.

In 2011, the Chicago Department of Aviation entered into an unprecedented twenty-year lease of concessions at O'Hare International Airport's Terminal 5. Like the parking meter deal, there was very little due diligence or information provided to the city council before they were asked to approve the deal.

In pitching the International Olympic Committee in 2009 to choose Chicago for the 2016 Olympics, the mayor secretly committed the city to the full cost of producing the games. This open commitment was made without the city council's knowledge or approval and would have obligated the city to billions of dollars in costs. Fortunately, Chicago lost to Rio de Janeiro to host the games.

Despite constant criticism of the city's tax increment financing (TIF) program, and despite vows by the mayor to phase it out, the program continues to siphon off hundreds of millions of dollars for special projects. In July 2017, it was revealed that TIF funds intended for a hotel at McCormick Place were secretly redirected to Navy Pier.[3] The original funding was approved 46–3 by the city council. What is the relationship between a rubber-stamp council and a sister entity with its own board? How can the council begin to oversee this money-losing enterprise?

This list of prominent city actions is but a sampling. Many other controversial matters large and small are handled in the same way: the mayor conceives the deal in private with vendors and interested parties, and then the city council approves it. In some cases, the matter is sprung on the city council with little information and no time for study. A vote is called, and the city suffers the consequences. In other cases, city behavior cries out for consistent oversight, but there is no effective mechanism within Chicago's governance structure to allow for it.

How the City Works: Strong Mayor, Weak City Council

The governance structure of a city determines how decisions are made and how things get done. In the parlance of local government law, there are two forms of municipal governance: a mayor-council form and the council-manager form. Smaller and newer cities often have a rather weak city council and mayor who in turn hire a professional city manager to run things. With the mayor-council form, the mayor can be either weak or strong relative to the council. As called for in the Illinois Constitution, Chicago has a strong mayor-weak council form of government, with each exercising appropriate power. Other major cities have either a weak mayor system or a strong mayor system with significant powers reserved to the council. It is this relationship between the mayor and city council that is at the center of the governance equation. Another key dynamic is the presence (or absence) of independently elected city officials who have substantial power over critical functions. In Chicago, mayors have hoarded power to themselves since the founding of the city. How is this done?

THE ALDERMAN AND THE WARD

The vocabulary of city government in Chicago reveals its structure. The word *alderman* is a variation on *elderman* and reflects the patrimonial village chief role played in traditional societies worldwide. As a verb, *to ward* is to protect or guard; as a noun, it is a place where people are protected, as in a ward in a hospital. In Chicago, fifty aldermen are elected from fifty wards. The city, therefore, is composed of fifty small villages, and the chief of each ward protects the inhabitants; he or she holds power over decisions within the village and tends to the needs of the people there. The alderman need not be qualified to vote on citywide issues of governance; the village chief leaves that to the big chief, the mayor.

The deficiencies of this structure are not unknown. In 1954, the Chicago Home Rule Commission issued a report titled *Modernizing a City Government.* That report states in part: "The ward system was established to enable aldermen to service their constituents. The nature of the service function has changed materially, however, in the last three decades as a consequence of the increased professionalization of social service work, the development of service activities by trade and labor associations, and the coming of the so-called 'welfare state.' . . . The consequence is a conclusion that the existing 50-ward system is an anachronism."[4] The ward system has not become any less outdated in the sixty-four years since that pronouncement.

A principal problem of the aldermanic system in Chicago is that aldermen hold important executive and administrative authority. All zoning and development decisions within a ward must carry the alderman's approval before being taken up by the full city council or even the planning department. Likewise, business signage and licensing is controlled at the ward level. The use of discretionary "menu" funds that average $1.32 million a year for local improvements allows aldermen to reward loyal voters and punish those who raise their voices or cause political trouble.[5] Chicago Inspector General Joe Ferguson has said that the removal of such executive and administrative powers from the aldermen's hands would do more than any other reform to check corruption in the city. This aldermanic privilege or prerogative is not written into the charter of the city; there is no such document. Nonetheless, the informal practice has persisted since the city was founded.[6] This practice was challenged in April 2018 by a real estate developer who was denied a zoning change. The city council's zoning committee rejected the developer's appeal, falling solidly in line supporting the continuation of aldermanic privilege.[7] The same scenario was playing out in the Second Ward, where the alderman was not ready to support a massive new development.[8] This arrangement is one of several that make for a weak city council. It is also unheard of in other major cities.

TOO MANY ALDERMEN

A problem related to aldermanic privilege is the number of aldermen and wards. That same Home Rule Commission report called for reducing the number of aldermen, at the time when Chicago's population had hit its zenith of over 3.6 million people; the population today is 2.6 million. Central to the argument for a reduction in the number of aldermen is the assumption that with aldermen having more constituents and the council having fewer members, the council would be more powerful. With more constituents it would be more difficult to serve them, forcing council members to focus more on citywide interests. Here, too, the commission speaks: "City-wide interests should have an opportunity to compete, in open council, with ward interests." Finally, some would argue that with fewer council members and more competitive races, the quality of candidates for that office would improve.

The argument against fewer council members with larger constituencies rests on the assumption that such an arrangement would make political contests more competitive, requiring more money and arousing the attention of special interests. Those special interests, however, are already at work on only one target, the mayor; and with more powerful council members, their work would be more complicated. An analysis of city council size undertaken in New York City at the time of its 1989 charter revision observed that party regulars want larger councils elected by districts; reformers, on the other hand, want smaller councils elected at large.[9] Another analysis concluded likewise that "the geometrical growth of the size of New York's Municipal Assembly was inversely related to the level of its prestige."[10]

How does Chicago stack up with the other cities that make up the top fifteen most populous in the United States? Table 1.1 shows that the city is certainly an exception, if not an outlier.

FILLING VACANCIES

The Illinois Municipal Code governs the filling of vacancies on the Chicago City Council. If the vacancy occurs more than 130 days from a general municipal election, then the mayor shall appoint an alderman. In most cases aldermen resign well in advance of the 130-day mark, and some negotiate their resignation for an unknown political promise. In 2016, shortly after he was reelected, Alderman Will Burns resigned to take a job with Airbnb, a position that would involve significant interaction with City Hall.[11] In April 2018 longtime alderman Michael Zalewski stepped down well ahead of the end of his term to start a political consulting practice. The mayor replaced him with an ally of Illinois House Speaker Michael Madigan.[12] This law assures that virtually all vacancies will be filled by the mayor. As of the beginning of 2017, twelve of the fifty sitting aldermen had ascended to office by mayoral appointment.

Once in office, aldermen obtain powerful benefits of incumbency; they exercise critical approval power, for example, in many business matters that attract support from interested parties; they are given an annual menu fund that they can use to enhance political support; and if the alderman supports

TABLE 1.1   Selected Governance Attributes, Fifteen Most Populous US Cities

	Population (2014)	Number of council members	Population per member	At-large offices	Term limits	Filling vacancies
New York	8,491,079	51	166,492	0	two 4-year	special election
Los Angeles	3,928,864	15	261,924	0	two 4-year	council president appointment
Chicago	2,722,389	50	54,448	0	none	mayoral appointment
Houston	2,239,558	16	139,972	5	two 4-year	council appointment
Philadelphia	1,560,297	17	91,782	7	none	special election
Phoenix	1,537,058	8	192,132	0	three 4-year	special election
San Antonio	1,436,697	10	143,670	0	two 4-year	special election
San Diego	1,381,069	9	153,452	0	two 4-year	special election
Dallas	1,281,047	14	91,503	0	four 2-year	special election
San Jose	1,015,785	10	101,579	0	two 4-year	council appointment
Austin	912,791	10	91,279	0	four 2-year	special election
Jacksonville	853,382	19	44,915	5	two 4-year	special election
San Francisco	852,469	11	77,497	0	two 4-year	mayoral appointment
Indianapolis	848,788	29	28,291	4	none	precinct committee appointment
Columbus	835,957	7	119,422	all	none	council appointment
Average			117,601			

the mayor, the mayor will throw the full weight of his political organization behind the alderman to defeat any challengers. In such an arrangement, the political future of an alderman is solely dependent upon the favor of the mayor.

REDISTRICTING

Chicago's municipal code, which is the closest the city comes to having a charter, governs the process of setting aldermanic district boundaries every ten years. The code reads: "In the year following the national decennial census, the City Council shall redistrict the City on the basis of such census. In the formation of wards in such redistricting, as nearly as practicable, each ward shall be compact, contiguous, and of substantially equal population with an acceptable deviation to respect established communities of interest or to achieve other legally valid and permissible objectives."

In 2012, the council set new districts based upon the 2010 national census. Alderman Robert Fioretti lost his district and has discussed the process publicly many times. According to Fioretti, three men sat down to draw the boundaries: Alderman Dick Mell, the chair of the Rules Committee; Alderman Ed Burke, powerful longtime head of the Finance Committee; and the mayor. In the absence of any other guidance in the municipal code, there was no way to tell what process would be legitimate; the municipal code makes no mention of the mayor's involvement.

The resulting ward boundaries included a crab-shaped Second Ward so devoid of compactness that it became a laughing stock in newspapers and among Chicago's citizens (fig. 1.1).[13]

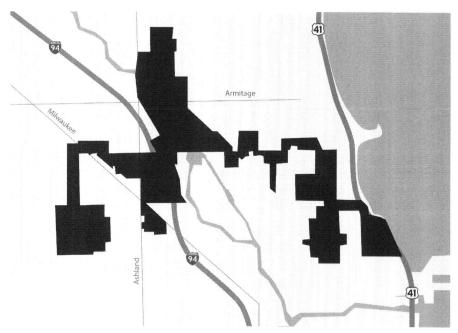

FIGURE 1.1. Chicago's Second Ward. Map by Thea Baldwin.

Statewide and national elections are partisan, so redistricting is all about securing an electoral advantage for a political party. Chicago's municipal elections are nonpartisan, so the control of districting by the mayor is another way of controlling the city council by rewarding friends and punishing enemies. Alderman Fioretti ran against the mayor, and redistricting cost him his seat on the council. The Second Ward was formerly his.

HOLLOW COMMITTEES AND COMMITTEE CHAIRS

The city council maintains a number of standing committees and is empowered to establish special committees, but with one exception they do not function well. Other than by a list of these committees, there is no way to determine from the Chicago municipal code how such bodies are to be administered. Although it is nowhere to be found in the code, the mayor appoints committee chairs, and such appointments are then ratified by the full council. Committees appear to be so meaningless that the average committee meeting attendance between May 2015 and May 2017 was 57 percent, and eight council members had attendance below 40 percent.[14]

The one powerful committee is the Finance Committee. Alderman Ed Burke has been the chairman of that committee since 1983, with the exception of two years in the tumultuous 1980s. The Finance Committee gets involved in aspects of city government that would logically be assigned to other committees. It oversees the workers' compensation system for the city in secret.[15] As the case of Scott Waguespack and the parking meter concession shows, the domination of the Finance Committee by its chairman was instrumental in quashing debate. In 2011 the council created the office of legislative inspector general to keep an eye on council members. Within two years the Finance Committee defunded the office and eventually completely eliminated it.

Creating a new committee or office with any power is difficult. In 2013, the city council voted to establish a City Council Office of Financial Analysis with its own independent professional staff. Eighteen months later, certain council members finally broke a logjam over whom to hire and filled the position to head the office. In early 2017, after another eighteen months, that person left the office. This new office has been adrift just as the financial woes of the city have worsened dramatically. Four years after the office was created, the council considered legislation, common in other cities, to require it to prepare an analysis of the cost of proposed ordinances and to do so in sufficient time in advance of votes so aldermen can be educated as to the impact of their decisions.[16] No analysis of the fiscal impact of legislation is currently being prepared, and no action has been taken on a measure to require such an analysis.

The council and its committees live up to their characterization as a rubber stamp. An analysis of the council's activities for the two years ended May 2017 shows that of 19,000 items or pieces of legislation considered, only 2 percent were substantive. While what are categorized as substantive ordinances numbered 307, grants of privileges numbered 4,730, handicapped parking permits numbered 4,364, and sidewalk café permits numbered 2,570.[17]

OTHER ELECTED OFFICES

In addition to the mayor, there are two other citywide offices that are elected and two crucial offices that are not elected. The city treasurer is elected to manage the city's cash. This position is more of a custodial function, since the treasurer has no authority over any other city assets nor any authority or even role in budgeting, borrowing, or finance. The treasurer sits on the boards of the four city worker pension funds, but cannot assure that the city will make sufficient contributions to any of them. The city clerk is also elected citywide, but, as the title implies, this is a strictly clerical office with no substantive authority. Don Haider, former city chief financial officer and onetime candidate for mayor, has observed that the city of Chicago is structured so that elected officials have no real power that could detract from the mayor.

To perpetuate mayoral control, two key offices remain appointed: the chief financial officer and the city attorney. All budgeting and financial management of the city is overseen by the chief financial officer and the budget director. It is the city attorney who advises the mayor on the legality of his or her actions. The law department oversees all Freedom of Information Act inquiries and fights lawsuits to disclose hoarded information. In the case of the Laquan McDonald video, it was the city attorney who led the fight to withhold the release of the video and who eventually was overruled in court. It is also the city attorney and the law department that handles any lawsuit brought against the city. These suits would include any manner of tort and especially charges of police misconduct. As noted in chapter 8 on policing, the choice by the city attorney to defend or settle suits can have material effect on the city's finances.

What about Other Cities?

In researching this book the authors studied the governance documents and practices of the country's largest fifteen cities by population. In addition we interviewed office holders, academics, or civic leaders in all of the cities. The results of that research for the two cities that are larger than Chicago—New York and Los Angeles—are presented below. The research for the remaining twelve cities is presented in appendix B. In all of the fourteen cities studied there exist some governance differences from what is experienced in Chicago. In some cases the differences are few and minor, but in many the differences are major and profound. In all of these cases the differences are the result of governance innovation undertaken by community leaders in the past hundred years who have sought to modernize the structure and functioning of government. The efforts of New York and Los Angeles have been the most sweeping and are considered by some to be the most effective.

NEW YORK

Over the years, New York City has suffered crushing challenges, both from external sources and those created internally, which have threatened its existence in many ways. It has always risen to these challenges and defied defeat. The Tammany Hall era made New York City the model for corrupt, big-city, political boss rule. In 1933, Mayor Fiorello La Guardia established a charter commission that ended the ward system, created proportional rule in the city council, and set up a board of estimate to run New York. In 1975, that city's home rule powers were limited by the New York State Emergency Financial Control Board. Some readers will remember the newspaper headline at the height of the New York's financial crisis: "Ford to City: Drop Dead." This brush with municipal bankruptcy brought much-needed financial reforms to city government.

Of all the efforts to modernize New York's governance, none is as comprehensive and relevant as the charter revision of 1989. In 1988 and 1989 Mayor Ed Koch created two successive charter commissions.[18] These charter reforms were precipitated by a lawsuit filed in 1981 by some Brooklyn activists challenging the board of estimate system. This case, *Board of Estimate of City of New York v. Morris*, claimed that the board of estimate system violated the Voting Rights Act of 1965. The board acted like an executive committee whereby the mayor, the city controller, and the president of the city council were allotted two votes each, while the presidents of the five boroughs each received one, though the largest borough, Brooklyn, had over two million people while Staten Island had only 350,000. The charter commission had the choice either to reform the composition of the board of estimate or tackle the entire governance structure of the city. It chose the latter.

The charter commission cited several reasons for completely overhauling New York City government. Although the *Morris* case was the politically recognizable reason, the commission noted other significant factors, including the underrepresentation of racial minorities, the domination of government by Manhattan, and the fact that New York had become an overwhelmingly Democratic, one-party city. In addition, the city had been lurching from one crisis to another; the board had become a "trading post" for deal making and did not give sufficient attention to underlying causes or policy.[19]

Although there have been several charter commissions since 1989, none has been as far reaching as that one. Today the New York City Council acts independently of the mayor. There is no formal manner whereby a council member can exercise executive authority over zoning, development, or any other matters within his or her district. There are fifty-one council seats in a city three times the size of Chicago. Vacancies that arise in the council are filled by a special election called within forty-five days of the vacation of the office. Council members' service is limited to two consecutive four-year terms. The New York City Council has a robust committee system that is supported by significant professional staff. In addition to the mayor and city council, New York City elects a controller and a council president, who serves primarily as a public advocate and ombudsperson.

LOS ANGELES

With the exception of the police corruption investigation after the beating of Rodney King and the Rampart anti-gang unit investigation, Los Angeles city government has faced fewer crises than most major cities. Los Angeles prides itself on being a good government city. Metrics from city finances to the murder rate compare quite favorably to Chicago. Even Los Angeles pensions, which are generally described to be in terrible shape, are 78 percent funded; Chicago's five biggest plans are below 50 percent. Every big city has big problems, of course, but Los Angeles seems to keep itself out of correspondingly big trouble. Does governmental structure play a role?

In the late 1990s the city underwent a contentious charter revision effort; it also had before it the threat of secession by activists in the San Fernando Valley area of the city. Like New York, this charter revision was one of many in a long history of striving for better government. An account of the charter revision contains a telling remark about Chicago: "The charter reformers are saying that 15 members each representing 230,000 people is too many. The example they give is that Chicago has 50 councilmembers each representing 60,000 residents. What reformers are really saying is that CHICAGO-STYLE POLITICS should be brought to Los Angeles. The nerve of the charter reformers to speak of CHICAGO-STYLE POLITICS and Los Angeles politics in the same breath, **that is ludicrous!**"[20] Los Angeles city government is very different from Chicago's. Mayoral control of the city council is modest, and vacancies are filled by the council president. In late 2016, the council president appointed himself to represent the suddenly vacated San Fernando district rather than hold a costly special election. He did not receive any more money and he did not gain a vote, but at least the San Fernando voters had interim representation. Both the mayor and council members serve for no more than two four-year terms. Council members do not exercise executive functions within their districts, but they do receive discretionary funds they can spend on local projects. In addition to the offices of mayor and council members, Los Angeles voters elect a city controller and a city attorney. The controller is the CFO of the city and is responsible for reviewing the budget, audits, and bookkeeping; the city attorney advises on matters and points of law. The work of council committees seems robust, and it is supported by the office and staff of the chief legislative analyst. In Los Angeles, the mayor is quite divorced from the responsibilities of policing. The mayor appoints the members of the police commission, and the commission runs the police department. If the mayor seeks to remove a commissioner, that person can appeal to the city council.

Solving Problems: A Better Governance Structure for Chicago

Sound thinking that would improve the governance of Chicago is not a new idea. Martin Kennelly served as mayor of Chicago from 1947 to 1955. He was considered a weak mayor, succeeding the scandal-plagued Edward Kelly, who was harassed and undermined by the city council toward the end of his term.[21] Kennelly had a clean government reputation, and among his many studies and reforms he created the Home Rule Commission. The commission's report, published in book form in 1954, describes the cumbersome manner in which the state of Illinois administers home rule and delegates powers to the city of Chicago. It recommended that the state legislature enact specific powers "permitting the Chicago City Council, or the Chicago electorate by the initiative process, to propose changes in the form and structure of city government, subject to referendum approval, but without the necessity of prior state legislative approval."[22] This thorough report goes on to describe specific and substantive changes in the governance of the city, including reducing the number of aldermen, stripping them of executive powers, and making the city council independent of the mayor. Although the commission's report has been shelved since 1954, it contains many truths that should not be ignored.

The improvements recommended by the Home Rule Commission are part of the routine process that New York City practices. New York City regularly and thoroughly revises its charter in an effort led by senior civic leaders. Many of the other top fifteen cities have excellent charters that have been regularly updated, but the account given by Schwartz and Lane of New York City's effort is as fine an example of good governance process and result as can be found. It is a model to emulate. The new charter that resulted from the New York commission's efforts addressed numerous essential points of city governance that Chicago should note:

- Expanding the power of the city council
- Size of the council
- Term limits
- Redistricting
- Other citywide elected officials
- Elaborate budget procedures
- Land use decision making
- Franchises, concessions, and licenses
- Procurement of goods and services
- An independent budget office
- Formal institutions to open city government

For Chicago's government to function properly, there needs to be a balance between the powers of the mayor and other elements of government.

To achieve that balance, the city must have a capable city charter arrived at with deliberation, supported by a popular vote, and regularly reexamined for intended effectiveness.

Chicago's governance structure lies somewhere between the large, more politically governed cities like New York or Los Angeles and the smaller, faster growing cities of the Southwest that have adopted the city manager form of government. Chicago needs better management, even if it may not be ready for a city manager. Other larger cities have created the position of chief administrative officer. In distributing the power of the mayor to other members of the government and by cutting the mayor's powers down to size, the mayor can be more manager than politician. Although the city manager form should never be ruled out for any city, it does not seem feasible for Chicago just yet. Before Chicago can even consider such a change, it must adopt the other changes in governance described in this study.

A charter for Chicago should address the current imbalance between the powers of the mayor and those of the city council. The council must become completely independent of mayoral control, must be structured to focus on big-picture, citywide policies, and must develop its own ability and authority to study issues in support of legislative decision making. Key to balancing the power is the elimination of the aldermanic ward system and replacing it with a smaller more robust city council. Changing the method of filling vacancies, revising how districting is handled, and imposing term limits will further bring Chicago into line with the norm in most big cities. The city council must be presided over by a council president, one of its own. The president can be elected by the council from among its members or, as with some cities, can be elected at large specifically for the function. The key is that the council not be presided over by the mayor. A critical but little known concept is that of residual powers. Should enumerated powers be given to the mayor with residual powers held by the council or vice versa? This issue was explicitly addressed in Los Angeles, and it should be explicitly considered during charter creation.[23]

In addition to the issue of council independence, the charter should consider the creation of other elected offices. Table 1.2 shows the manner of selection and accountability for both a city controller and attorney in the fifteen largest cities. Five of them have an elected financial officer with substantial power. In another five cities there is a city manager who is accountable to the city council and who hires the chief financial officer. Only in a minority of cases is the financial officer appointed by and accountable to the mayor. In Chicago in 2011, the mayor hired a comptroller who was already under investigation at the time he was hired.[24] Such failed vetting is much less likely when the candidate must run for the office. The enormous and growing fiscal problems in Chicago cry out for the election of such a position (see chapter 4).

Several large cities also elect their city attorney or the position is accountable to the city manager. Although more city attorneys report to the mayor than do city controllers, the number is still a minority within the top fifteen cities. Under normal circumstances, such a proposal would not be high on the list of changes for Chicago, but with all of the trouble that has recently plagued the city's law department, it must now be seriously considered (see

TABLE 1.2 Manner of Selection and Accountability of City Controller and City Attorney

	Independent elected controller	Selection of city attorney
New York	Yes	Mayor
Los Angeles	Yes	Elected
Chicago	No	Mayor
Houston	Yes	Mayor
Philadelphia	Yes	Mayor
Phoenix	Manager	Manager
San Antonio	Manager	Manager
San Diego	No	Elected
Dallas	Manager	Council
San Jose	Manager	Manager
Austin	Manager	Manager
Jacksonville	No	Mayor
San Francisco	No	Elected
Indianapolis	No	Mayor
Columbus	Yes	Elected

chapter 8). If these two positions were added to the other two elected offices, the treasurer and clerk, this book would be criticized for recommending a proliferation of elected offices. But the need for independent and elected financial and legal officials is more critical than retaining the treasurer and clerk; those elected offices could become mayoral appointments.

To accomplish these broad objectives, a new governance structure for the city would include the following changes:

- The city council should be reduced in size to include only twenty members, each elected from districts.
- The aldermanic ward structure should be eliminated. Specific provisions must prohibit council members from holding or exercising any executive functions that dispense any discretionary city budget funds within their respective districts. These provisions would prohibit any vestige of aldermanic privilege.
- Term limits should be enacted for both the mayor and council members. Two consecutive four-year terms would be an appropriate norm.
- The city council should elect a president who would preside over meetings, make assignments to committees, and assign committee chairs.
- Vacancies on the city council should be filled either by appointment, by the council itself, or at a regularly scheduled citywide election with the seat remaining vacant until then.
- The establishing of city legislative districts should be conducted by an independent districting commission of private citizens who have not held public office.
- The city council should allocate to itself sufficient funds to establish professional staff for its standing and special committees.
- The functions of chief financial officer and city attorney should become elected offices.
- The city council should commission a reexamination of the city charter every ten years.

Studying comparative governance structures in the large American cities, these recommendations seem obvious, but it is not enough merely for government to embrace these changes. The city of San Diego incorporated some of these features and still continued to make poor decisions. Observers of its challenges noted that in addition to correcting political institutions, there needs to be strong civic leadership and political culture.[25] The charter commissions in the other big cities were led from civil society, by professional leaders in business, labor, law, universities, and foundations. It is these leaders who must push for a city charter, keep an eye on the result, and engage in the inevitable subsequent charter revision. It is time for Chicago's leaders to stop acquiescing and take on the responsibility for governance reform.

CHAPTER 2

Discouraging Democracy

The vote is a trust more delicate than any other, for it involves not just the interests of the voter, but his life, honor and future as well.
—JOSE MARTI

⌒

The weather in Chicago on February 24, 2015, was not unusual. The low temperature was seven degrees at 6:00 a.m., just when the polls opened for the municipal elections. What was unusual, though, was that someone had hacked the election judge list the weekend before the election, and robocalls were sent to the judges asking them to attend a special training session at a fake location. The result? Hundreds of election judges did not show up for the actual election, and many polling places were understaffed.

If the weather was unexceptional, the election itself was not. The incumbent mayor had four challengers: William "Dock" Walls, former aide to Mayor Harold Washington; Willie Wilson, a businessman; Alderman Robert Fioretti; and Cook County Commissioner Jesús "Chuy" García. It was not unusual for the mayor to be challenged, but it was unusal for the incumbent not to receive the majority vote (50 percent plus one vote) required to avoid a runoff. The incumbent, Rahm Emanuel, received a little over 45 percent of the votes, García 34 percent, Wilson 11 percent, Fioretti 7 percent, and Walls 3 percent. Emanuel and García were forced into a runoff, which took place on April 7 and in which the incumbent received 56 percent to García's 44 percent. This was the first time since the mayoral election system had been changed in 1995 that a runoff was necessary.

Emanuel was admittedly chastened by the initial failure to achieve a majority and ran a humble runoff campaign. He received fewer endorsements than García, but they were powerful ones, including President Barack Obama, former mayor Richard M. Daley, Senator Dick Durbin, and the major newspapers. García, in turn, received the backing of several aldermen and county commissioners, national Democratic celebrities Bernie Sanders and Howard Dean, two locals of the Service Employees International Union, and a local of the Teamsters. García also received the endorsement of Karen Lewis, the powerful head of the Chicago Teachers Union, along with her ally Diane Ravitch, a national education policy analyst. Lewis, in fact, had urged García to run as the labor candidate. Those who opposed the idea of an elected school board worried that it could result in the democratic capture of the school district by the teachers' union. In the mayoral election of 2015, the union made a pretty good run at city hall.

Chicago Municipal Elections

Chicago is governed by electing one person, the mayor, who then appoints the remainder of the municipal administration. It is through that election that voters hold the mayor accountable and democracy works its magic. But what if democracy itself is discouraged in such events?

On a national scale, the question of voter disenfranchisement occupies a prominent place. The original US Constitution recognized three-fifths of the black slave population for the purposes of calculating representative government, but it did not allow them to vote. Women likewise were not given the vote until less than a hundred years ago. In the aftermath of protests by young men subject to the military draft during the Vietnam conflict, many states lowered the voting age from twenty-one to eighteen. Voter identification requirements remain a contested issue in many states and cities. The level of enforcement of the Voting Rights Act of 1965 is still debated, especially the redistricting called for every ten years. Some states allow former felons to vote, other states do not. But whatever their differences, all well-meaning sides of these important issues work to ensure that those entitled to vote can vote, that citizens can make their voice heard and influence lawmaking through their representatives. Discouraging voting is antithetical to the American spirit of democracy.

In Chicago, the more contemporary issues are of less civic import. Redistricting of aldermanic wards does not affect the partisan makeup of the city council; the office is nonpartisan and all public officials are Democrats anyway. The gerrymandering of aldermanic wards is, instead, a means whereby the mayor retains his control over aldermanic loyalty. Similarly, voter identification is not considered a pressing issue. The only time voter identification is a factor is during petition signature validation. When an entrenched politician is challenged by an outsider, he will try to throw his rival off the ballot. This is one definition of the Chicago Way.

In both Chicago and Illinois, a severe and overlooked voting problem is the timing and nature of municipal elections. The date for the first Chicago municipal elections in Illinois, misleadingly called the consolidated primary, is set by the state election code for the last Tuesday in February. If a candidate fails to receive 50 percent of the vote plus one, then the race goes to a two-candidate runoff on the first Tuesday in April. These municipal elections are for city offices. County elections—including the critical board president, assessor, district attorney, and sheriff—take place in November in even-numbered years with partisan primaries and a general election. It is probably a mystery to voters why there is such a difference between city and county elections.

What is the result of this unusual timing? Consider the election results for the past fifteen years in Chicago, shown in table 2.1. By setting the date for municipal elections in the middle of the winter in an odd-numbered year, state law explicitly discourages voting. The average voter turnout for those elections since 2000 has been 36.4 percent, less than half the average for the November presidential elections. No other major city in the United States works in this way to discourage voters from participating in democracy.

The timing of elections in Chicago is not a hapless misreading of the calendar. As Milton Rakove points out in his 1975 analysis of the Daley machine, the scheduling of the mayoral primary and the aldermanic elections in February of odd-numbered years was designed to serve a number of political purposes. First, it insulated the mayoral election from national, statewide, and countywide political trends, which at times could have been dangerous to the Democratic candidate. Second, horrible weather at the end of a long winter discouraged turnout among voters "not controlled by, indebted to, or subservient to the machine's precinct workers. The skewed turnout in a combined mayoral and nonpartisan aldermanic election yielded a number of positive results for the Democratic political organization. First, Democratic precinct captains at each polling place were able to note the relatively few

TABLE 2.1   Chicago Voter Turnout by Election, Comparing Municipal Elections to Statewide and National Elections, 2000 to 2016

Date	Winner of the highest office on the ballot	Winner's total number of votes	Total votes cast			Number of registered voters	Mayor's votes (% of registered voters)
			February municipal election	November midterm election	November presidential election		
November 7, 2000	Bush	163,610			955,261	1,472,534	
November 5, 2002	Blagojevich	548,035		693,073		1,364,931	
February 25, 2003	Daley	363,389	463,145			1,436,286	25
November 2, 2004	Bush	188,056			1,032,878	1,416,101	
November 7, 2006	Blagojevich	504,457		651,885		1,360,747	
February 27, 2007	Daley	324,519	456,765			1,407,979	23
November 4, 2008	Obama	930,866			1,089,879	1,497,292	
November 2, 2010	Quinn	520,413		689,951		1,334,807	
February 22, 2011	Emanuel	326,331	590,357			1,406,037	23
November 6, 2012	Obama	853,102			1,015,634	1,364,371	
November 4, 2014	Rauner	135,431		656,481		1,368,708	
February 24, 2015	Emanuel	218,217	478,204			1,421,430	15
April 7, 2015	Emanuel	332,171	590,733			1,441,637	23
November 8, 2016	Trump	135,317			1,090,343	1,570,529	
Average Votes			515,841	672,848	1,036,799	1,418,814	
Voter Turnout			36.4%	47.4%	73.1%		

Source: Chicago Board of Elections.

constituents that requested a Republican ballot and adjust their strategies accordingly. Second, a strong Democratic showing for the mayoral candidate would spill over into the aldermanic results, ensuring a heavily Democratic, though officially nonpartisan, majority in the City Council."[1]

While the Daley political machine receded long ago, the calendar that helped to cement its dominance remains.

Other Major Cities

Compared with timing of elections in other cities, Chicago is an outlier. Table 2.2 shows that no other major city holds its municipal election in February, even in the Sun Belt states. Ten of the large city elections are in November, and two of them follow the presidential cycle.

California and Los Angeles specifically are leaders in encouraging voting. In 2015 the state of California passed a law mandating that municipalities whose local elections receive 25 percent or fewer votes than the four previous statewide elections must change the date of such local elections to coincide with statewide elections.[2] By the time this measure passed, Los Angeles voters had already approved, on March 3, 2015, a special referendum on election timing changing over to the presidential election cycle. The vote total was just over 180,000, and the measure passed with more than 77 percent of votes cast. There was irony in the fact that about 10 percent of voters turned out for the referendum.[3] Those in favor of the measure quoted experts who showed that the date of elections was the major determinant of turnout. They also cited the cost effectiveness of consolidating elections and estimated that it might save the city $19 million. The *Los Angeles Times* endorsed the change: "Democracy is not served when so few Angelinos vote. Low turnout allows the few to make decisions for the many and gives extra power to well-organized special-interest groups that know how to get out their vote."[4] Those opposing the referendum argued that, instead of the proposed change, money should be spent on civic education and that elections could be moved to weekends, or that the city could even declare a voting holiday, giving citizens the day off to vote.

Other major municipalities have also addressed the issue of election timing. New York City holds its elections in November of odd years. In an editorial critical of this timing, the *New York Times* pointed out that even in November the turnout was recently 26 percent, compared to 56 percent

TABLE 2.2   Terms and Timing of Elections for Mayor and City Council in the Fifteen Largest US Cities

	Term length (years)	Month and year of most recent election	Partisan election?
New York	4	November 2017	Yes
Los Angeles	4	November 2016	No
Chicago	4	February 2015	No
Houston	4	November 2015	Yes
Philadelphia	4	November 2015	Yes
Phoenix	4	August 2015	Yes
San Antonio	2	May 2017	No
San Diego	4	November 2016	Yes
Dallas	4	May 2015	Yes
San Jose	4	November 2014	Yes
Austin	4	November 2014	No
Jacksonville	4	March 2015	No
San Francisco	4	November 2015	No
Indianapolis	4	November 2015	Yes
Columbus	4	November 2015	No

for the most recent presidential election. The newspaper also noted that the board of elections requested $42.5 million just for the separate municipal elections.[5] A report by Rice University's Kinder Institute for Urban Research produced similar recommendations for Houston after turnout in that city's most recent municipal elections hovered near 10 percent.[6] A report on San Antonio's municipal elections likewise estimates that turnout would double if the election was moved to November, and double again if moved to a national election year.[7]

The Literature on Turnout

Voter turnout has been widely studied by political scientists, and no one in the United States has studied this topic more than Zoltan Hajnal of the University of California, San Diego. His 2010 book *America's Uneven Democracy: Race, Turnout, and Representation in City Politics* takes an authoritative look at timing and turnout and their effects on municipal governance. One of the many examples he offers is the case of Ferguson, Missouri, which experienced widely publicized civic unrest in 2014 over the shooting of a black man, Michael Brown, by a white policeman, Darren Wilson. The city had a white mayor and a predominantly white city council, school board, and police force. Hajnal attributes this to the timing of elections, which discouraged voter turnout. One particularly important finding of Hajnal's work is that by timing municipal elections to discourage voter turnout, certain minority voices are suppressed. In a sophisticated experiment, he simulated who would have been elected mayor in ten big-city races if the vote had been held at a time with greater turnout. In three out of the ten cases (New York, Houston, and San Diego) a different mayor would have been elected.[8] He concludes that the timing of municipal elections is not a trivial matter. Another scholar, Sarah Anzia, has also written extensively about timing and school board elections. She corroborates Hajnal's findings; indeed, the title of her book tells the whole story: *Timing and Turnout: How Off-Cycle Elections Favor Organized Groups.*

Both of these works show the disadvantages of off-cycle elections from different perspectives. Hajnal makes it clear that such elections discourage democratic accountability. Anzia comes from the inside, showing how special interests—principally teachers unions and municipal workers—capture government by timing elections to favor themselves. While politicians and special interests may prefer off-cycle elections, one survey undertaken by Anzia, the Cooperative Congressional Election Study, polled a spectrum of voters and found that nearly 70 percent preferred to vote for municipal offices on the same day they vote for statewide and national office.[9] Those excluded from the process are primarily the disadvantaged and people of color. Although these studies do not overly concern themselves with the cost of elections, they show that including municipal races at the time of statewide or national elections saves money.

Those who defend February elections claim that early and absentee voting allows all voters to participate in democracy. Northwestern University professor Mary McGrath led a study of early voting and found that it favors partisans and older voters but that extending the window for voting does not do much for voter turnout.[10] The votes for mayor shown in table 2.1 include early and absentee votes, yet participation remains low.

Partisan Elections

Another discouragement of democracy is the nonpartisan election. It is no secret that Chicago residents, like those in most northern and eastern urban areas, are predominantly Democratic Party voters. Although Chicago's last partisan mayoral election was in 1995, the last Republican mayor of Chicago was William H. Thompson, whose final term ended in 1931. The same state law that sets municipal elections in February also calls for municipal elections to be nonpartisan. Chicago's mayoral race had long been an exception.

Just after the 1995 municipal election, the Republican-controlled state legislature and the Republican governor passed a change that made the mayoral race nonpartisan in order to conform to aldermanic races. At the time, Mayor Richard M. Daley stated that he was ambivalent about the change, indicating a standoffish indifference.[11] Other commentators claimed that he actually pushed for the legislation so that he would not be vulnerable to a party primary repeat of 1983, when Harold Washington was nominated by the Democrats and assured the election.[12] In that 1983 election, Washington received 37 percent of the vote in the primary, defeating incumbent Jane Byrne with 33 percent and Richard M. Daley with 30 percent. In typical Chicago political style, the change from partisan to nonpartisan municipal elections was enacted with no forewarning, debate, or deliberation.

The idea of a nonpartisan primary election with multiple candidates, followed by a runoff if no candidate receives a majority, gives a loser time to form a coalition against a minority, most likely African American. It would make a "divide and conquer strategy by a black candidate against a white incumbent no longer feasible."[13] Since 1995, the race has gone into a runoff only one time, when García seriously threatened Emanuel. Here, then, was a white incumbent defending himself from a Hispanic challenger.

Although Chicago is Democratic, the idea of offering voters a Republican candidate should not be dismissed. In that fateful 1983 election, after the Democrats had chosen Harold Washington, a relatively unknown Republican, Bernard Epton, received 48 percent of the vote in the general election, coming close to Washington's 51.7 percent. In recent years, the statewide and national elections have resulted in Republican candidates garnering between 17 and 21 percent of the vote in the city of Chicago. In other heavily Democratic cities, the election of a Republican mayor is more common. In New York, Republican

Michael Bloomberg was elected three times, and in Los Angeles, Republican Richard Riordan was elected twice.

What do others say about partisanship in municipal elections? The National League of Cities summarizes findings from a handful of sources. The reasons supporting nonpartisan elections are that (1) parties are irrelevant to providing services and (2) cooperation between elected officials from different parties is more likely. The counter arguments they offer are that (1) the absence of party labels confuses voters; (2) voters then turn to whatever cue is available, often ethnicity; and (3) nonpartisan elections tend to elect leaders more representative of upper socioeconomic status, which only aggravates bias.[14] As table 2.2 shows, eight of the fifteen largest cities in the United States hold partisan municipal elections.

There is little academic literature on partisanship in municipal elections, but one persuasive article is "Teams without Uniforms: The Nonpartisan Ballot in State and Local Elections." From their study of selected races, the authors found that "nonpartisanship depresses turnout and that in nonpartisan contests voters rely less on party and more on incumbency in their voting decisions."[15] While it is not an academic study, the New York Charter Commission cited the fact that New York City is a one-party polity as another reason for a revised charter.

What is the point of offering Republican candidacies in Chicago when the city will likely go Democratic anyway? One advantage is to allow a different policy voice to enter the public debate. While many question whether Republican governance results in improved fiscal order, candidates from that party are more likely to campaign on fiscal issues than Democrats. Republicans who know they have long odds to win might be more likely to challenge the established municipal order than Democrats whose past and future are intertwined with the party organization. There may be, moreover, pockets of voters within the city who might actually prefer a Republican. In the 2014 election, while Illinois gubernatorial candidate Bruce Rauner received only 20.6 percent of Chicago votes, he received a majority in the Forty-Second Ward and came within a fraction of a percentage of winning the Forty-Third Ward. Some claim that the reforms initiated by political activist and later Illinois governor Pat Quinn in 1980, which eliminated three-member districts in the state legislature, were the death knell of the Republican Party in Chicago. Whether it was that reform or the subsequent 1995 change in municipal elections, the result is that Chicago does not host a meaningful Republican organization for any elections.

The consideration of partisan primaries brings up two additional issues that plague Chicago elections. If Chicago is to return to partisan municipal elections, it must reconsider the open primary voting system. Currently, voters need not register their party affiliation and can choose at the polls whichever party ballot they wish to vote. If parties other than the Democrats are to be given a chance to compete, they must be protected from excessive gaming of the elections.

The other matter that is more of a county and statewide problem is the holding of public office by the head of a party organization. Until 2018, Cook County Assessor Joseph Berrios was concurrently the chairman of the Cook County Democratic Organization. In the Illinois House of Representatives, Speaker Michael Madigan is also the chairman of the state Democratic Party. In the past, both Mayor Richard J. Daley and his son Richard M. Daley held party offices. When the office holder also heads the party organization, he or she controls the distribution of campaign funds to other party candidates and, in the absence of a robust primary election, dominates slate making. This practice confers powerful advantages to the incumbent. That is why, when New York City rewrote its charter in 1989, it made it illegal for elected officials to hold party leadership offices.

Encouraging Democracy in Chicago

The timing of municipal elections in Chicago is critical to both democracy and good governance. Not enough deliberation has been given to the effects on voter turnout of a February election in an off year. Voters must brave some of the coldest weather of the season, and the snowbirds—Chicago residents who spend the winter in the Sun Belt—must either vote absentee or skip the election altogether. This latter group is likely to pay higher-than-average taxes and use fewer-than-average city services.

Discouraging turnout encourages special interests. As table 2.1 shows, it takes about 258,000 votes to elect a Chicago mayor (a little over half of the average voter turnout of 515,841). This is less than 10 percent of the people living in Chicago, where five of the six largest employers are units of government. Two of them, the city and the Chicago Public Schools, are local. Between those two units of government alone there are over 80,000 employees, and a similar number of retirees depend upon city pensions for their income. Not all of these retirees still live in Chicago, but there are over 170,000 active and retired participants in the city's pension funds. The potential for Chicago to validate Anzia's assertion that public employee unions hold disproportionate sway is undeniable.

If public employees are disproportionately enfranchised, Republicans are not. As noted above, over time, Republican candidates for governor, senator, or president have received between 17 and 21 percent of votes cast in Chicago. The last time a Republican ran for mayor, however, was 1995, and that candidate was a professional clown. Republicans are certainly discouraged from participating in municipal government, and as a result, the policy differences among Democratic candidates are often smaller than if a minority opposition candidate was on the ballot.

If Chicago is to achieve better governance with more citizen participation, if it is to consider elected school governance, if it is to reform the city council, if it is to vote on bonds and taxes, if it is to elect a city attorney and controller, then it must not work to discourage democracy. Instead, it should change election laws to encourage every voter to participate:

- Change the date of municipal elections to coincide with November general elections in even years or, preferably, the presidential election years.
- Reinstate partisan municipal elections with primaries and general elections at the same time as statewide races.
- Reconsider continuing to allow open primary voting.
- Prohibit office holders from heading party organizations.

These changes would do more to encourage democracy than all the voter registration drives and voter identification initiatives so hotly debated now. Modernizing governance without election changes could destabilize democracy, leave the government open to further capture by special interests, and make matters worse than the present status quo.

CHAPTER 3

Governing the Schools and the City

The citizens of Chicago tax themselves heavily in the interests of public education, and as a body they are honest in their desire for good schools. Why then do their efforts terminate occasionally in such a miserable fiasco as that which has recently attracted the attention of the world? Any attempt to answer this question must carry the inquirer into that complicated and restless sea of social forces which perpetually surround and condition the public schools.
—GEORGE S. COUNTS, *SCHOOL AND SOCIETY IN CHICAGO*, 1928

The setting for the first of three town hall meetings was appropriately chosen and well prepared. Outside Chicago's Malcolm X College, it was a calm and balmy August day. Inside, the gymnasium was set with folding chairs, microphones, and a platform for the mayor and his financial executives from which to listen to comments from the community about the city budget for 2016. There was a security station for those entering and a sign-up sheet for those wishing to speak for the two-minute limit. The meeting plan matched the low-key modesty the new budget would need to embody.

This was the first public town hall budget meeting in three years, an event that had been a tradition under Mayor Richard M. Daley, and it did not go well. Fran Spielman, writing in the *Chicago Sun-Times*, noted: "After his first budget season as mayor, Emanuel had replaced the public hearings with focus groups stacked with sycophants. But this time, he will just have to sit there and take his punishment."[1] The crowd was filled with angry activists pushing for the reopening of Dyett High School in the South Side Washington

Park neighborhood; the school had been closed in the spring, and now Dyett supporters, chanting for its reopening, filled the line of speakers at the microphones. Only a few precious comments about the budget for the City of Chicago got through.

The plan to reinstate these public town halls did not survive the first encounter with the enemy. Three days later, on September 2, 2015, the second meeting was held at the South Shore Cultural Center. Inside the ornate Paul Robeson Theatre, the Dyett activists had a home field advantage, and before the meeting could even get under way, they stormed the stage, causing the mayor's security detail to whisk him away and cancel the meeting.

In a free society, all forms of communication must be tolerated, but the City of Chicago was facing dire financial problems and could ill afford to squander the opening moments of its first town hall meeting in four years on comments, however important, about a separate unit of government with problems of its own. What did the schools have to do with the city's corporate fund or its pensions?

This mayor, who was fresh from a bruising runoff election with a candidate heavily supported by the Chicago Teachers Union, had become quite unpopular during his first term. Coming into office in spring 2011, Mayor Rahm Emanuel faced many critical problems with the Chicago schools. The school district had mounting fiscal problems and a stubborn structural deficit. Changing neighborhood demographics and declining enrollment had left many schools with low occupancy rates. The pension plan had been decimated by years of pension holidays, and in just seven years its funding ratio had plunged from almost 90 percent to below 60 percent. Student achievement, which had been declining, had leveled off but was now languishing, and graduation rates that appeared to be improving would later be found to be inflated by a statistical error. The mayor needed all the political capital he could muster to negotiate a new collective bargaining agreement with teachers when the old one would expire in 2012.

Faced with these problems, the mayor's first initiative was to push for a longer school day and a lengthened school year. Rather than take this up in negotiations for the 2012 contract, he went around the union and, with incentives offered directly to school principals, tried to convince them to go along with the change a year early. The principals agreed, but all the time added to the day ended up in lunch hour and recess. The teachers union was enraged and went on strike the next year, winning a new contract that many considered mayoral capitulation. An ambitious project of the previous mayor had been Renaissance 2010, a plan to rapidly expand charter schools in Chicago. The new contract with the teachers union put an end to the expansive spirit of Renaissance 2010. Later in Emanuel's first term, he closed nearly fifty schools, including Dyett, and incited a firestorm of community grievance and teacher protest.

The mayor was able to set the agenda for the schools because he controls the school board and appoints the chief executive officer for Chicago Public Schools (CPS). The board members and CEO are to pledge loyalty to the mayor, not to the schools.[2] Is it beneficial to the schools that the mayor controls them? Is it beneficial to the city that a mayor can spend his political capital on the schools?

Chicago's School Problems

This book is about the structure of Chicago's government, not about education policy. This chapter is about whether the way Chicago's schools are governed is good for the schools and good for the city. In order to better evaluate structural changes, we must look at the problems that the schools face today and what the foreseeable future holds.

Chicago's schools are a twisted mess of fiscal, demographic, and sociopolitical problems, some of which are self-inflicted while others are universal problems faced everywhere. As of this writing, the Chicago Public Schools are in dire financial condition. Tables 3.1, 3.2, and 3.3 tell the story from 2007 to 2017 and show chronic structural deficits that have been papered over with borrowing. Meanwhile, many recent years of pension holidays have decimated the funding level of the Chicago Teachers' Pension Fund. Ratings agencies have downgraded CPS debt, and bond buyers, if they can be found, are demanding interest rates that are several percentage points (several hundred basis points) above investment-rated municipal bonds. The debt is not being repaid, and the district has failed to make pension payments on time. Tables 3.1 and 3.2 show that grim picture, together with the history of the Chicago Public Schools' financial condition.

The constant struggle of the district to find money merely to operate has taken its toll. In recent years it has lurched from one short-term crisis to another and has failed to implement sustainable long-term financial planning.

TABLE 3.1   Financial Data for Chicago Public Schools: Revenue, Expenditures, and Debt

Fiscal year	Total revenue	Total expenditures	Year end surplus (deficit)	Debt service	Outstanding debt
2007	4,820	4,832	−12	342	4,092
2008	5,018	5,118	−100	260	4,277
2009	5,020	5,692	−673	301	4,222
2010	5,304	5,972	−668	384	4,905
2011	5,660	5,805	−145	332	5,249
2012	5,760	5,840	−79	374	5,594
2013	5,388	5,830	−442	390	6,058
2014	5,437	6,505	−1,068	468	5,945
2015	5,437	6,529	−1,092	534	6,073
2016	5,273	6,136	−864	481	6,579
2017 (end of year estimate)	5,474	5,363	111	n/a	7,700
2018 (proposed)	6,447	6,478	−31	n/a	n/a

Note: Total revenue and expenditures include operating, debt, and capital. Outstanding debt is for general obligation bonds. All figures are dollars in millions.
Source: Greg Hinz, "The Data behind CPS' Hemorrhaging Finances," *Crain's Chicago Business*, August 22, 2017, http://www.chicagobusiness.com/article/20170822/BLOGS02 /170829978/the-data-behind-cps-hemorrhaging-finances.

The mishandling of a lawsuit by the district's CEO gave rise to ethical concerns and cost him his job. Meanwhile these distractions may have caused the district to neglect other problems. In 2018 the State of Illinois found that the district was mishandling its special education practices and took over the administration of this function. At the same time the *Chicago Tribune* uncovered the mishandling of sexual abuse by both employees on students and students on other students.

This critical state of affairs raises two categories of questions: First, is the financial condition a direct result of mayoral control of the schools and would a change in that structure guarantee better fiscal management? Second, what fiscal structures, policies, and practices must CPS consider adopting, whether

TABLE 3.2   Pension Data for Chicago Public Schools

Fiscal year	Student enrollment	Total CPS employees	CPS employer pension contribution ($ millions)	Actuarial unfunded pension liability ($ millions)	Actuarial funded ratio
2007	413,694	Not reported	168.8	2,920	80.5
2008	408,601	44,806	229.3	3,130	79.4
2009	407,955	44,021	263.1	4,140	73.6
2010	409,279	42,942	355.8	5,370	67.1
2011	402,681	41,444	208.6	6,800	59.9
2012	404,151	40,668	203.7	7,980	54.1
2013	403,461	41,827	207.7	9,590	49.7
2014	400,545	39,414	650.4	9,420	51.7
2015	396,683	39,393	708.7	9,590	52.0
2016	392,285	37,921	635.1	9,620	52.5
2017 (end-of-year estimate)	381,349	37,087	680.4	n/a	n/a
2018 (proposed)	372,684	36,511	719.4	n/a	n/a

Source: Greg Hinz, "The Data behind CPS' Hemorrhaging Finances," Crain's Chicago Business, August 22, 2017, http://www.chicagobusiness.com/article/20170822 /BLOGS02/170829978/the-data-behind-cps-hemorrhaging-finances.

or not mayoral appointment is ended? These questions will be considered later in this chapter.

The demographic challenge for the schools is twofold. First, student enrollment is declining. Second, the gap between those who pay for the schools and those who attend is widening. A *Chicago Sun-Times* study showed that just eight wards in or near downtown provide over 50 percent of tax revenue, and just one ward, the Forty-Second, provides a full 25 percent.[3] These taxpayers include urban professional workers who have no children attending Chicago Public Schools, retirees, and businesses employing a large proportion of suburbanites.

The sociopolitical problem has to do with school choice. Within the boundaries of the Chicago Public School District, the past two decades have seen the emergence of dozens of charter and magnet schools. These schools are allowed by their charters to operate differently and often receive significant funding from philanthropists, some of whom live outside the school district. Parents have favored many of these schools and students have flocked to them while the Chicago Teachers Union, along with other teacher unions in the state and nationally, have stiffened their opposition to the charter movement. Meanwhile, the past fifty years have seen a 25 percent decline in Chicago's population, from over 3.6 million to near 2.7 million. Much of the out-migration has been to the suburbs, and much of it has been driven by parents' desires for better schools for their children.

The political debate centers on whether primary and secondary education is a right, a public good, or a private good. While it is beyond the scope of this book to argue the different sides of that debate, the choices that are being made by parents nationwide provide a practical answer. The majority of parents in all socioeconomic groups think that education for their children is what economists call a superior good, a good whose consumption increases as income increases. It stretches this definition a little to say that parents are less concerned about what specifically their children learn as long as their education is superior to that of others. They want the best education they can afford. They consume this education by moving to communities, often suburbs, where the taxes are higher but the schools are superior. Or they send their children to private or parochial schools. A growing number devote significant personal effort to homeschooling. For the same reasons, parents who live in Chicago and want a superior education for their children will choose a charter or magnet school. This demand for superior education is a worldwide phenomenon in the modern age.

Set against this private and fundamental urge is the political notion that education for our children is a right. This is why governments around the world seek to offer public education, and why state constitutions like the one in Illinois explicitly address this matter. The Illinois Constitution states that educational development is a goal; the state shall provide it free for secondary students, and the state shall have primary responsibility for financing it. As a result, there are constant efforts to reform education funding in order to make it equitable for all students in the state. At the local level, the fight is against special treatment of charter schools at the expense of public schools.

Here, then, are three significant challenges that the Chicago public schools must grapple with: failing finances, multiple demographic discontinuities, and the socioeconomic problem of school choice. Over the coming decades, other challenges will surely emerge, and Chicagoans might see hints of them even today.

Not all of the news for CPS is negative. A 2017 study by a Stanford University group found meaningful improvement in test scores at CPS for the lower grades.[4] Still, scores are below the national averages, and it remains to be seen if the district can maintain the current rate of improvement in an atmosphere of turmoil and challenge.

The Immediacy and Imperative of Fiscal Improvement

The dire fiscal condition of CPS casts an oppressive shadow over everything affecting the schools. Even if there is no change in governance, the schools struggle to operate under financial pressures; any change in governance will be doomed to failure if it is greeted with unresolved fiscal problems. These problems are nothing new, but what must be new is their sustainable resolution.

For much of the past one hundred years, CPS has struggled with fiscal problems. In the depths of the Great Depression, teachers were given promissory scrip instead of paychecks, only then to endure payless paydays.[5] In 1980, the State of Illinois took over the schools to remedy fiscal distress. It created a state School Finance Authority (SFA) so that banks would lend to the schools. "The SFA was empowered to abrogate labor contracts, downsize the central office, and even close schools in order to force a balanced budget."[6] Although the SFA was meant to operate for three years, it held on, but it made little fiscal progress until 1995, when the schools were turned back over to Mayor Richard M. Daley. As of this writing, a gaping deficit in the CPS budget seems to have been partially filled by a state education funding bill that provides temporary but illusory relief. A structural deficit remains, and the bond rating agencies have not upgraded the district's debt.

In chapter 4 we discuss the structural deficit and poor fiscal practices of the City of Chicago. Those same practices and lack of discipline are contagious, having infected the budget of the school district. The structural deficit is created by significant expenses that are unpredictable, rising, and out of control, together with revenues that are not allowed to keep pace with the normal growth of spending. Table 3.3 provides an eight-year look at this condition.

There are five conditions whose trends contribute to the CPS structural deficit: pensions, charters, debt service, local revenue, and teachers' salaries.

TABLE 3.3   Selected Chicago Public Schools Financial Information and Enrollment

		2008	2012	2016	Percentage change, 2008–16
Total revenues		$5,018	$5,760	$5,273	5
	Local	$2,296	$2,859	$2,911	27
	State	$1,846	$1,965	$1,552	−16
	Federal	$876	$936	$809	−8
Total expenses		$5,118	$5,840	$6,136	20
Selected expenses	Teachers' pension	$350	$335	$811	132
	Charter school payments	$189	$424	$705	273
	Debt service	$282	$374	$480	70
	Teachers' salaries	$1,885	$2,027	$1,870	−1
Selected characteristics	Total enrollment	408,601	404,151	392,285	−4
	Charter school enrollment	22,484	49,005	57,519	156
	Remaining CPS enrollment	386,117	355,146	334,766	−13

Note: Dollars in millions.
Source: *CPS Comprehensive Annual Financial Reports*, https://cps.edu/About_CPS Financial_information/Documents/FY16_CAFR.pdf; and Illinois Network of Charter Schools from Illinois State Board of Education Fall Enrollment Counts, https://www. incschools.org/tableau/?post=32&type=enrollment_facts&index=2-1.

Pension payments are the blob that is consuming the CPS budget and crowding out expenditures for current operations. Table 3.3 shows the effect that pension holidays have had on expenses. The teachers' pension fund has now been depleted to below 50 percent, a calculation made with optimistic discount rates. The popular complaint about the sad state of pensions is that the government just did not keep up its funding between 2007 and 2016. Funding for that period would have required an additional $7 billion, which, when combined with the total $9 billion of deficits for that period, amounts to $16 billion that would have been required to properly manage finances for the nine-year period. CPS would have needed an additional $1.8 billion a year. With approximately $2.3 billion in local taxes for 2006, this would mean that taxes should have been raised by about 78 percent in that year. This is the financial pain that was deferred, and which future generations will have to pay for.

Catching up the pension debt is problematic. When the pension holiday ends, CPS must catch up funding to 90 percent over the next forty years. The schedule for these payments is calculated as 43 percent of current year payroll, which is assumed to be increasing every year. As a result, the lion's share of pension catch-up payments is made in the later years of the schedule and causes the burden to be significantly back loaded. This funding method is dishonest, because teacher salaries are not increasing. A more realistic policy would be a level dollar amount of annual funding, which would require annual payments by CPS of about $1.5 billion. Even then the amount might have to be adjusted upward if discount rates or mortality tables are negatively revised. This is more fully discussed in the chapter on pensions, but even these brief comments show that the funding problem must be addressed now in order to correct the persisting structural problem. Even if the numbers become more honest, the catch-up funding dumps a huge legacy cost onto the young and unborn.

CPS is caught in a charter bind. The government pays CPS to educate children in Chicago. CPS in turn charters schools to operate and is itself the paymaster for these charter schools. Currently, CPS is expected to reimburse charter schools for approximately the same per student cost that it incurs for the total school population based upon its budget. This rather new formula is called student-based budgeting (SBB). Under this arrangement, CPS estimates the total cost of educating each student but only receives outside aid for a portion of that cost. It must, however, forward to the charter school the full cost per student. With the decline in enrollment in CPS schools due to charter growth, CPS increasingly will be forwarding more money than the costs it is incurring. The result is that CPS revenues are increasing at the rate of 5 percent over eight years at the same time charter expenditures are rising 273 percent. CPS is still on the hook for high fixed costs as the charter payments siphon off significant marginal revenue.

The third destabilizing expenditure on CPS books is debt service, which constitutes mostly annual interest costs since no debt is being retired. Interest costs on general obligation debt incurred because of prior deficits are the empty calories in the budget. They contribute nothing to education but consume precious resources. Since they represent the wages of prior sins, they must be paid for with local taxes. Neither the state nor federal government wishes to subsidize this continually rising expense. As the numbers show, debt service, like unfunded pensions, if left unchecked, will eventually devour the budget.

The only source of revenue that CPS currently has control over is local property taxes. As of 2016, these revenues have risen imperceptibly just as state and federal aid has declined. In 2017, a significant increase in local property taxes championed by the mayor went into effect as major education funding reform was passed at the state level. This was a huge legislative undertaking that cost state legislators significant political capital. It is not likely to be repeated anytime soon. Nevertheless, the relentless pressure from pensions, charters, and debt service will require significant new local revenue. The 2017 action was a temporary patch; the structural deficit remains.

Teacher salaries are the district's largest expenditure and drive the structural deficit. Looking solely at the numbers, the total dollars spent on teachers' salaries has remained stable. The mirage here, though, is that over the eight-year period, the same amount of money is being spent to teach 13 percent fewer students. If teachers' salaries had kept parity with the decline in enrollment, salaries would have decreased $243 million. Either the number of teachers was not reduced or the rate of compensation increase nullified any productivity increases implemented by the school administration. According to statistics compiled by the National Council on Teacher Quality, Chicago teachers are some of the highest paid in the country, higher than the similarly large school districts of New York and Los Angeles.[7] Somehow CPS is not managing to reduce expenditures as net enrollment declines. On the other hand, a look at the annual report of the Chicago Catholic Schools shows an organization that has managed a more drastic decline in enrollment while maintaining fiscal health and strong student achievement.[8] This report even claims that the Chicago Catholic Schools have saved CPS $532 million in the 2015–2016 school year by educating Chicago children. The management of CPS teachers' salaries is a major factor that contributes to the structural deficit with, as elsewhere, a multiplier effect on teachers' pensions.

When the same deficits, debt, pension trouble, and structural problems that plague the city also plague the schools, it is difficult to argue that mayoral control has helped. State control of the schools helped by granting the School Finance Authority powers that CPS does not currently hold. Whether the city were to move to elected control of the schools or retain mayoral control, there are certain fiscal changes that must be implemented to give CPS a fighting chance of staying out of fiscal trouble.

The pension problem must be resolved. The city needs either to get out from under the obligation for the plan or to secure dedicated funding for honest and level annual payments that will not present the budget with nasty surprises. The Chicago Teachers' Pension Fund is the only teachers' pension fund in Illinois that is funded from the local school budget. All other school districts have their pension liability funded by the State of Illinois. If CPS could transfer this obligation to the state along with accepting a commensurate decrease in state aid, it would rid itself of a volatile component of the structural deficit. If CPS cannot muster the formidable political forces to accomplish this, it should reschedule its pension debt to provide for level dollar amounts of payments each year and then assess a special dedicated fixed-dollar tax to cover these payments. The use of dedicated revenue streams to retire legacy debt, while undesirable, is not uncommon. In 1975, when New York City got into severe financial trouble and formed the Municipal Acceptance Corporation, it imposed stiff taxes for a limited period of time to pay down the unsecured debts that had accrued. In Chicago in 2017, the city refinanced $3 billion of debt and dedicated sales tax revenue to improve the debt's rating and lower interest costs. We shall call this plan defeasance. The level dollar pension payment and tax should be considered in the context of a long-term financial plan for CPS, one that reduces the remaining tax burden for current operations and other long-term needs of the district. In the pension chapter of this study, other solutions for the city's pension problems are discussed more fully; the solutions discussed here should be considered in light of those other proposals.

The outsized general obligation debt of CPS must be eliminated in the same manner as the pension debt: with defeasance. Keep in mind that this debt is not like normal school debt, where taxes are raised (generally with voter approval) to fund a new school and then, when the bonds are paid off, the taxes go back down. The current debt was incurred without raising taxes. It is time to raise those taxes, pay off the debt over a short period of time, perhaps ten years, and then free the district of this drag. To pay down a debt of

$7.5 billion over ten years at a 6 percent rate will require annual payments of approximately $1 billion. If current debt service costs are around $500 million, then amortizing the debt will require another $500 million of new taxes.

CPS must plan better for the funding of charter schools. It must work out a long-range financial plan that involves both teachers and charter schools. Such a plan must look ten years out and incorporate charter growth, declining enrollment, and teacher and classroom planning. Such a plan will be painful to develop, and it will not come about without conflict. The teachers' labor contract signed in 2017 included a rare cap on the creation of charter schools, but many think that this limit will not hold forever. Rather than an annual crisis of school closings, layoffs, deficits, and battle with the charter schools, a long-range plan would allow all parties—children, parents, teachers, and charters—to see their choices into the future. If charter schools are allowed to grow, their expansion must be controlled and guaranteed so that CPS can plan reductions in capacity accordingly.

Making headway in tackling the fiscal problems of the district must take into account at least two practices that are widespread in other major cities and districts: obtaining the approval of voters for taxes and bonds and the outlawing of teacher strikes. Most other school districts are required to obtain voter approval before they can raise taxes or issue bonds. Granted, it may prove impossible to get voters to approve raising taxes dedicated for pension and debt defeasance, in which case state legislation might be required. Beyond that, however, future debt or tax action should be approved by the voters.

A central element of the relationship between the district and the CTU is the teachers' strike. Illinois is one of the few states where such strikes are legal, and it is second only to Pennsylvania in the number of teachers' strikes between 2010 and 2015.[9] Table 3.5 shows how few school districts allow strikes at all. Many think that recent teacher contracts that are entered into after a strike (or even on the brink of a threatened strike) have not satisfactorily bargained in the interest of taxpayers and students. Chicago and the State of Illinois must look at their labor laws to see if these laws contribute to high education costs and budget instability.

Controlling costs, managing a decline in enrollment, and dealing with the disruption of charter schools will involve, and have a direct impact on, the CTU. Such dealings are best undertaken in an atmosphere of mutual trust and respect. For all the reasons discussed elsewhere in this study, the governance of the entire city of Chicago has not contributed to such trust. It is the authors' overarching premise that a different governance structure would contribute to developing such trust. Whether or not governance changes take place, and whether or not CPS can generate sufficient trust with the CTU, it will still need to work out the long-term fiscal plan described above. The Chicago Public Schools cannot afford annual crises, and it cannot afford *not* to tackle the big problems.

The aforementioned problems and solutions are not easy. Any leader who says that correcting for decades of poor fiscal practices can be solved simply or that the burden should be put on only one party is posturing, not leading. The example of New York City in 1975 is illustrative. As discussed earlier, New York City reached the end of its fiscal rope after decades of the same practices that now plague CPS. Solving the problem required outside intervention: the creation of entities like the Municipal Acceptance Corporation (MAC), the imposition of new taxes dedicated to paying off legacy debts, and the overriding of labor contracts and collective bargaining rights. If the city and CPS can take action before a crisis, it can better manage the pain all will have to endure. If the crisis comes first, before measures like these are taken, the school district will lurch from one disingenuous temporary patch after another. The measures imposed in that situation would also likely have to come from outside. Only when the fiscal house is in order should the schools consider changing its governance structure.

Other Cities and the Largest School Districts

The question, then, is what structure will best serve the decision making that will manage the many challenges that the Chicago schools face. What can we learn from other cities? A glance at selected characteristics of other big-city school districts, shown in table 3.4, places Chicago among its peers. The source for this data is the school districts' fact sheets. There are no standards for preparing these documents, so there are some inconsistencies among them. What these comparative data show, though, is how diverse the job of management is for the top fifteen cities that are the subject of this book.

A look at the nation's top school districts (table 3.5) shows a different set of circumstances. These data are older than those in table 3.4, and some inconsistencies remain; nevertheless, the numbers reflect broad trends and governance features. In many cases, large cities do not have the largest school districts.

TABLE 3.4   Selected Data for Schools, Top Fifteen US Cities

	Population, 2014	Total students	Total teachers	Ratio	Total staff	Teacher/ staff ratio	Student racial makeup		
							Hispanic	Black	Other
New York	8,491,079	1,038,727	92,624	11.2	116,000	0.80	49.9	30.3	19.8
Los Angeles	3,928,864	734,641	26,556	27.7	60,191	0.44	72.3	9.6	17.8
Chicago	2,722,389	381,349	19,757	19.3	29,476	0.67	47	37.7	15.8
Houston	2,239,558	215,627	11,854	18.2	29,402	0.40	62.1	24.5	13.4
Philadelphia	1,560,297	131,362	18,390	7.1	N/A	N/A	20.0	50.0	30.0
Phoenix	1,537,058	—	—	—	—	—	—	—	—
San Antonio	1,436,697	55,086	3,437	16.0	7,632	0.45	7.4	89.5	4.1
San Diego	1,381,069	131,252	6,000	21.9	13,559	0.44	46.5	10.2	43.3
Dallas	1,281,047	160,253	10,518	15.2	20,757	0.51	69.8	23.4	6.8
San Jose	1,015,785	33,184	1,750	19.0	3,000	0.58	8.0	53.0	39.0
Austin	912,791	82,776	6,244	13.3	12,227	0.51	58.1	7.5	34.4
Jacksonville	853,382	128,702	8,284	15.5	11,876	0.70	10.0	44.0	46.0
San Francisco	852,469	55,613	5,174	10.7	9,992	0.52	27.0	7.0	66.0
Indianapolis	848,788	30,097	2,579	11.7	4,090	0.63	N/A	N/A	N/A
Columbus	835,957	50,809	4,166	12.2	6,571	0.63	6.7	58.0	35.3

Note: Phoenix does not have a unified school district. *N/A* = information not available.

TABLE 3.5   Selected Data for the Top Twenty US School Districts, by Enrollment

School District	Enrollment	Total expenditures ($ millions)	Expenditures per student ($)	Appointed school board	Elected school board	Voter approval on bonds and taxes[a]	Teacher right to strike[b]
New York City	990,145	24,814	25,061	x		Yes	No
Los Angeles	659,639	8,898	13,490		x	Yes	No
Chicago	403,004	5,741	14,246	x		No	Yes
Miami-Dade	350,239	3,407	9,729		x	Yes	No
Las Vegas–Clark County	313,398	2,860	9,125		x	Yes	No
Broward County, Florida	258,478	2,318	8,968		x	Yes	No
Houston	203,066	2,356	11,601		x	Yes	No
Hillsborough County–Tampa	197,041	1,917	9,728		x	Yes	No
Hawaii State	182,706	2,345	12,833	x		No	Yes
Orange County–Orlando	180,000	1,768	9,824		x	Yes	No
Fairfax County, Virginia	177,606	2,575	14,495		x	Yes	No
Palm Beach County, Florida	176,901	1,777	10,045		x	Yes	No
Gwinnet County, Georgia	162,370	1,590	9,794		x	Yes	No
Dallas	157,575	1,901	12,061		x	Yes	No
Philadelphia	154,262	2,814	18,241	x		Yes	Yes

TABLE 3.5 (*continued*)

School District	Enrollment	Total expenditures ($ millions)	Expenditures per student ($)	Appointed school board	Elected school board	Voter approval on bonds and taxes[a]	Teacher right to strike[b]
Wake County–Charlotte, North Carolina	148,154	1,353	9,135		x	Yes	No
Montgomery County, Maryland	146,459	2,646	18,073		x	No	No
Charlotte–Mecklenburg, North Carolina	141,728	1,242	8,763		x	Yes	No
San Diego	131,044	1,429	10,904		x	Yes	No
Jacksonville, Florida	125,429	1,132	9,024		x	Yes	No
Average expenditures per student ($)				17,595	10,922		

[a] "State by State Comparison of School Bond and Tax Laws," Ballotpedia, https://ballotpedia.org/State-by-state_comparison_of_school_bond_and_tax _laws. Note that all cities in Illinois require voter approval except Chicago.

[b] "Teachers' Unions/Collective Bargaining: State and Local Laws," FindLaw, http://education.findlaw.com/teachers-rights/teacher-s-unions-collective -bargaining-state-and-local-laws.html.

Source: "Analysis of School District Spending 2011–2012 School Year," Ballotpedia, November 17, 2014, https://ballotpedia.org/Analysis_of_spending_in _America%27s_largest_school_districts.

Table 3.5 tells many stories. Not all large cities have large or unified school districts; smaller cities (and even one entire state) often contain unified school districts. It is customary in the southern United States for the county to house one such unified school district, while in the western states there are often multiple school districts in a large city. Table 3.5 conspicuously illustrates how only a minority of school districts are appointed by either a mayor or governor. Also conspicuous is the significant difference in overall expenditures per student between the average appointed board and the average elected one. Although the literature on school governance claims that mayoral control of schools results in lower per student costs, the evidence clearly contradicts this claim. Table 3.5 also shows which school districts allow teachers to strike. Although not unheard of elsewhere, teachers' strikes such as those experienced by Chicago are not widespread.

Aside from these cursory observations it is difficult to make a comparative study of governance structure in education; there is simply too much diversity. Instead, there is a modest amount of literature on school governance that is worth consideration.

Scholarship on Mayoral Control of Public Schools

In 2007 and 2008, there were a number of studies by scholars looking at what was called mayor-centric governance of public education. Most of these studies recite a history that begins in the nineteenth century, when urban public education grew with the migration of Americans off the farms and into cities. Like every aspect of urban life at the time, education was dominated by corrupt and ineffectual political machines. As the Progressive movement at the beginning of the twentieth century sought to clean up government, it successfully advocated for school systems run by elected school boards, which subsequently became the norm. By the end of the twentieth century, urban public schools had taken a political beating, and the narrative of elected but dysfunctional school boards gained acknowledgment. By 2007, mayors and state governments had taken control of some key big-city school districts, or at least tried to do so. Scholars looked at this trend as perhaps inevitable and felt there had been enough experience to attempt some objective conclusions.

Perhaps the best overview of the research on school board governance is by Frederick M. Hess, director of Education Policy Studies at the American Enterprise Institute. Hess quotes Eli Broad (2003): "I believe in mayoral control of school boards or no school board at all. We have seen many children benefit from this type of crisis intervention." Hess also quotes Chester E. Finn Jr.: "Schools boards are an aberration, an anachronism, an educational sinkhole." Nevertheless, Hess finds that "those who have studied mayoral board appointment are generally equivocal about the idea."[10] He finds that much of the research replicates or repurposes a limited number of case studies that often focus on racial composition, not on other aspects of the public education enterprise. From his review, Hess identifies five common criticisms of elected boards and five criticisms of mayoral appointed boards.

According to Hess, elected school boards often fail to provide accountability because elections are rigged, being held at times to minimize turnout; this results in public apathy. This apathy in turn allows mobilized constituencies, especially teachers' unions, to exert a disproportionate influence. Elected boards can lack coherence and continuity, as members "feel they must undertake everything all at once."[11] The boards themselves lack discipline and tend to micromanage, not focusing on essential tasks. And finally such boards operate in isolation from both the mayor and city political and civic leadership.

On the other hand, mayor-appointed boards have their own disadvantages. Politically self-conscious mayors seek to control data, and as a result such boards can lose transparency. Voices are likely to be silenced as collegial boards may be reluctant to ask uncomfortable questions or raise unpleasant issues. Appointed boards may "go native" as politically savvy mayors reach comfortable accommodations with unions and major service providers. Mayors may get caught up in politicizing school boards or ignore schools altogether as they pursue other pressing concerns. And it is not clear that elected boards are as dysfunctional as feared. "Skeptics acknowledge that urban school governance is troubled but argue that mayoral control is unlikely to help and may bring unwelcome side effects."[12]

In 2004, Jeffrey R. Henig and Wilbur Rich, from Columbia University and Wellesley College respectively, devoted an entire contributed volume to mayoral control of schools, *Mayors in the Middle: Politics, Race, and Mayoral Control of Urban Schools*. This work centers its analysis on case studies of six cities: Baltimore, Chicago, Boston, Detroit, Cleveland, and Washington, DC. At the conclusion, Kenneth J. Meier analyzes them, questioning the very logic of mayoral control. What are the reasons for a change to mayoral control, and why may those reasons not be valid? The reasons echo those of Hess. Meier's discussion involves cities moving to mayoral control; as Chicago has always had such control, some of the arguments should be viewed inversely as reasons to move away from mayoral control. Meier makes the following suggestions:

- An increase in mayoral control must adjust to the local politics. Mayoral control does not remove politics from school governance.
- To the extent that politicians are interested in goals other than educational quality, mayoral reform is likely to produce results that do not affect the school system's performance, or that affect performance at best only indirectly and with a higher probability of unintended consequences. If a mayor's goals include avoiding tax increases, then burdening the schools with deficits, debt, and unfunded pensions are the unintended consequences.
- Simply changing a structure is no assurance that school leaders will be more competent or less corrupt than the representative of the smaller constituency.
- Mayor-dominated structures interact and are affected by the personalities and tactics of the specific mayor.
- In education policy, the sustained effort necessary to reform a school system might well be too long for any politician's term in office.

Meier is one of those skeptics: "These practical limitations imply that structural reforms may not produce the benefits that advocates suggest. The relationship between greater mayoral control over education and the quality of education remains, at best, and empirical question, and at worst, a major risk."[13]

A 2008 book edited by Thomas L. Alsbury contains two concluding chapters on the issue of mayoral control.[14] Both chapters are unequivocal in their support for mayoral control. The first of these, written by Thomas E. Glass, recites the benefits of mayoral control mostly in terms of the failures of elected boards. Glass does not evaluate the failure of mayoral boards or the many reasons that elected boards are so dysfunctional and ineffective. The other chapter, by Kenneth K. Wong and Francis X. Shen, is also unequivocal in its support for mayor-centric school governance. Wong and Shen go further and introduce what they call "integrated governance," which suggests that government must take into account all stakeholders in a holistic manner; elected boards and interest groups are too fragmented to do so. The centerpiece of this article is an empirical analysis of 104 school districts in forty states. The analysis sought to correlate two factors of school district performance with the level of mayoral control: elementary school reading performance and per-pupil revenues. The study showed quite modest improvement of reading performance in mayor-centric systems and lower per-pupil revenue. Wong and Shen sum up: "Synthesizing the findings of our analysis of mayors and school finances, we believe that the big picture story is one in which new style mayors are being more strategic in prioritizing their resource allocation and management. Central to this strategy is the notion that fiscal discipline is constraining labor costs."[15]

After this flourish of studies, the topic does not appear to have been revisited by scholars. Likewise there has been no new case where a major city switched from an elected board to mayoral appointment. Los Angeles tried this over ten years ago, but the plan was rejected by the courts.[16]

If the trend toward mayoral control was so inevitable and favored by so many influential philanthropists and thinkers, why did it stall? The only plausible explanation is that public education was just beginning to be disrupted by the charter school movement. A battle had broken out on a new front.

What Should Chicago Do?

Chicago's school board and the CEO of the school district are appointed by the mayor. Only four of the largest twenty school districts in the United States are governed by appointed boards of education; the remainder are elected. Repeatedly over the years, there have been calls for Chicago to change to an elected school board. As recently as January 2017, legislation was introduced yet again in the Illinois General Assembly to elect Chicago's school board.[17] Opinion polls and advisory ballot referendums have overwhelmingly favored such a change. As of this writing, a major civil rights lawsuit initiated by the former governor of Illinois that was wending its way through the courts seeking a change to an elected board has been dismissed.[18]

While other cities are newcomers to mayoral control of the schools, Chicago schools have been overseen by the mayor in one form or another since public education began in the city. The 1870 Illinois Constitution provided for Chicago schools to be governed by a state law that put jurisdiction for schools in the mayor's hands. Over the years, there have been many variations of such mayoral control. In 1980, in the midst of yet another fiscal crisis, Chicago schools were taken over by the state-appointed Chicago School Finance Authority (CSFA). Another reform in 1988 gave some power to local groups in the form of the local school councils (LSCs), but the CSFA stayed in the picture. By 1995, the state had tired of its responsibility and turned the schools over directly to the mayor of Chicago, who then appointed the board and hired the board president.

The issue of mayoral control of Chicago schools may yet change dramatically. The lawsuit that was making its way through the courts may resurface. Even if that does not happen, the introduction of legislation in the Illinois General Assembly to switch to an elected board is a perennial affair, and it might very well find a sufficient backing. If nothing happens on either front, we are still faced with determining the best governance structure.

From the scholarly literature and conventional wisdom there are a handful of reasons that an elected board should be avoided. These reasons deserve a closer look and can be easily challenged.

Elected boards fail to provide accountability because elections are rigged, voter turnout is abnormally low, and voters become apathetic. This is a real problem, but it already exists in Chicago. As we have seen, municipal elections in Chicago are held the last Tuesday in February of the odd year, and turnout is historically the lowest of any elections. This must change, regardless of school governance structure.

Election of school board members can leave the schools vulnerable to control or capture by the special interests, especially the teachers' union. In the 2015 mayoral election the teachers' union handpicked their candidate, Jesús "Chuy" Garcia, to run for mayor. The union encouraged him to run, becoming one of his biggest campaign contributors. In the February election, his candidacy was successful at depriving the incumbent mayor of the 50 percent plus one vote majority needed to avoid a runoff. With low voter turnout, sympathetic support from other public- and private-sector unions, and no other organized civic group to oppose them, the teachers' union could easily capture the schools and the city to boot.

Elected boards micromanage the schools, introduce du jour changes, and lack the discipline to tackle essential tasks. A new mayor undertaking as his first initiative to lengthen both the school day and the school year—at a time when finances and pensions are crumbling—demonstrates that elected school boards do not hold a monopoly on such behavior.

A separately elected board may operate in isolation to the city and civic leadership. The case of the Dyett school protests, which drowned out dialogue about the city budget, demonstrates that a greater degree of isolation could benefit both the schools and the city. The erosion of the political capital of a mayor because of controversial school decisions, mismanagement, or corruption can impair that mayor's ability to manage other city affairs satisfactorily. Two of the three school CEOs appointed by the current mayor have resigned over ethical concerns, and one has been sentenced to prison. In Washington, DC, the troubled popularity of a controversial schools chancellor, Michelle Rhee, was identified as the primary reason for the failure of the mayor who appointed her to win reelection.[19]

Mayoral appointed boards are more capable and more likely to practice fiscal discipline and control labor costs. The mayor of Chicago has governed the city's schools as long as there have been public schools in Chicago, and for just as long there have been chronic fiscal problems. The appointed board has not proven that it can balance budgets, and in recent years the tolerance for fiscal irresponsibility on the part of the city seems to have infected sister entities, most notably the schools.

Although these observations all seem to point toward moving to an elected school board, such a change would be quite a departure from what Chicago residents and government are accustomed to. There is much more to municipal governance than just this one issue; such a decision should be placed in the context of other measures.

There are two areas where changes should take place before school board governance is considered. Some of these changes should accompany a change in governance if it is forced by a court or state legislation. Before the city tackles the school board issue, it should undertake the fundamental changes in city governance discussed elsewhere in this book: it should make reforms to the city council, make the city controller an elected position, demonstrate control over city finances, and make the municipal elections more competitive to increase turnout. Then certain changes need to be made at CPS, regardless of whether it goes from mayoral control to an elected board. The changes to financial practices, solving the pension problem, and adopting certain changes to labor practices, including outlawing teacher strikes, will contribute to a healthier state of affairs and give elected school governance a fighting chance of success.

The literature concerning school governance speaks of many appointed and electoral configurations that have been tried over the years. These include a nominating committee to present board candidates to a mayor for appointment, election of board members either by district or at large, or some combination of appointed and elected board members. The latter may very well be the governance structure that results from pending litigation or proposed legislation.

On the other hand, there is an untried structure that might be worth considering. In Chicago, citizens may wish to elect just one person, as is currently the practice with the mayor, and hold him or her accountable for the schools. This could entail electing a single school overseer or elector who would in turn appoint school board members. Such an elector would be independent of the mayor's office and board members could not, once appointed, be removed until the end of their term except for cause. If there is concern that adopting a full-scale elected school board might open the schools to governance capture by the unions, then restricting governance to one elected person who is not the mayor might be a way to prevent such an outcome. There could be a requirement that those running for overseer never have had an affiliation with the teachers' union, take no campaign support from the teachers' union, and appoint no board members that have a like affiliation. Electing one school authority could satisfy the desire voters have for the one-person accountability some profess with the current mayoral arrangement. At the least, it might serve as a transitional arrangement on the way from an appointed board to a fully elected school board.

As compelling as a change in school governance might seem, it must not be taken lightly. The conservative approach described above might well be necessary to minimize unintended consequences and build confidence in independent decision making.

Disruption

Recent years have been described as the age of disruption, most conspicuously seen in shopping, transportation, and hotels. Public education, especially in urban school districts, has also been significantly disrupted. Decades ago, public education was a rather homogenous middle-class undertaking. This equilibrium was first disrupted when families in more established cities fled to the suburbs, leaving the urban areas with a concentration of problems. For many years, it was the government, foundations, and philanthropists who took an active interest in reform and innovation to help those urban areas. Then, about twenty years ago, another phase of disruption dawned.

Four major upheavals to public education emerged. First and foremost was the advent of charter schools, which began two decades ago in Minnesota. Along with charters came talk of vouchers, which have been adopted in several major cities. Both charters and vouchers represent school choice. The former is a seamless opportunity for students to choose another government-funded school within their district. Vouchers give students portable money which they can spend at either private or religious schools. Homeschooling, a third disruption, grew rapidly, especially in suburban and rural areas; it seems, however, to have plateaued. And finally, the proliferation of testing, measuring educational performance, and rating of schools and education has changed the way public education is conducted.

Charter schools have proliferated in Chicago. Enrollment has grown from zero to over 57,000. All of the top Chicago high schools are either charter schools or have selective enrollment. Students must apply to these schools; by definition, therefore, they are chosen by students. Charters are more popular with high school students, who can use public transportation to get to school on their own, as compared to elementary schools, where charter schools are fewer.[20] A recent study by a University of Chicago Consortium found that charter high schools in Chicago compared favorably to district schools on several measures, but there was significant variation in the quality of those high schools.[21] The growth and popularity of charters in Chicago mirrors the nationwide trend.

Disagreement over whether charters are superior to public schools, and whether the existence of charter schools is good for public schools, is perennial. Charter operators claim that, while some of their peers fail to do an adequate job, the vast majority result in significantly better outcomes. Opponents led by the teachers' union attempt to indict all charters with the failure of the few and claim that the disruption from charters dumps financial and social burdens onto the public schools. Many independent studies find that charters are on balance better both for charter and district students; indeed, the competition they provide improves the public schools themselves. The one unassailable fact is that charters are very popular with parents who do not have the means to move out of the city and cannot afford private or religious schools.

Charter schools are authorized by the Chicago Public Schools, but they differ from district schools in several ways. They are not covered by the same collective bargaining agreement that covers CPS schools. Some charters have unions, some do not. Some charter schools do not offer participation in a retirement comparable to that of CPS. And charter schools are governed by state requirements for the length of the school year, not Chicago mandates for the length of the school day and school year. If a charter application to CPS is denied, the school may appeal to the Illinois State Charter School Commission. In the discussion of school finances, we saw how the fiscal dynamics of payments to charter schools is harmful to the budget. The fact that charter schools have this troubled arrangement with CPS creates a battleground in the halls of the district offices between the teachers' union and charters.

From the time that charters were introduced and during the Renaissance initiative of the preceding mayor they experienced rapid growth that is now in jeopardy. In 2016, a school strike was averted at the last minute by a contract that put a cap on the number of charter schools and students in Chicago. After the contract was signed, there was disagreement over what the terms actually allowed.[22] This cap could be lifted when the next contract is negotiated, but once it has made its way into contract language it will be difficult to remove. That same year, charters sought approval to open twenty-one new campuses, yet none were approved by CPS. More permanent and ominous for charters is the pending combination of independent charter unions with the Chicago Teachers Union. Some feel that the capture of charter growth by the union could spell the end of improvement and opportunity for Chicago students and their schools.

Charters have clearly disrupted the Chicago Public Schools and have created a further problem for a district that was ill-equipped to deal with them. In other states and cities, charters are overseen by a university or state board. Such a governance structure might be desirable for Chicago, but there is one major obstacle: revenue. Unlike those other states and cities, local property taxes are levied by CPS and represent well over 50 percent of total revenue. Charters put CPS in a real financial difficulty, and this is a chief reason for teachers' union resistance. With demand for charters growing, and with a resistance that is effectively placing a moratorium on expansion, it is becoming both obvious and urgent that a more capable governance structure be found to channel disruption in a sustainable manner, one that addresses the educational appetites of parents. Solving the fiscal problems and developing a more trusting and collaborative relationship between CPS and CTU must go hand in hand with a change in governance.

Another development that has disrupted the public schools in the past twenty years is the proliferation and publication of school-level performance data, together with a corresponding influence of the state and federal government over public education. Teachers abhor testing requirements that force them to teach to the test instead of what they feel the students need. Administrators fear the consequences of poor test results and find that testing pits them against the wishes of teachers. Parents and students who care find the time and effort spent on testing annoying. The public, on the other hand, finds that measures of performance are essential to good management and spending. Testing is a disruption and a cause for conflict that will not go away and will not be influenced by a change in governance structure.

One positive result of the measurement era is the acknowledgment that standardized test scores for selected CPS students have experienced remarkable improvement from 2009 to 2014. A study by Stanford University's Center for Education Policy Analysis has found that for third through eighth graders scores improved dramatically over the five-year study period.[23] While these students still score below the national averages, they are not nearly as far below grade level as they once were. The study did not separate charter students from the rest, so it is unclear whether the growth of charters during this time period had any effect on test scores.

The disruption that digital technology has spawned in so many commercial endeavors has been slow to disrupt Chicago schools. In the past several years, the budgetary and operational appearance of the schools remains relatively unchanged. This echoes the experience of school districts nationwide. Nevertheless, good governance calls for thinking deeply about the digital phenomenon and preparing to adapt to yet another disruption.

The Chicago Public Schools and its board must prepare for the continual disruption that characterizes our age. It must view its governance structure both as a board and in its relationship with state government with deliberation and sober judgment, so that ill-conceived governance changes do not distract from the real and seemingly insurmountable challenges it faces. It will need to experiment and catch up to best practices elsewhere, but with care.

Disaggregation

The Chicago Public Schools, the nation's third-largest unified school district, must think about its geographic and functional scope. There is no other public school district within city limits. The charter schools are not currently organized into a separate school district. The Archdiocese of Chicago oversees Catholic schools in both Cook and Lake Counties. This configuration is over a hundred years old and arose at a time when the city underwent massive annexation and expansion. Since then, the boundaries and configurations of school districts have hardened and stabilized. The same is true for the most part across the entire country. The question for the school district is whether on a proactive basis it might consider some other configuration or whether on a defensive basis it should be alert to forces that might pressure for some other arrangement.

Not all school district boundaries in the United States have remained unchanged. Since 2000, seventy-one communities in the country have attempted to withdraw from their school districts. Of these, forty-seven have succeeded, and many more attempts are still under way. Only nine secessions have been prevented.[24] One of the more conspicuous cases was that of Gardendale, a suburb of Birmingham in Jefferson County, Alabama, where a more affluent white community sought to withdraw from a poorer, predominantly black community. In a dramatic challenge, a court finally ruled to allow the secession to proceed.[25] Another conspicuous attempt was that of the communities in the San Fernando Valley to secede from the City of Los Angeles, primarily to avoid paying to support schools in the rest of the city. The threat of this secession sparked a chaotic effort at charter reform for the entire city, which ultimately swayed enough voters to squash the withdrawal.

In Illinois, school district withdrawal and secession are not allowed, and so it would appear that the issue is moot. Nevertheless, in a city where taxpayers are concentrated in a central area and are mostly white and childless while the school district is 85 percent people of color, the demographic tension for change exists and is increasing. School enrollment is declining faster than the city population, so younger workers with higher incomes continue to move to the suburbs as they form families. Placing their children in a unified school district, even one that has charter and magnet schools, is not attractive enough to reverse this trend.

CPS should think about disaggregation. From a defensive perspective, there is the possibility that a wave of withdrawal and secession might sweep the country, which could threaten the status quo. Proactively, CPS should consider the benefits of multiple school districts. The district is already divided into thirteen networks with their own chiefs. In 1988, while the Chicago schools were still under state supervision, the district implemented local school councils to select school principals. This attempt at distributing power to the local level has atrophied and is no longer widely practiced; still, the desire for more decentralization in the district remains a driving force for parents and their neighborhoods. It was neighborhood parents who led the opposition to the recent closing of fifty schools.

Is there some way that disaggregating the school district could serve larger societal interests? Splitting the school district on a geographical basis need not be the only criterion. As mentioned earlier, one possibility could be the formation of a separate charter school district with a chartering agency that is not CPS. Other approaches to creating districts may be able to accomplish goals that have eluded CPS for decades. Is there some configuration that could serve to integrate one of the most segregated schools districts in the United States? Special needs schools have been taken over temporarily by the State of Illinois, but could the creation of a special needs school district better address the problem of adequately serving this particular population?

A central argument against disaggregation is that smaller districts would lose the economies of scale that the large district enjoys. Yet seeing how smaller cities run their schools at lower per-student cost gives pause to that argument. There is literature on school consolidation, especially with rural or smaller districts, but no study of large urban school districts.

With all the reforms that CPS must begin to undertake, disaggregation might be out of sight at the moment; it should, however, be kept in mind.

The Urban School System of the Future

The raging battle between charter schools and the teachers' union, together with the growing chasm between taxpayers and consumers of public education, has created the opening for a new way of thinking about urban education.

Into this opening has come education expert Andy Smarick, whose 2012 book, *The Urban School System of the Future*, looks at the problem of troubled urban schools, both public and charter, through a different frame of reference, that of quality improvement.[26]

Smarick repeats the laments that urban school districts have been left with a disproportionate number of lower income and minority students, have experienced consistently poor results, and have failed to respond to attempts at reform and improvement. Instead of looking at aggregates and arguing whether or not the average public school does a better job than the average charter school, he shows that both sectors, as well as the private and faith-based sectors, have a broad distribution of quality. Some charter schools are superior and some are failing. The same is true for public schools. However, the chartering and renewal process induces the charter authorizer to close underperforming schools, just as it allows for successful schools to expand their coverage or replicate their models. The problem with public schools is that it is difficult to close them, with the result that disproportionate amounts of effort and money are poured into failing schools with no measurable benefit.

The future of urban education, Smarick says, might revolve around the management of a portfolio of public, charter, and perhaps even private schools, which is constantly managed by expansion, replication, and closure. A successful elementary school, public or charter, might be allowed to expand to serve higher grades or an adjoining neighborhood. A good organization that is providing superior education might replicate its efforts elsewhere in the system. Schools that fail would be closed on a regular basis rather than throwing good money after bad. This is the social Darwinism that characterizes the business sector of the US economy, where creative destruction and innovation provide continuous improvement. Why not apply this approach to one of the most critical needs of our society? Such a system would be overseen by a chancellor of the city school system, who would have authority over a separate authorizing organization for each sector. In this system, public schools would operate more like the charter sector, and funds could go directly to one school or to a group of schools rather than to an administration-heavy central school district.

CPS officials are not unfamiliar with the benefits of continuous renewal. In December 2017 the district's chief education officer, Janice Jackson, was appointed chief executive officer. She is a product of CPS and rose through the ranks as a teacher. She helped secure funds from the Gates Foundation to open Al Raby High School in 2004 and was appointed the first principal at Westinghouse High School, which opened in 2009.[27] Jackson has been involved in every aspect of recent school closings. More than any previous education official at CPS, she has seen new school startups and closings up close.

If this type of system was found to be desirable, it would take several big changes to make the leap from today to tomorrow. The first order of business would be to find new authorizers. As Smarick notes, "districts are often unwilling authorizers, viewing charters as competition."[28] This is certainly the case in Chicago, where the Chicago Teachers Union holds sway over CPS and its charter decisions. Other states have turned to universities, nonprofit organizations, or state-level authorizers for independent measurement and decision making. In a conversation with the author, Smarick indicated a general preference (not specific to Chicago) for a state-level charter board as his first choice. His second preference is a state's General Board of Education. Surprisingly, his third choice would be the mayor (personal communication, December 13, 2017).

Smarick avoids any discussion of the cost of opening and closing schools on a regular basis. This is a central issue in Chicago. Parents fight the closing of neighborhood schools, and the union fights the opening of charter schools. If the Chicago schools ever hope to achieve the flexibility to open and close schools, both district and charter, on a routine basis based on performance and not utilization, it will require a change of mindset by all parties. Having such flexibility as a goal gives more urgency to finding a way to eliminate the immense burdens of legacy costs sooner rather than later.

While not central to Smarick's argument, he makes a persuasive case for the inclusion of private and faith-based schools in the system. The obstacle to integrating faith-based schools within a portfolio system involves the precedence of court cases and government funding of faith-based schools, which is constrained by state laws. Other states are overcoming these obstacles, and the creation of tuition tax credits in Illinois in 2017 might be a step in the direction of relaxing such restrictions. As the Catholic Archdiocese, the largest operator of private schools in Chicago, acknowledges, private schools are already educating city children, saving CPS hundreds of millions of dollars each year.[29]

The ideas that Smarick proposes seem to solve many of the problems that are hampering progress with Chicago schools and schoolchildren. His proposal provides a regular and orderly method of closing and opening schools rather than wildly unpopular mass closings followed by moratoriums on both closings and openings. It resolves the conflict between public and charter schools and addresses disaggregation by providing an integrating yet liberating governance structure. Has it been tried? Nowhere formally. Nevertheless, aspects of his proposal are already popping up in jurisdictions all over the country. Anyone serious addressing school progress cannot avoid this valuable contribution to understanding.

A Homework Assignment for Chicago Public Schools

Like many other areas of Chicago government, the Chicago Public Schools are hampered by crushing legacy problems at a time when adapting to demographic, political, and social changes has never been more urgent. It has its work cut out for it. The way forward is to put its house in order and then consider a more capable governance structure, in that order. Here is the assignment:

- CPS must tackle the crushing pension debt that will conservatively absorb more than 34 percent of teacher salaries. It must either negotiate a state takeover of this burden or, failing that, impose a dedicated tax that funds the liability in accordance with the pension recommendations laid out in chapter 5.
- CPS must likewise assess a tax to fund and extinguish the general obligation debts of the district over a reasonable time period, perhaps ten years. The amount of this tax will be approximately $500 million.
- These two measures will be painful and seem draconian to some, but they are what would ensue if the schools were taken over by the state. This is the type of approach that the Municipal Acceptance Corporation enacted when it took over the City of New York in 1975. If it is what would be done with a state takeover, why wait?
- Develop a ten-year financial plan that is honest, practical, prudent, and holistic. An honest plan takes into account conditions that actually exist and looks at trends that are under way, including the decline of enrollment and the rise of charter demand. A prudent plan takes care of the future and not just the present; it does not put off problems, it faces them. A practical plan contemplates actions that can actually be

implemented, not just wishful thinking. And a holistic plan takes into account all the moving parts of a complex and dynamic school system. This ten-year plan should be revised annually, but that revision should be an update and should not be a revelation of painful surprises that could have been addressed at the outset.

- Once the debt and its extinguishment is brought under control, and once a solid ten-year plan is implemented, it is time for CPS to enact state legislation that gives voters the authority to approve tax increases and borrowing.

- None of these measures will be possible without finding balance in the relationship between CPS and the Chicago Teachers Union. The CTU has good reason to feel aggrieved and distrustful of a district that has run roughshod over some of the interests of teachers. The abuse of the Chicago Teachers' Pension Fund is the most egregious example. Once this has been satisfactorily addressed, it is time for the teachers' union to become a partner rather than an adversary. And it is time for CPS to balance better the interests of teachers, students, parents, and taxpayers. Such balance will include measures that are almost universal in other parts of the United States, including the prohibition of teacher strikes. As justified as the grievances of teachers may be, Chicago cannot remain an outlier.

- The actions listed above must be undertaken whether or not the school board remains appointed. By the time this book is published, CPS governance might be on its way to radical change. Either way, a new governance structure must be considered—but if and only if the City of Chicago has made other changes to its governance structure suggested here. These changes involve empowering the city council, electing a controller, bringing order to city finances, and making elections more competitive and enhancing turnout. If CPS attempts to change its governance structure in isolation from the city without having stabilized its finances, it will be doomed to failure in short order.

- Assuming that the time will come to consider bringing elections to the school district, it will need to find a governance model that is prudent and effective for both the schools and the city. While the most obvious structure might be a board of manageable size elected from districts, the authors believe that electing just one person, an overseer or elector, might make for a better transition.

- To bring balance and reduce the inherent conflicts of interest between public and charter schools, the community should look for a chartering agency more neutral than CPS.

CPS may not be looking for change, but change is looking for it. The pace of demographic, social, and technological change will not slow, it will accelerate. Continuous disruption is here to stay. Only a fiscally healthy and stable system that has the trust and vote of all parties to the school enterprise can face these changes with deliberation, realism, and courage.

CHAPTER 4

Chicago's Fiscal Ruin

*Government is like a baby; an alimentary canal with a big appetite
at one end and no sense of responsibility at the other.*
—RONALD REAGAN

∽

"Surrounded by grinning labor leaders, Mayor Richard M. Daley on Tuesday announced an unprecedented 10-year contract with city building trade unions that will last until after—and may help the city attract—the proposed 2016 Summer Olympics," declared *Crain's Chicago Business* columnist Greg Hinz on August 7, 2007. "The deal means that a mayor who often has had acrimonious relations with union chiefs will enjoy peace with a key faction of organized labor as the city's campaign to win the Olympics proceeds."[1] Not only did the mayor make peace with the building trades, but he also made long-term agreements with a wide swath of city workers. It was not until ten years later that most Chicagoans got a glance at what was in those contracts.

On May 31, 2017, Chicago's inspector general issued a report on all city collective bargaining agreements as the ten-year period of labor peace was coming to a close.[2] The report contained a detailed list of provisions that individually cost the city sometimes thousands, sometimes hundreds of millions of dollars.[3] Here are just five such provisions:

- Traditional work: Any work that has traditionally been done by union employees must continue to be done by union employees. When a work group goes to a work site, they must be driven by a Teamster driver, who does not do any of the underlying work. The report estimates that this provision cost $200 million over ten years.

- Prevailing wage: The contract for construction workers requires that they be paid the prevailing wage. This wage is based on the highest hourly rate paid to similar workers in the private sector for any amount of work, even a half day or just a few hours. City construction workers are then paid at that rate for all their work week after week, even though they enjoy a far more secure annual income than their private sector counterparts.

- Health care employee contribution caps: The city employee contribution to health-care plans for family coverage is capped at $2,229 per year, whereas the comparable national rate for employee contribution is $4,917. Applied to 10,000 employees, the difference is about $27 million per year.

- Contracting out for fire department employees: The fire department contract prohibits contracting out work that it currently provides. This is why a fire truck is dispatched along with an ambulance if there is the possibility that CPR will be administered. This costly practice was questioned by Monica Eng on WBEZ's *Curious City* program.[4]

- Detail pay for policemen assigned outside their district: The police contract provides that if sergeants are assigned duty outside their district, they are paid time and a half for it.

When taken altogether, these contracts—signed to limit the leverage of government employee unions in advance of an event that never happened—have burdened the city with inflexibility and costs that run into the hundreds of millions of dollars. They are just a few of the many poor decisions that have ruined the finances of Chicago.

Can these findings be dismissed as just the usual mismanagement and waste that accompanies all government, or do they manifest themselves in costs that are bloated out of proportion to the standards of municipal management of other large US cities? Many of the large cities in the comparison group for this study are still relatively small. Half of the cities have a population less than 50 percent of Chicago's. Los Angeles, on the other hand, has a population that is nearly 50 percent larger than Chicago, and it has a land area that is more than double Chicago's. It would seem a good choice to compare Chicago's municipal costs against. Table 4.1 is a snapshot of the

TABLE 4.1   Police and Fire Spending in Context, Chicago versus
Los Angeles

	Chicago	Los Angeles
Land area (square miles)	234	503
Population, 2017	2,716,450	3,999,759
Fire department budget, 2018 (in $ millions)	633	657
Police department budget, 2018 (in $ millions)	1,552	1,576

Source: City of Chicago, 2018 Budget Overview, pp. 114, 119, https://www.cityofchicago.
org/content/dam/city/depts/obm/supp_info/2018Budget/2018_Budget_Overview.pdf;
City of Los Angeles, 2017–18 Budget Summary, p. 21, http://cao.lacity.org/budget17-18
/2017-18Budget_Summary.pdf.

two public services with the highest cost in those cities: the fire department
and the police department.

The comparison shows that Los Angeles is able to operate at about the same
cost that Chicago incurs, even though it is much larger in both population
and area. Is this a fair comparison? Los Angeles, like Chicago, is a strong
union town, heavily Democratic in a heavily Democratic state. But the fire
department deals with brush and forest fires, a much higher demand for services than anything Chicago has seen since it went up in flames back in 1871.

What is the cost difference? If Chicago has 69 percent of the population of
Los Angeles, and that percentage is applied to its costs, the resulting reduction
would be $648 million a year for these two departments combined. If the two
largest costs of municipal government are this excessive, can we assume that
many other costs incurred by the city likewise are excessive by comparison?
One certainty is that these departmental costs are mostly compensation; the
excess, therefore, has a multiplier effect on city pensions.

Chicago's Fiscal Problems: Seen and Unseen

All economics and finance are based upon scarcity and the fact that resources
are limited. If resources were unlimited, there would be no reason to worry
about or even keep track of them. Municipal finance is governed by these
economic laws. Governments rely on taxpayers and users of public goods
for their resources. They can only spend the money they receive. Likewise,

the amount of money that taxpayers and users have, or are willing to pay, is limited. In theory, politicians know how much they can tax people, and they know how much they can in turn spend for public goods. They must divide those limited resources among all the competing demands from the public. When politicians budget, and when governments operate, they decide how much money is available and how it will be spent.

There is one loophole, one escape hatch, in this theory of government finance: municipal borrowing. If government can borrow, it does not have to tax its citizens, and it does not have to constrain its spending, at least for a while. This is why all the talk about the fiscal health of a unit of government revolves around a four-letter word: debt. And like an iceberg, there is debt that we can see and debt we cannot.

Every Chicagoan knows from repeated news reports that the finances of the city are in horrible shape. This is the visible debt. The credit rating agencies have downgraded their scores for the City of Chicago and Chicago Public Schools (CPS) to at or near junk status. Think tanks like the Civic Federation, the Better Government Association, the Illinois Policy Institute, and the Center for Tax and Budget Accountability regularly report on the poor condition of finances in the city, CPS, or both. The daily and weekly newspapers keep up the drumbeat on deteriorating finances, as do the television and radio stations. Even international news magazines are keen to weigh in on Chicago's woes.[5]

Since everything is relative, how does Chicago compare to the largest US cities? As table 4.2 shows, only New York City rivals Chicago in debt per resident. Both cities, in fact, leave the rest of the pack in the dust. This comparison to New York City, however, is not strictly equivalent. New York's numbers include many public functions that Chicago's does not, and it includes about every department of city government. Chicago government, in contrast, is divided into what former Chicago Chief Financial Officer Donald Haider calls the "seven sisters," the seven separate units of government that show up on Chicago property tax bills. These include the Chicago Public Schools, the Chicago Park District, the City Colleges, Cook County, the Metropolitan Water Reclamation District, and the Cook County Forest Preserve District. According to Haider, the seven sisters were set up separately decades ago to make it easier for each to borrow money. And it worked. The City of Chicago owes $15.3 billion in business-type activity bonds such as water, sewers, and the airports. It also owes over $9 billion of general obligation debt. CPS owes over $7.3 billion of such general obligation debt, and one affiliate that is not a part of the seven sisters, the Metropolitan Pier and Exposition Authority (MPEA), owes $4 billion.

There are many problems associated with this debt. First and most obvious is the cost of debt service. For just the formal city corporate fund, which pays for vital public services, general finance costs are projected to be $813 million for 2017, or nearly 22 percent of the budget, eclipsing every other department except the police. For CPS, the 2016 interest expense was 10 percent of revenue. For the MPEA, the total interest and amortization of debt was 65 percent of its total revenues. For these operating budgets, debt service is crowding out

TABLE 4.2   Comparison of Bonded and Pension Debt, Top Fifteen US Cities

	Population, 2014	City bonded debt (in millions)	Pension debt (in millions)	Combined debt (in millions)	Debt per person
New York	8,491,079	$126,658	$55,876	$182,534	$21,497
Los Angeles	3,928,864	$24,725	$8,172	$32,897	$8,373
Chicago	2,722,389	$24,374	$33,846	$58,220	$21,386
Houston	2,239,558	$13,027	$5,341	$18,368	$8,202
Philadelphia	1,560,297	$9,742	$9,405	$19,147	$12,271
Phoenix	1,537,058	$6,705	$3,876	$10,581	$6,884
San Antonio	1,436,697	$11,684	$1,343	$13,027	$9,067
San Diego	1,381,069	$2,516	$1,721	$4,237	$3,068
Dallas	1,281,047	$5,256	$5,602	$10,858	$8,476
San Jose	1,015,785	$2,660	$2,278	$4,938	$4,861
Austin	912,791	$6,343	$1,290	$7,633	$8,362
Jacksonville	853,382	$7,752	$2,455	$10,207	$11,961
San Francisco	852,469	$13,217	$2,326	$15,543	$18,233
Indianapolis	848,788	$1,125	$944	$2,069	$2,438
Columbus	835,957	$4,248	$1,315	$5,563	$6,655

Source: "City Chart," State Data Lab, https://www.statedatalab.org/state_data_and _comparisons/citychart#cafr1_anc.

core services. These deficits and their resulting debt pile up and constitute "legacy costs." This is a seventy-five-cent word for the accumulation of prior expenses that have been financed with borrowing. It is the municipal equivalent of credit card debt.

What fiscal problems are unseen? The first that comes to mind, and one that is widely discussed, is the structural deficit of all these Chicago public entities. A structural deficit is defined as a budget deficit that results from a fundamental imbalance between government revenue and expenditures. This is different from a cyclical deficit, where receipts and expenditures alternate in exceeding each other through an economic cycle. A structural deficit is not an occasional deficit caused by isolated one-off factors that will not recur. A structural deficit persists for many reasons. Sometimes government has entered into long-term contracts that impair its ability to control expenses. In other cases it is constrained legally or politically in raising revenue. In all cases these governments run chronic budget deficits that are financed by general unsecured debt that accumulates and burdens future generations.

It is this concept of structural deficit that is foremost in the minds of the credit rating agencies assigning ratings to municipal bonds. The rubric in figure 4.1, which is published by Moody's, spells out what they are looking for. When there is a weak ability to raise revenues and a weak ability to reduce expenditures, the result will be a rating on the right side of the grid. When the sources of revenue and major expenditures are unstable and unpredictable, ratings are driven lower.

Chicago has seen regular instability with its revenues and expenditures. As described in an earlier chapter, by 2012 most of the money received up front for the parking meter concession had been taken into the general budget as occasional revenue.[6] In the aftermath of the financial crisis of 2008, the city also received over $2 billion from the American Recovery and Reinvestment Act, the stimulus package enacted in 2009.[7] Here were just two large unpredictable and unstable sources of revenue. When this money ran out, the city opted to control expenditures by taking a pension holiday with several of the city and school district pension plans. In addition, since 2004 Chicago has seen a recurring pattern of settlements for police misconduct claims that have now totaled over $662 million.[8] The union contracts described above are not the sole problem; they are just one of many poor decisions that make up the pathology of Chicago's fiscal problems.

Operating Revenue Flexibility

Revenue Predictability / Revenue Raising Ability	Strong ability to raise revenues	Moderate ability to raise revenues	Weak ability to raise revenues
Major revenue sources tend to be highly stable and predictable	Aaa	Aa	A
Major revenue sources tend to be moderately stable and predictable	Aa	A	Baa
Major revenue sources tend to be somewhat unstable and unpredictable	A	Baa	Ba or B and Below

Operating Expenditure Flexibility

Expenditure Predictability / Expenditure Reduction Ability	Strong ability to reduce expenditures	Moderate ability to reduce expenditures	Weak ability to reduce expenditures
Major expenditures tend to be highly stable and predictable			
Major expenditures tend to be moderately stable and predictable			
Major expenditures tend to be somewhat unstable and unpredictable			

FIGURE 4.1. Moody's institutional rating rubric. Courtesy of Moody's Analytics.

Another unseen source of debt is the permanent impairment of sources of revenue from concessions like the parking meter and parking lot deals, as well as from abnormally long-term leases and contracts. These are sources of revenue for the use of public property that have, in effect, been given away and are not available now for public purposes.

Even more invisible is the burden of deferred maintenance. When government postpones the maintenance of capital items—large long-term infrastructure improvements—those capital items deteriorate. Not only does government postpone the expenditure, but the cost to make repairs increases and property is rendered unusable. Deferred maintenance is quite visible to city residents as they drive and walk the streets, attend schools, and use other public services. Unlike monetary debt, though, there is no single reliable number that can gauge this invisible debt.

And finally, an even more invisible debt is the city's failure to keep up with the modern world. Whether it is technology or infrastructure or modern public services, a government that is paying too much for the past is robbing from its own future. The fact that the city did not separate its storm water sewer system from its sanitary sewer system a century ago is now costing billions of dollars to rectify—and both the river and Lake Michigan are still taking in raw sewage when big storms occur. Chicago also has more lead water pipes connecting homes to street mains than any other city, with nearly 80 percent of the city's homes using a lead service line.[9] In 2013, a US Environmental Protection Agency study of Chicago homes found that if those lines are disturbed by street work, high levels of lead can flow from household taps for months on end.[10] What modernizations is the city currently failing to undertake because of financial constraints?

How City Finance Is Supposed to Work

City financial management is, surprisingly, rather simple. Like our households and businesses, the municipal entity must estimate revenues for a future year, appropriate funds to be spent, and control spending to balance the two. The budget is prepared in advance of the year, is approved by authorities, with the government then operating within the budget through the fiscal year. Of the two sides of the budget, revenues and spending, the government can only directly control spending within a given year. If the revenues fall short of expenditures, there is a deficit; if they exceed spending, there is surplus.

Some governments wait until the fiscal year is over to see how they did; others take stock during the year and adjust spending based on interim revenue. Revenues typically include taxes, fees, and other revenue or grants. Normally, the spending for a city includes all expenditures: salaries, benefits, purchases of products and services. In this simplified description, the expenditures are for city services that provide no lasting benefit. There is nothing permanent about these expenditures.

Big capital expenditures, however, require a different financial treatment. On an annual basis, governments can have a small and regularly recurring expenditure for capital items of equipment, repairs, or minor improvements to public property. These expenditures are typically included in the operating budget for the year. Occasionally, though, a government may wish to make a major expenditure for a school, a sewer project, a new road, or other major public work that has a useful life of many years.

Government typically finances these expenditures with bonds that are issued outside of the annual operating budget. If the improvement is expected to generate revenue, whereby the improvement, such as a sewer project, would be paid for by increased fees, then the municipality would issue revenue bonds and the increased fees would be legally dedicated to paying off the bonds. If the improvements are to be paid for by taxes, the government imposes a special tax or increases an existing tax and issues a general obligation bond to be paid off by the incremental tax legally dedicated to pay off the bonds. In both cases it is customary for the government to require the approval of voters before the bonds may be issued.

Conscientious governments discipline themselves to pay off capital debts. Often they create a separate fund or account for bonds that are to be paid with taxes. The incremental or separate taxes that were approved to pay for the bonds are put into the fund, with the interest and eventually the principal of the bonds paid off from these segregated funds. Since tax revenue can fluctuate according to economic conditions, these bonds are backed by the full faith and credit of the issuing unit of government; if there is a shortfall from the special tax, other tax revenue is available to pay off the bonds. That is why these are called general obligation bonds.

In certain cases the interest received from owners of municipal bonds is exempt from federal income taxes. As a result, the buyers of these bonds will accept a lower interest rate because they do not have to pay income taxes.

Such bonds must be issued to finance capital improvements that provide a public good. If there is no underlying new project, for example, if the bonds are being issued to cover ongoing current government operations or to pay pensions, the interest is not exempt from income taxes on the part of the bond owner. To compensate the owner, the interest rate on these taxable bonds will be higher so that the recipient will have enough money to pay the taxes.

There are many books and organizations that describe good city financial practices. The Government Finance Officers Association (GFOA), a national organization, does a particularly fine job and offers many publications that are easy to understand.[11]

One critical element of government accounting has to do with what are called generally accepted accounting principles (GAAP). Businesses in the private sector that produce financial statements audited by a CPA include with their financial statement an accountant's opinion that the statements are presented fairly in accordance with GAAP. This requirement has existed for decades. In recent years, the Government Accounting Standards Board (GASB), an accounting industry standards committee, has worked hard to bring the quality of governmental accounting up to the level of its corporate counterpart. Although the quality of municipal financial statements is improving, cities are not required to use GAAP for budgeting or any other governmental or statutory functions.

How Chicago Has Worked

For many years, Chicago has conducted its finances far differently than the norm described in the previous section. The City of Chicago, together with most of its affiliated units of government (the schools, parks, CTA, MPEA, etc.), has been careless in defining, counting, and estimating anticipated revenues. Although these entities are required by law to approve a balanced budget, when the year is over and the government releases its *Comprehensive Annual Financial Report*, the numbers invariably show a sizeable deficit. One analyst has reported that the difference between the budget and actual results was over $11 billion for the years 2012 through 2017.[12] These chronic deficits have been financed by general obligation borrowing that is not tied to any dedicated new revenue or capital project. The focus of the press and think tanks on balanced budgets is obviously misguided. While they mention balanced budgets, these critics are really referring to the actual deficits incurred and the borrowing required to finance them. Meanwhile increasing debt affects the bond ratings and debt service costs gobble up the budget.

The structure of fiscal governance in Chicago is complete mayoral control, and this is the source of fiscal irresponsibility. The financial work of the City of Chicago is conducted by the chief financial officer (CFO) and the Office of Budget and Management on the fifth floor of city hall. The CFO and budget director are both appointed by the mayor. The city treasurer is an elected office but functions merely as a custodian of the city's money. On the city council, there is both a Committee on Budget and Government Operations and a Finance Committee. Each committee has thirty-five members with no significant independent staff; they act, consequently, more like a committee of the whole rather than as a working committee. Although the chair of the Finance Committee, currently Ed Burke, is individually quite powerful in the council, the committee itself is not, with the exception of its secretive administration of the city's $100 million workers' compensation program. The home rule powers of the city allow the mayor with city council approval to levy taxes of all kinds and to borrow money without voter approval. As noted in chapter 1, the city council created the Council Office of Financial Analysis in 2013 to assist council members with independent information when considering specific legislation. That office initially experienced delays in filling the director position, has since experienced turnover, and has yet to make a significant contribution to debates on the budget or other issues.

With such a structure, how does the city function? The two chief fiscal players are the Office of Budget and Management and the Department of Finance. The staff in the budget office has been dealing with deficits of all kinds for so long that very few can recall how to develop and operate within a balanced budget without incurring additional debt. As required by law, the office develops a proposed balanced budget that is submitted to the city council for approval. But, as noted above, these budgets are not prepared with the same accounting principles (GAAP) that will show up at the end of the year when the city publishes its *Comprehensive Annual Financial Report*. In 2015, the budget office proposed a budget that listed $297.3 million of measures that would close the gap.[13] It has not closed that gap since. By 2017, the city needed to find money to close a gap of only $137 million, but the Civic Federation projected that the gap would increase to \$233 million for 2018 and \$342 million for 2019; these numbers, moreover, do not include most pension payments.[14] Long-term planning consists of deficit projection.

The current mayor has made it clear that he is not interested in city fiscal policy. In a July 19, 2018, talk at the Economic Club of Chicago he derided finances when he said, "A fiscal policy is not an economic policy." A prime example of how the mayor's office abuses the budget came to light in August 2018 when the city reached a settlement with ridesharing companies and received \$10.4 million. Along with the announcement of the settlement the mayor said he would spend the windfall on a youth mentoring program. At the same time, the city regularly settles police misconduct cases, the costs of which are just a negative variance from the budget. If the city wins, it spends the money. If it loses, it still spends the money. This mentality and practice is the backbone of structural deficit.

By far the most dominant function in city hall is the Finance Department. These are the people who have to take action to keep the city afloat. Most of their effort is directed toward financing and refinancing the city's debt. At the end of 2015, the city's *Comprehensive Annual Financial Report* stated that the general revenues available for government operations increased by \$780.3 million, due primarily to drawing from the line of credit and issuing general obligation bonds.[15] In other words, the annual deficit was being paid for by borrowing. In addition to this new borrowing, necessary to pay for deficits and lawsuit settlements, the finance department must also refinance the existing debt. The popular phrase for refinancing general obligation debt is "scoop and toss," whereby the unpaid debt and accrued interest are bundled together and replaced by a new loan or bond. Newspapers and think tanks use the phrase to criticize this element of fiscal management, but despite the mayor's commitment to end it, the practice continues.

On the fifth floor of city hall, these two offices tolerate ongoing deficits and remain powerless to impose sufficient discipline to produce and operate a true balanced budget. Elsewhere on the same floor, offices are swarming with interest groups. This includes vendors who can sell the city revenue-raising schemes, for example, red-light cameras and plastic bag taxes, as well as equipment, such as hundreds of millions of dollars of LED lights, that is financed off the books in the Infrastructure Trust. Also located there are the investment bankers who finance the ongoing deficits with loans and bonds and real estate interest groups who offer the mayor new real estate tax revenue and fees in exchange for unplanned development, a state of affairs described very thoroughly by Hunt and DeVries in the book *Planning Chicago*.[16]

Complicit in this fiscal behavior is a city council that is powerless to change the course of the budget. Although recent councils have not rubber-stamped the budget and several members have even voted against it, there is no robust capability outside the mayor's office to effect change. The Council Office of Financial Analysis has existed now for several years but has yet to provide any support to the council in making fiscal decisions.[17] Without a strong council committee or independent budget office, individual decisions about contracts and policies are not scored to assess their impact on finances. And finally, unlike other municipalities, voters do not approve taxes, fees, or bond issues.

This fiscal pathology is contagious. Some of the city's other governmental units that are controlled by the mayor, such as the Chicago Public Schools, also run chronic and structural deficits.[18]

How Other Cities Work

Pressure from interest groups for more money is a natural feature of the municipal landscape. Over the years, though, most cities have developed the governance muscle to manage these pressures and keep financial trouble at bay. In some, it has been relatively easy for the political process to exercise prudent financial control; in other cases, however, it has come with wrenching crisis and the imposition of controls from above. Table 4.3 compares the presence of some of the elementary governance structures that aid such control. As the table shows, the only city that lacks fiscal control across the board is Chicago.

What has been the experience of other major US cities? Appendix C tells brief stories of the fiscal experiences, governance structures, and practices of the largest fifteen cities, excluding Chicago. Some are big cities that faced enormous challenges and surmounted them. Some are small towns that were fortunate enough to grow into big cities but retained the city manager form of government and small-town fiscal mentality. In all cases these cities take their finances seriously, keep their house in order, and look out for taxpayers. The stories presented in the appendix are enlightening and far from boring.

TABLE 4.3   Fiscal Control Features, Top Fifteen US Cities

	Population, 2014	Independent elected controller	Robust council involvement	Voter fiscal constraints
New York	8,491,079	Yes	Yes	No
Los Angeles	3,928,864	Yes	Yes	Yes
Chicago	2,722,389	No	No	No
Houston	2,239,558	Yes	Yes	Yes
Philadelphia	1,560,297	Yes	Yes	Yes
Phoenix	1,537,058	Manager	Yes	No
San Antonio	1,436,697	Manager	No	Yes
San Diego	1,381,069	No	Yes	Yes
Dallas	1,281,047	Manager	Yes	Yes
San Jose	1,015,785	Manager	No	Yes
Austin	912,791	Manager	No	Yes
Jacksonville	853,382	No	Yes	Yes
San Francisco	852,469	No	No	Yes
Indianapolis	848,788	No	No	Yes
Columbus	835,957	Yes	No	Yes

Institutional Safeguards

Chicago is an outlier in many respects, and its poor finances stand out. This book has described some of the actions that have led to this condition, and these examples are merely a sampling of the many decisions over the years that have led to deficits (both occasional and structural) and to debt and the crowding out of vital services by the demands of creditors.

Chicago is also an outlier in its institutional and structural financial functioning. In short, a government that has always been totally dominated by a mayor has lacked the checks and balances and depth of deliberation to make better decisions. It will take a city charter to produce the changes that better functioning requires. These changes are necessary, but Chicagoans should not fool themselves into thinking that they will be sufficient to right the financial ship. These changes must also be predicated on the other modifications examined elsewhere in this study. Just as New York City devoted a significant part of its charter to finances, it also addressed many other government functions that have a bearing on finances. Adopting a charter typically entails also adopting the habit of periodically reconsidering the charter, and those involved in the process must keep in mind the primacy of financial health, which is so vital to civic life.

What are some of the changes Chicago must consider? The following are some obvious recommendations which we can surmise from a cursory look at other city governments:

- Robust city council functioning. In chapter 1, we showed that an independent city council with robust committees staffed with sufficient expertise are vital to better decision making. Nowhere is this more sorely needed than in the areas of budget and finance. These two functions are separate, and the extent to which the budget committee can eliminate structural deficits and bring about healthy financial operations, the city will be able to rely less on the finance function. These two committees should study the operation of their counterparts in other cities and look for best practices to adopt. The current Council Office of Financial Analysis is not sufficient to provide sufficient oversight of the city's finances. The committees of the council should have independent professional staff and sufficient budget resources to be an effective check on the elected financial official.
- Independently elected financial official. A city charter should create a new elected position of city controller or even create an independent budget office. This official must wield the same level of control and authority over the budget that the city council and mayor do. Like the vigorous city council committees, this new official must have access to sufficient funding to do a thorough job of vetting budgets, contracts, and any other financial plans and commitments. With this office in place, does the mayor still need a budget and finance department, or can this new official fulfill all those duties?
- Voter approval for all borrowing and taxes. Like so many other cities, the new charter must call for voter approval of taxes and borrowing. This discipline must also extend to all other affiliated city entities. Such voter approval will require a level of longer-term planning which has not

been on display in Chicago; it should be sought in advance of specific borrowing and not used simply to ratify previous bank borrowing by converting such debt into bonds. If balloting and elections are no more frequent than every two years, government officials will have to do a better job of managing and forecasting needs. Measures must be put in place so that officials cannot work around the clear requirement of discipline that voters impose.

What is less obvious than these three recommended governance changes are the specific practices that so many other cities have adopted, either in their charters or their ordinances or in the office of the city manager. These recommendations are as essential as the more obvious practices outlined above:

- Generally accepted accounting principles. The budget and financial statements of the city and affiliated entities must be prepared on the basis of generally accepted accounting principles (GAAP) which are inclusive of all items of expense, including pension accruals; this will reflect the true condition of the city's finances. "In 1975 the state [of New York] required New York City to move to GAAP for budgeting purposes. The city achieved budget balance within three years; and in the thirty years since then, the credibility of the city's budget balance has not been questioned."[19]
- Easy financial information. In writing this chapter, one of the authors, who is a CPA, examined years of budgets and financial statements and still found them opaque. The city must be required to provide information that is easy to find and easy for the average person to understand. The New York City charter commission spent considerable time addressing the issue of more openness. "All budget documents under the Charter had to be public and widely available."[20] The charter commission went so far as to quote James Madison that "popular government, without popular information, or the means of acquiring it, is but a prologue to farce, or a tragedy, or perhaps both."[21]
- Independent decision scoring. All decisions considered by the mayor or city council must be scored by independent officials to quantify their impact on city finances. This would include budgets, taxes, contracts, leases, concessions, collective bargaining agreements, changes to pension plans, and other similar commitments.

- Performance audits. Regular performance audits of city and governmental departments are a key ingredient of prudent financial management. Such audits are not something that just anyone in government can do; they must be authorized by charter. A charter for Chicago should authorize the independently elected financial officer to be the one who conducts performance audits.
- Long-term financial planning. The active use of long-term financial plans that show how the condition of the city will unfold for at least the next ten years is essential to providing decision makers and the public with context. This practice is a staple of the federal government and most other large cities.
- Disciplined decision making. The foregoing structures and practices would considerably aid government in making sound decisions, but without a commitment by officials to put themselves under such discipline, the measures will remain hollow. Establishing a culture of discipline will require both city officials and civil society to elevate their financial prudence. If they wish to spend money or incur obligations, they must pay for it in the current year by raising taxes and not push the tax increase into the future by borrowing for the expenditure. It is up to everyone to hold government accountable.

Additional Measures

Institutional changes will be necessary if Chicago is to operate in a fiscally sound manner; in and of themselves, however, they will not be sufficient. If the city is merely to correct for the disparity with Los Angeles, as shown in table 4.1, changes in governance will not be enough. They will not solve the structural deficit that chronically undermines the ability of the city to balance its books. If those measures were adopted, the city would still project deficits and debt as far as the eye can see. The root of the structural deficit is the very complex interrelationship with the provision of city services and the people employed to do so. Running a city is a very labor-intensive service business. The lion's share of the cost of government is employee compensation and benefits.

Chicago finds itself in a very difficult and constrained position with respect to labor. It has entered into collective bargaining agreements with the principal public employee unions for compensation and benefits that it has not raised the funds to pay for. This is the source of the structural deficit.

Over the years, the city has sought to keep current costs down by promising retirement benefits in the form of pensions and retirement health care and then not paying for those benefits either. It has also agreed to work rules that make running the city less efficient. Meanwhile, the world of work is changing, and there are new ways of working that could make providing city services more efficient and effective.

One way the city can keep up with productivity is to engage in what is called new public management (NPM). This concept has grown out of the National Partnership for Reinventing Government, an initiative led by former vice president Al Gore in the 1990s.[22] For local government, one option that has been pursued is gainsharing or productivity bargaining. With gainsharing, management and labor work cooperatively to find more efficient ways to work and then share together in the savings generated. This approach is new and has had limited success; it requires trust and a cooperative labor relations atmosphere.

Trust in labor relations is in very short supply in Chicago. In recent years, the police have felt besieged by the community and that City Hall does not have their back. This lack of trust has translated into collective bargaining contract clauses that protect police from the level of oversight that many reasonable citizens and experts believe is called for. Teachers have gone on strike in recent years, and the resulting contract has been considered overly generous to compensate for trying to go around their union to lengthen the school day and year. Across the board, the extreme underfunding and deterioration of pension plans erode confidence in government. Poor labor relations are costing the city dearly in both the short and long run.

It is not within the purview of this book to recommend the steps that should be taken to bring those relations to a satisfactory level. Such improvement must come from leadership, from government treating all parties with transparency and dignity, and from government action in all forms that is fair to both employees and taxpayers. Nevertheless, it is a reality that other major cities have effective civil service and labor relations committees of their city councils.

Richard Kearney and Patrice Mareschal, in their book *Labor Relations in the Public Sector*, have written about these complex issues. In a passage about government response to the increases in public sector compensation costs, they list nineteen measures that government can take. Some of these are the same poor efforts that have become Chicago's bad habits: borrow money, raise user fees, divert other government money, etc. Many other measures on the list, however, are reasonable, but they depend on a better relationship between management and labor than the one currently existing in Chicago. Toward the end of the list are three that deserve reproducing:

> 17. Refuse to fund negotiated payroll or benefit increases, making the argument of inability to pay. Collective bargaining laws in at least 11 states offer this final option to public employers. For example, the Iowa law provides, "No collective bargaining agreement or arbitrator's decision shall be valid or enforceable if its implementation would be inconsistent with any statuary limitation on the public employer's funds, spending, or budget or would substantially impair or limit the performance of any statutory duty by the public employer." The efficacy of this strategy may be questioned, however, because courts generally have affirmed the obligation of public employers to implement agreed-on compensation increases.
> 18. Reopen labor contracts and negotiate union giveback.
> 19. Declare bankruptcy.[23]

The chronic structural deficits across Chicago governmental entities is so critical that some additional measure along the lines of the recommendations 17 and 18 must be considered in reforming the budget habits of such a profligate city. Omitted, the city will come face to face with the last item on the list—bankruptcy.

The Problem of Legacy Costs

Legacy costs are the accumulated debt for the failure of government to pay for what it used in prior periods. For Chicago, this debt is in the form of general obligation debt and underfunded pensions. There are two problems with the legacy costs, one moral, the other equitable.

Before addressing the different problems associated with legacy costs, leaders, taxpayers, and citizens must ask a simple question: Do we intend to pay off legacy costs or merely to keep them at a specified level? To keep the costs level requires only that the interest cost of the debt be paid for with current revenues. If, however, the debt is in the form of bonds that mature at a point in the future, is it the intent to refinance these bonds at such time? Would new bondholders be found for such bonds and at what interest cost? If the intent is to pay off the legacy costs, the annual charge against the budget will be significantly greater than the interest costs. Is this a decision that the mayor should make? The council? Voters?

Politicians and some policy thinkers don't like to equate personal financial practices with public finance. However, it helps to understand the City of Chicago's debt policy if we think of it in terms of individuals' credit card debt. Citizens should ask municipal leaders if it is their private practice to never reduce their personal credit card balance and to die with a peak level of such personal debt. If they don't engage in such a practice in their private life, why should they do so with public finances?

"Scoop and toss"—the popular phrase for refinancing general obligation debt used by newspapers and broadcast media—has been picked up by the politicians who engage in the practice. Now whenever a refinancing takes place the current mayor vows to end the practice. Such vows are meaningless unless there is an explicit plan to pay off or amortize the general obligation debt. If there is no plan to pay down the debt, then every time a bond comes due, it must be scooped and tossed. Chapter 5 describes the amortization or catching up of pension debt for the city's defined-benefit retirement plans, but there is no comparable thinking about paying off, catching up, or amortizing the general obligation legacy cost debt of the city. Instead, when the city finds itself with even a modest windfall of surplus money, there is a feeding frenzy for the funds. In early 2017, the city found such a surplus when taxpayers failed to claim a low-income property tax rebate of $25 million. Instead of holding the surplus or even paying down debt, the race was on to spend the money.[24] Without a plan to reduce general obligation debt, any unexpected negative budget variance gets rolled into the next round of borrowing and the debt continues to grow.

The morality of legacy costs is that they ask those who did not consume city services to pay for them. It is like eating at a restaurant and, at the end of the meal, being presented with a check for the meals eaten by all those who sat at your table in the past. It is like asking a newborn child or a new immigrant to the United States to pay reparations for a wrong done to a group of people generations ago. This shifting of a burden into future years and decades has been described as a huge intergenerational fraud. To borrow Hayek's term and redefine it, legacy costs reflect the fatal conceit by government that what it spends money on today is more important than what was or will be done by all leaders past and future. It stretches the imagination of those bearing this burden and the credibility of those who impose the cost to explain how paying today for the ephemeral benefit of past deficits provides a benefit for those who bear that burden today. Put more plainly, we must pay for today so that our children can pay for tomorrow.

Seeing the same problem in more practical terms calls fairness into question. Is it equitable when ongoing annual legacy cost obligations that are funded in current governmental budgets crowd out expenditures for vital services, capital expenditures, and modernization? There is no question that this is happening today, given that the second-largest category of expense in the Chicago general fund is debt service.

If Chicago undertakes the institutional reforms and additional measures described in this chapter, it will still be handicapped by legacy costs. Other cities have tackled this problem in one way or another. Detroit and others have done so through bankruptcy proceedings. In the 1970s, New York City did so with special limited-term taxes that were dedicated to extinguishing the debt. In these and other cases, it took a crisis for government to take action to remedy the condition.

If Chicago were to choose to amortize and pay off its approximately $10 billion of general obligation debt in one generation, twenty years, it would require payments of about $725 million a year at a 4 percent interest rate. These payments would exceed the simple interest on the debt by about $325 million a year. In addition to balancing the budget so that no additional debt is taken on, these payments would require a matching $325 million tax increase. The choice of one generation as a pay-off period is predicated on the idea that the burden would not be imposed on those unborn when the plan is adopted. The adoption of and compliance with such a plan would restore confidence in the financial management of the city.

Will it take a crisis for Chicago to act on its legacy costs? Can Chicago, as a part of reorganizing government under a charter commission, peacefully tackle its legacy costs without a crisis? Can Chicago truly make any civic progress without addressing these costs?

Conclusion

A new mayor of Chicago was elected in 2011 on a platform that included solving the financial problems of the city. As has been pointed out here, Rahm Emanuel's first term was spent pursuing other matters, and it was not until his reelection campaign that finances moved to the forefront. From the end of 2010, just before he was elected, until the end of 2015, the general obligation debt of the city rose by $1.9 billion, nearly 25 percent. During the same period, the business-related debt also rose by $2.1 billion, or almost 20 percent. Debt at sister agencies and entities rose along with the city's, and the most dramatic deterioration was seen in pension funding. More than any mayor in recent memory, Rahm Emanuel has belatedly tried to tackle this problem. He had to. But despite taking painful first steps, the financial decay has merely decelerated in some areas. Depending on the entity, some are getting worse at a slower pace. This is a testament to how intractable the problems have become.

Solving the city's fiscal problems starts with honestly balancing its financial performance, not its budget, every year. This means eliminating the structural contributors to chronic deficits. Some policy analysis focuses on the city's proposed budgets and not actual performance, concluding that there is a revenue problem and discussing various tax and revenue measures. One such analysis is *Chicago Is Not Broke*, edited by Tom Tresser and self-published by his Civic Lab.[25] The book surveys the city budget and then addresses three areas where the city wastes money: corruption, bank dealing, and police abuse. A virtue of the book is that it focuses some attention on spending, but it doesn't look deeply enough. Like other attempts at analysis, the book identifies sources of revenue that it feels are sufficient to right the fiscal ship. Those sources include a progressive income tax for the state, a financial transaction tax for Chicago, and a public bank. While there are points to agree with in Tresser's book, it does not comprehend the magnitude of the city's fiscal challenges, and it does not address the apparent substantial bloat and excess spending for core city services that pervades every corner of city government.

In writing this book the authors sought to avoid specific policy recommendations, including targeted spending reductions or the merits of certain revenue sources. We show that billions in expenditures for legacy costs must be paid down but stop short of saying how the city must pay for them. It is our expectation that with the changes in governance and practices discussed here an independent city council and financial officer along with voter involvement will make a big contribution to better performance. As noted throughout this book, the proposals we describe are necessary to change the direction of city government, but it will take much more specific struggle and pain to make up for past mistakes. If the measures described herein are not considered, the city is vulnerable to spendthrift, unaccountable actions of a mayor acting on whim. Even a mayor committed to improving the city's financial picture and bond ratings faces formidable obstacles. It will require embracing structural and institutional changes, measures to correct for structural deficits, and the significant reduction of the burden of legacy costs for the city to regain meaningful financial soundness and credibility. Only then can it face a rapidly changing future with strength and resilience, not weakness and vulnerability.

CHAPTER 5

Pension Apocalypse Now, Not Later

We cannot solve today's problems with the same level of thinking that created them.
—ALBERT EINSTEIN

෴

The Holiday Habit

Everyone loves a holiday. We take time off from work or school, we play, we celebrate. Often we are meant to commemorate some event or some person, but seldom are we so conscious of the meaning of our days off. Here, then, is the tale of three peculiar holidays.

In April 2009, with no study and little notice, the Illinois General Assembly passed pension legislation that granted the Chicago Public Schools a pension holiday. Rather than pay the ever-increasing required contribution to the pension plan, CPS was allowed to pay a fraction of the dollars owed and the forty years required to achieve 90 percent funding was extended an additional fourteen years, to 2059. Once again, CPS was under severe financial strain and needed a break from pension obligations. Funding of the pension plan which once hovered near 100 percent was now headed for 50 percent.

On June 9, 2014, the Illinois General Assembly passed legislation to modify the pension plan provisions for the city's municipal employees and laborers. The changes would have reduced some benefits, increased employees' contributions, and obligated the city to catch up funding for the plans to 90 percent by 2055. The city had been contributing to plans on the archaic basis of a multiplier framework, whereby the employer contributes a multiple (generally approximately two times) the amount of employee contributions. The contribution required by this formula is woefully inadequate to keep the plans funded. With this new legislation, the city would finally have to catch up to 90 percent funding, but only after enjoying a holiday at the old and lower multiplier rates until 2020. This legislation was struck down two years later by the Illinois Supreme Court, and so the Municipal Employees' Annuity and Benefit Fund of Chicago was, according to its 2016 annual financial report, headed for the complete extinction of its assets.

On May 30, 2016, the state legislature again passed a law dealing with the pensions for Chicago policemen and firemen. This law granted the city reduced pension payment obligations until 2021 and extended the time to catch up to 90 percent funding by fifteen years, now to 2055. The policemen's fund alone projected that the difference between incoming contributions and outgoing benefits and expenses would amount to a deficit of $681 million by 2021.

What all three of these particular holidays commemorate is the inability of Chicago government to raise the revenue to pay for obligations that it has haplessly undertaken. As of the end of 2016, the pension obligations of the City of Chicago were larger than that of any other major city and greater than that of forty-four of the nation's fifty states. When the pension holidays end, the increases in taxes, fees, and charges will be a rude awakening and a painful shock for taxpayers and citizens.

A Chicago Pension Snapshot

A look at various pension facts tells the Chicago story. The most widely used measure of pension health is the unfunded accrued liability of the pension fund, otherwise known as pension debt. It is calculated by subtracting the pension fund assets from total accrued liabilities. Table 5.1 is a snapshot of the condition of seven major pension plans in Chicago.

What is the meaning of these numbers, and what is their context? Looking at them in different ways shows how outsized they are. First, the unfunded liability divided by the population of Chicago shows that this pension debt is equal to more than $15,300 for every man, woman, and child in the city. When this number has been presented in focus groups, participants immediately dismiss it: surely every man, woman, or child cannot possibly pay so great an expense. Such dismissal highlights the severity of the problem because someone sometime will have to pay this money and more. By contrast, the

TABLE 5.1   Funding of Local Pension Plans in Chicago, 2017

Pension fund	Total assets	Accrued actuarial liability	Unfunded liability	Funding level (%)
Teachers	$10,113	$21,125	$11,012	48
Municipal employees	$4,554	$16,282	$11,728	28
Police	$3,122	$13,454	$10,332	23
Firemen	$1,126	$5,746	$4,620	20
City laborers	$1,268	$2,630	$1,362	48
Chicago Park District	$398	$1,624	$1,226	25
Chicago Transit Authority	$1,752	$3,338	$1,586	52
Total	$22,333	$64,199	$41,866	35

Note: Dollars in millions.
Source: Comprehensive annual financial reports or actuarial reports of the plans.

state of Wisconsin has 5.8 million people, a little over twice the population of Chicago. The total pension liability for state-level plans in Wisconsin is $90.1 billion, which is only 1.3 times the liability of Chicago. Wisconsin's pension plans, however, have assets of $88.5 billion, so the unfunded liability is a mere $1.6 billion compared to the $41.9 billion in Chicago.[1] Compared to Wisconsin, Chicago's liability is much higher and its assets are less than one-fourth those of Wisconsin's.

The pension problem is affecting every area of municipal government. As will be shown later in this chapter, the average planned contribution to the Chicago pension plans to catch them up over the next forty years would require about $4.5 billion per year. Keep in mind that the total budget of the city, excluding pensions and debt service, is about $4 billion, and that the average CPS budget is likewise a little over $4 billion, excluding pensions. For the same amount of money, the city could employ tens of thousands of additional employees—teachers, police officers, and others—per year, perhaps doubling the current city workforce, or build 1,500 schools at $3 million each, more than doubling the number of schools in the district. These numbers illustrate what has been reported repeatedly in the newspapers: the pension debt is crowding out vital public services.

Pension matters are in fact much worse, though, because these are not real numbers; they are fabricated using a variety of actuarial assumptions that make them much smaller than the actual dollar amount will eventually be paid to retirees. The assets are real, but the accrued liabilities are calculated assuming a certain life expectancy of retirees and a certain rate of return that the funds might earn until they are called upon to pay the pension. As a result, the pension funds are able to discount or only report a fraction of what they will be required to pay out to retirees. The amount that will eventually be paid to pension plan participants is much higher than the $64 billion shown in table 5.1, and it will only grow much larger in the coming decades. This is an overwhelming problem.

The data in table 5.2 show further adverse trends. The ratio of active employees to retirees is called the maturity ratio of a pension plan. Chicago has an overall ratio of 1.1, compared to a national average of 1.65.[2] There are more than 170,000 active and retired public employees, many of whom are living in Chicago, who are counting on their pension every month or at retirement. The pension plans are currently paying out over $3.5 billion in benefits annually, and this amount rises every year. This source of income is a meaningful contributor to the Chicago economy. In 2017, the five largest pension plans were

TABLE 5.2   Selected Beneficiary Data on Chicago Pension Plans

Pension fund	Active employees	Pension beneficiaries	Total annual pension payments (in thousands)	Pension per retiree
Teachers	29,543	28,298	$1,346,532	$47,584
Municipal workers	30,296	25,236	$813,092	$37,243
Police	12,177	9,603	$678,819	$70,688
Fire	4,757	4,306	$258,446	$60,020
City laborers	2,816	3,769	$145,577	$49,062
Chicago Park District	3,114	2,870	$71,030	$24,749
Chicago Transit Authority	8,204	8,869	$234,641	$26,456
Total	90,907	82,951	$3,548,137	$42,774

Source: Comprehensive annual financial reports or annual reports of the plans.

TABLE 5.3   Pension Debt, Top Fifteen US Cities

	Population, 2014	City pension debt (in millions)	Per capita city pension debt
New York	8,491,079	$55,876	$6,581
Los Angeles	3,928,864	$8,172	$2,080
Chicago	2,722,389	$41,866	$15,380
Houston	2,239,558	$5,341	$2,385
Philadelphia	1,560,297	$9,405	$6,028
Phoenix	1,537,058	$3,876	$2,522
San Antonio	1,436,697	$1,343	$935
San Diego	1,381,069	$1,721	$1,246
Dallas	1,281,047	$5,602	$4,373
San Jose	1,015,785	$2,278	$2,243
Austin	912,791	$1,290	$1,413
Jacksonville	853,382	$2,455	$2,877
San Francisco	852,469	$2,326	$2,729
Indianapolis	848,788	$944	$1,112
Columbus	835,957	$1,315	$1,573

Source: Truth in Accounting; https://www.statedatalab.org/state_data_and_comparisons/CityChart.

to receive contributions from the city and CPS, as well as from employees, of just over $1.8 billion, leaving a current deficit of $1.7 billion.

How does Chicago's pension debt compare with other large US cities? Table 5.3 puts the pension debt into further context.

How Are These Pensions Supposed to Work?

To understand how this problem has grown to such proportions, let us look at how an individual pension is calculated and then at how the actuaries deal with the numbers. Table 5.4 illustrates the facts for a single employee who began work in 1987, retired at the end of 2016, and is expected to live in retirement for thirty years. This employee's pension plan calls for a starting pension that is 75 percent of ending compensation, a provision not uncommon in Chicago public employee pensions. Assume that this employee received a constant 3 percent raise every year while he worked. When he retired, his pension plan increased his pension payment by a 3 percent compounded cost of living adjustment (COLA) every year. Some of the pension plans for the city have this provision, while others call for a simple (not compounded) 3 percent increase or some other equivalent of COLA.

What does this table illustrate? First, the employee earned a little over $1.4 million in his working career, and he will receive pension payments in retirement of over $2.5 million. Next, the COLA provision adds almost $1 million to his pension payments over the thirty-year period; it is a very expensive feature of the pension plan. The last column in table 5.4 shows how the present value of this series of pension payments is discounted by the actuaries. Thus, if the pension fund were to earn a constant 7.75 percent on its assets every year, then this is all the money that would have to be set aside to provide for the employee's pension payments. If the fund earned more, it could set aside less money; if it earned less, it would have to set aside more money. This is the fabricated number we referred to earlier. Our example uses the 7.75 percent rate, the same rate that is used by the Chicago Teachers' Pension Fund. The annual report of that fund revealed that if the rate used was 1 percent lower, the net liability would increase from a little over $11 billion to $13.7 billion. The fund's presentation of these facts is confusing. The estimated earnings rates used by plans and actuaries have been declining and are expected to continue to do so.[3] This will cause unfunded liabilities to increase regularly. Why not just report the total dollar amount that the plan is obligated to pay out, together with a table of discounted amounts, so that the reader could see the impact of expected earnings rates? This would be a much clearer presentation, but it would also cause the reported liability for the teachers' plan alone to be more than $50 billion before subtracting the value of the assets. Perhaps this is just too frightening a number.

What is missing from this presentation entirely is any discussion of whether there should be accrued pension liability or pension debt in the first place. When pension plans were first created, they were considered a fringe benefit of employment; they can hardly be called fringe now. As an employee benefit, the cost of providing for pensions was incurred by the employer— the city or one of its governmental units—at the time that the individual was working. If the cost was incurred at the time of employment, then the

TABLE 5.4 Example of a Typical Employee's Earnings and
Pension Benefits

Career salary		Pension payouts			
Year	Annual compensation	Year	Annual payout (no COLA)	Annual payout (3% compounded COLA)	Present value (at a 7.75% discount)
1987	$30,000	2017	$53,023	$53,023	$53,023
1988	$30,900	2018	$53,023	$54,614	$50,686
1989	$31,827	2019	$53,023	$56,252	$48,451
1990	$32,782	2020	$53,023	$57,940	$46,315
1991	$33,765	2021	$53,023	$59,678	$44,274
1992	$34,778	2022	$53,023	$61,468	$42,322
1993	$35,822	2023	$53,023	$63,312	$40,456
1994	$36,896	2024	$53,023	$65,212	$38,673
1995	$38,003	2025	$53,023	$67,168	$36,968
1996	$39,143	2026	$53,023	$69,183	$35,338
1997	$40,317	2027	$53,023	$71,258	$33,780
1998	$41,527	2028	$53,023	$73,396	$32,291
1999	$42,773	2029	$53,023	$75,598	$30,868
2000	$44,056	2030	$53,023	$77,866	$29,507
2001	$45,378	2031	$53,023	$80,202	$28,206
2002	$46,739	2032	$53,023	$82,608	$26,963
2003	$48,141	2033	$53,023	$85,086	$25,774
2004	$49,585	2034	$53,023	$87,639	$24,638
2005	$51,073	2035	$53,023	$90,268	$23,552
2006	$52,605	2036	$53,023	$92,976	$22,514
2007	$54,183	2037	$53,023	$95,765	$21,521
2008	$55,809	2038	$53,023	$98,638	$20,572
2009	$57,483	2039	$53,023	$101,598	$19,665
2010	$59,208	2040	$53,023	$104,645	$18,798
2011	$60,984	2041	$53,023	$107,785	$17,970
2012	$62,813	2042	$53,023	$111,018	$17,178
2013	$64,698	2043	$53,023	$114,349	$16,420
2014	$66,639	2044	$53,023	$117,779	$15,697
2015	$68,638	2045	$53,023	$121,313	$15,005
2016	$70,697	2046	$53,023	$124,952	$14,343
Total career earnings	$1,427,262	Total pension payments	$1,590,690	$2,522,591	$891,766

Note: The starting pension in 2017 is 75 percent of the employee's 2016 salary of $70,697, a provision common in public employee pensions.

money to fund the pension should have been contributed to the pension fund at that time; it would then have been fully set aside in the plan the day the employee retired.

The term *intergenerational equity* refers to the desire for the full cost of public services, including pensions earned by public employees, to be paid by those receiving the benefits of those services.[4] The plans accounted for this expense by accruing the liability, but the government did not set the money aside. The Society of Actuaries takes the position that all pension plans and all pension funds should be 100 percent funded all the time.[5] That is why the measure of the health of a fund's finances is its funding ratio. The further away from 100 percent it wanders, the more trouble it is in. Consider this statement from the Municipal Employees' Annuity and Benefit Fund of Chicago's 1999 *Comprehensive Annual Financial Report*: "The ideal ratio is 100%, and represents a professional assessment that all actuarial obligations will be met assuming contributions are received for current service cost each year."[6] The Chicago Teachers' Pension Fund says something similar: "The funding policy of the Fund provides for employer contributions, when added to contributions received from employee members and earnings on investments, will be sufficient to meet the actuarially determined obligations of the Fund. . . . The Illinois Compiled Statutes (Public Act 89–15) provide for an actuarially determined funding plan intended to maintain the assets of the Fund at a level equal to 90% of the liabilities of the Fund."[7] The federal Employee Retirement Income Security Act of 1974 (ERISA) requires private sector plans to maintain 100 percent funding and includes penalties, some of which are criminal, for not complying. That law did not cover public sector pension plans, although the case for full funding is overwhelming.

Beyond the funding ratio, there are other norms for sound management of pension plans. In 2013, the Society of Actuaries established a Blue Ribbon Panel to study funding for public employee pension plans. In February 2014, the panel issued its report. This thorough study articulated all of the norms for how pension plans should be funded and how they should prepare their reports.[8] In addition to advocating 100 percent funding, the society's report describes the intergenerational equity concept, explains the effect of funding on cost stability, and discusses amortizing unfunded amounts, the selection of discount rates, and the smoothing of assets, together with many other crucial aspects of pension management.

How Have Pensions Worked in Chicago?

Pensions were not always a costly matter. They began in Chicago in the early twentieth century, long before Social Security, and grew out of the informal practice of helping poor retired teachers and other workers in the few years they had to live between retirement and death. At that time, life expectancy was much shorter than present estimates, and retirement was not a widespread practice. When the benefit was formalized in the Illinois Pension Code, the funding arrangement had the employee contributing a set percentage of his or her paycheck to the pension fund while the employer would match this with a contribution that was a multiple of that amount—the old percent-of-payroll multiple formula, or multiplier framework.

From the early 1900s to midcentury, this arrangement worked well. Conditions, however, have changed. Chicago's population grew from less than 1.7 million in 1900 to over 3.6 million in 1950. Life expectancy and retirement periods were short, benefits were modest, and the public workforce was growing by hiring more and younger workers. Then, in the last half of the century, some trends caught up with the city. Population peaked and then declined more than 25 percent. The number of retirees relative to active employees (the maturity ratio) began to grow. Public employees formed unions and gained collective bargaining rights. One of the many benefits that the unions bargained for was early retirement, so just as retirement years were lengthening due to increasing life spans, workers were beginning to retire earlier. The hyperinflation of the late 1970s induced workers to bargain for enhanced COLAs for their pensions.

Well before 1970, the multiplier framework for funding pension plans had run into trouble. Concerned about the security of their pensions, the public employee unions pushed the 1970 Illinois Constitutional Convention delegates to provide an unconditional constitutional guarantee for their pensions. The current Illinois Constitution states that "membership in any pension or retirement system of the State, any unit of local government or school district, or any agency or instrumentality thereof, shall be an enforceable contractual relationship, the benefits of which shall not be diminished or impaired."[9]

Government leaders could see trouble coming. At the national level, President John F. Kennedy formed a committee in 1963 to study corporate pensions, which resulted in the 1974 enactment of ERISA. Back in Chicago, city leaders and their financial officers knew of the actuarial concepts the new law embodied and sounded an alarm. In a combined report of the four major city pension funds for 1980–1981, it was noted that the relatively small funds had already fallen behind, having an unfunded accrued liability of $1.8 billion and being close to only 50 percent funded.[10] The report went on to explain carefully the alternative methods of catching up the funding, but even then, the plan was to amortize the debt over forty years. It would not be until about the year 2000 that the inferior funding habits of the city inevitably affected the large Chicago Teachers' Pension Fund. Although city leaders bear responsibility for the dire straits Chicago finds itself in, the actuaries have been complicit by allowing catch-up funding on an unsound basis since at least 1981.

Taxpayers and residents of Chicago now owe nearly $41.9 billion. We say taxpayers and residents because in recent years the City of Chicago, like many other cities, has resorted to all manner of fees and charges to avoid property tax increases. Residents who might not pay real estate taxes but who have a telephone or pay a water bill in Chicago pay an excise tax just so the city can make its pension payments.

What does the future look like? In recent years, the five large pension funds in the city (teachers, police, fire, municipal workers, and laborers) have been reporting on funding progress. This reporting projects what contributions the plans will need to receive in the future to bring the level of funding up to 90 percent. This is called the amortization of the debt, or less technically, the "ramp."

All these plans have been using the percentage-of-payroll method with a goal of catching up to only 90 percent of the accrued liability over periods that end between 2055 and 2065. Table 5.5 and the accompanying graph (figure 5.1) show the combined effect of this approach. The contributions from the city and CPS required to catch up the unfunded liability will rise from $1.835 billion in 2017 to $5.712 billion in 2055. To meet these contributions, revenue from taxes or fees will have to increase approximately $100 million every year for the next forty years. With this inexorable march of increased contributions, the liability will still rise to a peak of over $54 billion in the year 2036. Even then, it will require enormous contributions in the 2050s to bring the funding percentage up to 90 percent.

But beware. There are several actuarial and accounting problems with these dire projections that, when taken into account, make the picture even

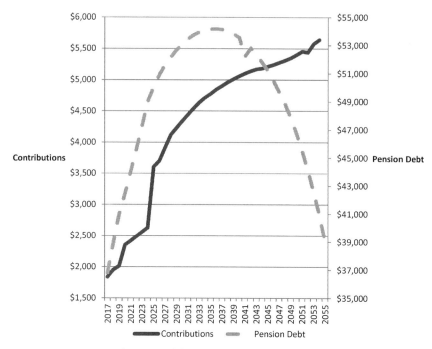

FIGURE 5.1. Forecast of pension debt and contributions. Dollars are in millions.

worse. For example, table 5.5 does not include funding for the Chicago Park District and Chicago Transit Authority; those plans do not publish this funding amortization, or ramp.

These projection tables are recalculated by the actuaries every year and seem to get worse with time. For instance, in 2014 the Chicago Teachers' Pension Fund calculated that the unfunded liability at the end of year 2036 would be $12.2 billion, and the required contribution for that year would be $1.078 billion. Then, just two years later, the actuaries recalculated the table, and their new projection for the same year, 2036, called for an unfunded liability of $13.5 billion and a required contribution of $1.179 billion. There was no change in the discount rate being used, but the projected numbers worsened by 10 percent in just two years. This shows how uncertain these pension calculations can be.

Another actuarial factor is life expectancy. Every ten years, when the US census is taken, actuaries update their mortality tables, which project life expectancy. Invariably, every decade has seen a rise in life expectancy. This

TABLE 5.5 Combined Required Annual Contributions and Unfunded Liability, Five Largest Pension Plans in Chicago, 2017 to 2055

Year	Combined annual contributions	Accumulated subtotal of contributions	Combined unfunded liability
2017	$1,836		$36,785
2018	$1,948		$38,890
2019	$2,011		$40,939
2020	$2,352		$42,467
2021	$2,418		$44,018
2022	$2,486		$45,616
2023	$2,556		$47,271
2024	$2,626		$48,988
2025	$3,604		$50,065
2026	$3,703	$25,540	$50,917
2027	$3,914		$51,623
2028	$4,119		$52,179
2029	$4,229		$52,672
2030	$4,338		$53,097
2031	$4,443		$53,452
2032	$4,544		$53,733
2033	$4,636		$53,939
2034	$4,715		$54,074
2035	$4,778		$54,152
2036	$4,844	$70,100	$54,164
2037	$4,905		$54,110
2038	$4,961		$53,989
2039	$5,011		$53,800
2040	$5,058		$53,542
2041	$5,100		$52,212
2042	$5,138		$52,812
2043	$5,170		$52,342
2044	$5,182		$51,800
2045	$5,211		$51,200
2046	$5,240	$121,074	$50,480
2047	$5,273		$49,694
2048	$5,309		$48,814
2049	$5,348		$47,834
2050	$5,397		$46,739
2051	$5,451		$45,515
2052	$5,438		$44,153
2053	$5,573		$42,635
2054	$5,639		$40,951
2055	$5,712	$170,213	$39,080

Source: Comprehensive annual financial reports and annual reports of the plans.

means retirees will live longer and the pensions they receive will be greater than previously projected.

Perhaps the most troublesome feature of the ramp tables is that they are developed using a constant percentage of compensation. What happens if total compensation does not rise as projected? We have seen this with the schools, where total compensation for CPS teachers has been level for the past eight years. It is unclear whether the pension plans and their actuaries, when faced with stagnant compensation increases, will adjust to a more level amount of funding. If they do not, then chronic underfunding will be aggravated.

The foregoing are reasons that most independent policy analysts conclude that the elements of the pension funding ramp, the required contributions and the continuing growth of liability, will be worse than even these most unfavorable projections. This is the best case scenario, and still taxpayers are on the hook and beneficiaries are at increasing risk of not receiving their pensions. In the 1960s, a cigarette advertisement asked, "Are you smoking more and enjoying it less?" As we look to the future of pensions, we must ask if those who shoulder the burden are paying more and making less progress.

If one merely accepts the funding projections as currently published, there are still a couple of serious problems. The first is back loading. The dollar amount of contributions for the thirty-nine years in table 5.5 adds up to a staggering $170 billion. Of this amount, more than $100 billion will be required after 2036, or during the last nineteen years of catch-up funding. This is 59 percent of the required funding, and it is contributed during the last half of the ramp. Actuarial reports use various methods of amortization, and the two most widely accepted are the level-dollar amount and the percentage of payroll. A level-dollar amount of catch-up funding would provide more than half of the required funding in the first twenty years. With the percentage of payroll method being used by the five pension funds, the required funding in the first twenty years is only 41 percent.

Yet another problem with the amortization of the pension debt is that the city and CPS budgets are always catching up with ever increasing pension obligations. There is a chronic lag built into the ramp, which leads to several undesirable government behaviors. Leaders are reluctant to raise taxes and revenues early and often enough to provide for the increased required pension contributions. Thus the government experiences chronic deficits, the permanent structural deficit described elsewhere in this book. When these deficits are paid for by borrowing, then the pension debt is contaminating the already precarious financial health of the city and CPS. As the government struggles to balance budgets, expenditures for current operations, vital public services, infrastructure, and even debt service for general obligation borrowing is crowded out. Chronic lag keeps the city and its sister entities trapped in a vicious cycle.

Our government leaders, our politicians, dread this nasty predicament. To escape from the vicious cycle, what do they always do? They take a holiday. In the past twenty years, as politicians at both the city and state levels have attempted to reform pensions, they often created a second tier of beneficiaries with slightly less expensive pension promises. In order to obtain union approval for these changes, the government gave something in return: they exchanged the statutory obligation to contribute a multiple of employee contributions for the acceptance of the full actuarial liability. Before each trade, the government could hide behind its limited liability. After the trade, they were on the hook for the complete pension debt. That is why they began amortizing it. But every time they agreed to such an amortization—a ramp—they took a holiday. The length of the holiday often coincided roughly with the remaining number of years in the politician's term in office. The taking of a pension holiday is one of the most consistent political and policy behaviors in both Chicago and Illinois government. What are the chances that, when the city arrives at the beginning of the next steep slope of the amortization schedule, it will take another holiday?

The Unfairness of Pension Debt

The discussion in the press of the size and impact of pension underfunding has not considered the fairness of paying it off. Those who criticize underfunding use various terminology: some say the government is incurring pension debt; others say it is stealing money from the pensions for other purposes. Since underfunding incurs a liability that will be paid in the future, it is, arguably, a misappropriation of government funds. These are not mere words to be debated; this debt will have real and severe financial implications for taxpayers and citizens twenty, thirty, and even forty years from now. It is the transfer of an immense burden onto the young and the unborn. Here is why.

As we saw with the hypothetical individual employee in table 5.4, the pension benefit earned by the employee was a significant cost for employing that person to do the work. Just because the payment for that benefit stretches decades into the future does not mean that the cost can be shifted to the future. Actuaries calculate for each employee the value of future pension benefits that the employee is entitled to receive at the end of each year of employment. If the employee is entitled to receive 2.5 percent of his projected retirement for each year of service, then the actuary will estimate the total future benefit and will add 2.5 percent to the liability for that employee at the end of the year of service. This cost for the employee is called the current service cost.

Private sector employers are allowed to account for and fund pensions differently than public sector employers. In the private sector employers who use the accrual method of accounting charge the current service cost as an expense on their financial statement. The private sector employer is required to pay the current service cost into the pension fund every year. It is unlawful under ERISA to dodge funding a private sector pension fund. If the employer does not offer a pension benefit, it must still participate in Social Security and must deposit with the federal government both the employer and employee portions of the contribution to Social Security, and not annually but after every payroll. Employers fully fund Social Security every payday. Governments, however, account for much of their operations on a cash basis, so they only have to charge the amount that they actually disburse on their financial statements. And, as we have seen, governments are often only liable for some formulaic contribution that is unrelated to the growing pension liability. This difference allows units of government to fall behind in funding. A government that fails to pay in the full current service cost every year will be catching up by owing for prior service costs.

On the pension plan side of the transaction, the failure to receive adequate annual funding causes the accrued liability to grow faster than the assets. If a fund is severely underfunded and the benefits that are paid out exceed the contributions received, the resulting deficit cannot be made up with earnings on fund assets. Table 5.6, from the Chicago policemen's pension fund report, illustrates this concept with real numbers. With only $3.1 billion in assets, it has been difficult for this fund to meet the deficit with earnings.

Funding this deficit is an unfair practice. Under normal pension operations, the earnings on assets must grow to meet the comparably growing liability. When earnings are used to subsidize the net cash flow deficit of an underfunded plan, funds are being appropriated from the future to pay for current benefits. In other words, an additional contribution from the government and

TABLE 5.6   Calculation of Payment Deficit, Policemen's Annuity and Benefit Fund of Chicago

Payment year	City contributions	Member contributions	Benefits and expenses	Net cash flow
2016	$420	$100	$696	−$176
2017	$464	$10	$717	−$143
2018	$500	$113	$748	−$135
2019	$557	$116	$782	−$109
2020	$579	$119	$816	−$118
Total	$2,520	$558	$3,759	−$681

Note: Dollars in millions.
Source: Policemen's Annuity and Benefit Fund of Chicago, GASB Statements Nos. 67 and 68 Accounting and Financial Reporting for Pensions, December 31, 2015, p. 4, http://www.chipabf.org/ChicagoPolicePension/PDF/Financials/actuarial/2015_GASB6768_PABF_Final.pdf.

ultimately the taxpayers in the future will be required because a deficit was run in the past. If that additional contribution comes in twenty-five years and from a twenty-four-year-old taxpayer, then someone who is unborn today is paying for a benefit that was paid out last year, perhaps to a beneficiary who died that year. Lawrence McQuillan, Senior Fellow at the Independent Institute, states the situation plainly: "The injustice and immorality of using millennials as piggy banks should be apparent to all but the willfully blind."[11]

Hold on, some might say. Is this not the way Social Security works? The answer is no—and yes. First of all, Social Security is really not the same kind of defined-benefit plan that a pension in Illinois is. Social Security benefits and taxes can be changed easily by congressional action and even by the flexible operation of the law. The federal government sets the COLA by administrative action of the Social Security Administration. In 2016, the Social Security Administration did not increase benefits and so the COLA was zero.[12] In the previous year, the taxable income base for Social Security taxes increased from $117,000 to $118,500, which increased the tax paid by employees and employers. Social Security is really more like a defined-contribution plan. The federal government can manage the plans to avoid running a deficit when revenues from taxes are not forthcoming. And there is another feature of Social Security that is absent in city pensions: a cap on benefits. Whether a person has earned $25,000 a year or $25 million a year during his working life, the retirement benefit is the same and will be a little over $30,000 a year. The pension benefits in the Chicago plans have no such cap.

On the other hand, yes, Social Security is not a prefunded plan as it should be, and it regularly comes in for criticism for this shortcoming. Nevertheless, every few decades Congress rights the ship by increasing taxes, decreasing benefits, or both. Ultimately, the federal government, the printer of money, has a much greater power to finance its own debt than a state or municipality, especially ones with the fiscal problems of Chicago.

As previously noted, of the $170 billion that is currently required to catch up the five Chicago pension funds, $100 billion will be contributed after the year 2036. This is the magnitude of current pension debt that is being dumped on the heads of the young and unborn. When all the wrinkles of underestimation are ironed out, the amount will likely be much more. This is no abstraction being floated by a "fiscal hawk." These are hard numbers calculated by the pension plans themselves. They are real benefits that are being paid out every month to actual retirees. And the real money has to come from somewhere. If the young people refuse to pay for these pensions or if they move away before the bill comes due, then the funds will dry up and the active employees will have no retirement to look forward to.

The argument for backloading pension debt boils down to asking current citizens to pay for sins committed in the past. Many current citizens may not have been alive when those sins were committed, and many had parents who came to this country from elsewhere long afterward. Asking that the crushing legacy costs that the city of Chicago has incurred—pensions, debt, and police settlements—be paid by taxpayers and citizens decades from now is nothing short of theft from the future of Chicago.

Solving the Pension Problem: Pain, Suffering, and Riddance

The pension problem presents an enormous and untenable economic conundrum. If you ask the beneficiary of a Chicago pension plan whether he expects to receive his full, promised pension, even when his plan is currently only 20 percent funded and is projected to get worse, he will answer affirmatively with confidence. After all, his pension is guaranteed by the Illinois Constitution. If you ask a young person whether he plans to spend the next forty years paying off pension debt incurred before he entered the workforce, he likely would dismiss the notion with just as much confidence. As the numbers show, both cannot be right. The city's leaders try to minimize, obfuscate, or avoid talking about the problem, while in fact many of them do not really understand it. Nevertheless, the numbers present a pension apocalypse. It is coming straight at us and we cannot avoid it.

From the foregoing, citizens and leaders should draw two conclusions. First, the City of Chicago and its patron, the State of Illinois, have managed their pension plans egregiously. They have proven time and again that they are not capable of offering such an employee benefit nor of managing the resulting funding. The Illinois General Assembly, for example, enacted a 3 percent COLA in 1983 for the Municipal Employees' Annuity and Benefit Fund of Chicago without so much as a study or calculation of the implications. Then, in 1998, the same legislature made the COLA compounding. These measures increased the costs by over 67 percent and were enacted, moreover, when the funds were already chronically underfunded. Pension holidays were then likewise granted with no deliberation or study. The Society of Actuaries' Blue Ribbon Panel "strongly recommends that proposed plan changes be considered over two consecutive legislative sessions (or their equivalent). The Panel believes experience has shown that this will improve the degree to which changes are thoroughly evaluated, in part by improving public awareness and discussions prior to the irreversible adoption of changes."[13] Chicago government, which negotiated the local pension plans enacted in the state pension code, has been consistently careless in managing pensions.

The second conclusion to be drawn from this study is that the amortization of the pension debt over forty plus years is too long, too unfair, and too insecure for beneficiaries. Again, the Blue Ribbon Panel has addressed this by recommending an amortization period of fifteen to twenty years. With the current amortization schedule, the level of underfunding does not peak until twenty years from now. For the next forty years, plan benefits will be in jeopardy, city government will be handicapped by overhanging pension debt, and taxpayers will see no end in sight for tax increases. No government should allow such a debilitating problem to linger for two future generations.

These conclusions point to the only obvious solution to this massive problem, short of a constitutional amendment to allow reforms to pension benefits:

the taxpayers must pay off the debt and discontinue offering such benefits. The City of Chicago, the taxpayers, and its citizens must amortize the pension debt in as short a period as possible, not to exceed twenty years. And such funding must be on a level-dollar basis, not as a percentage of payroll. This will cost the city and its inhabitants an additional $4 billion to $6 billion a year depending upon when action is taken and the level of pension debt. The authors calculate that to do so immediately will cost the city and its inhabitants an additional $2.35 billion a year, starting on top of the current $2 billion of contributions. This amount is based on the assumptions incorporated in current pension calculations in the annual reports for the various pension funds. It does not address the shortcomings of those assumptions. Figure 5.2 illustrates how the unfunded liability decreases over the twenty years as the plans' assets increase, putting level contributions to use, to match the increasing pension liabilities.

In exchange for accelerating the burden of paying for these legacy costs, taxpayers must demand that the city and all its sister entities discontinue offering

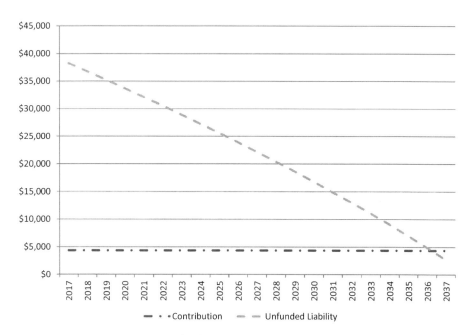

FIGURE 5.2. Decrease in unfunded pension liability with level pension plan contributions. Numbers in millions.

such defined-benefit plans. Specifically, they must freeze and discontinue the defined-benefit plans for employees and either replace them with defined-contribution plans of modest cost or enroll new hires in Social Security.

To fund these significantly larger pension contributions, the city and its entities should assess a separate and dedicated property tax. If the city is discontinuing the plans, then it must give the pension funds and the pension beneficiaries actual security, not mere assurance, that the money will be provided to pay for the pensions. A separate tax, moreover, would avoid having pension payments gobble up the municipal budgets.

There is nothing pleasant or fair to most taxpayers and citizens about these solutions. They did not enjoy the public services for which the benefits were accrued, they did not vote for the benefits they are paying for, and they did not even vote for the hapless and careless leaders who brought about the problem. If the city is to ask for billions of additional dollars immediately from citizens, it must give something in return. Before levying additional taxes, policymakers should do everything within the law to minimize the future pension obligations. Where law prohibits reasonable changes, they should do everything in their power to change the law. This could include calling for an amendment to the Illinois Constitution to protect benefits already earned but allow changes in future, unearned benefits.[14]

Freezing and discontinuing the plans is not a punishment for public employees; it is a recognition that the city has proven time and again that it is incapable of offering such plans with financial integrity. The law says, nevertheless, that the pensions must be funded, and the problem only gets worse with delay.

Freezing and Discontinuing the Plans

Ever since the 1974 passage of ERISA, corporate America has been steadily getting out of the defined-benefit business, and the federal government has been administering such terminations. Currently, only 4 percent of workers in the private sector have defined-benefit plans, down from 60 percent in the early 1980s.[15] Under ERISA, the several types of terminations and freezes can be boiled down to two choices: soft and hard. When new employees are not allowed into the plans while benefits continue to accrue unchanged for existing employees, it is called a soft freeze. When all employees stop earning additional benefits but are entitled to benefits already earned, it is called a hard freeze. In between are versions of partial freezes.[16] Whether a plan is voluntarily terminated by a private sector employer or is the result of financial distress or bankruptcy, benefits are always frozen in some manner.

The Illinois Constitution guarantees that benefits from pension plans will not be diminished or impaired. In the May 8, 2015, Illinois Supreme Court ruling nullifying a proposed change in state pension laws, the court strictly interpreted the constitution. It said, "Accordingly, once an individual begins work and becomes a member of a public retirement system, any subsequent changes to the Pension Code that would diminish the benefits conferred by membership in the retirement system cannot be applied to that individual."[17]

The constitution states that participation in a plan is a contractual obligation but does not say that employment by government guarantees participation in a plan, although state law does so stipulate. For municipalities outside Chicago, these provisions affect primarily policemen and firemen; teachers outside Chicago participate in the statewide Teachers' Retirement System of the State of Illinois, and municipal workers participate in the statewide Illinois Municipal Retirement Fund. There are some small municipalities that do not offer defined-benefit pension plans in Illinois, and state law only requires that a plan be offered if the population of the municipality exceeds five thousand.[18] Since current state law requires municipalities larger than that to offer their police officers and firefighters a pension, it would require state law to discontinue such a plan. Nevertheless, it would seem that, should the city seek state legislation authorizing discontinuation of a plan, it would not violate the state constitution.

Discontinuation of the plan would be the surest way to put this liability in the city's past. Should this prove difficult politically, an easier route might be to create a tier of plan participation for new hires which would provide no defined-benefit pension and which might spell out an alternative manner of providing for other retirement benefits. This would be a discontinuation of a benefit without a termination of a plan. Several of the city's plans already have tier 2 participation with reduced benefits, so the template for such action is in place.

In the event of a discontinuation, how would the current benefit be frozen? The wording in the constitution would call for a softer freeze, whereby those already participating in a plan could continue to accrue benefits. A city or some other unit of local government that finds itself unable to amortize a crippling pension debt might argue for a harder freeze, although it is difficult to predict how the court would review such a plea.

Taking an action as radical as discontinuing defined-benefit plans and thus providing for the tax revenue to accelerate the funding of the beleaguered plans would call for significant study and should not be undertaken with the casual approach with which prior benefit increases and pension holidays have been adopted. With the onerous burden that paying off the pensions will place on taxpayers, leaders must be assured that the cost of retirement benefits for new hires is modest. To replace an expensive defined-benefit plan that politicians would not pay for with a different costly retirement plan would completely subvert the goal of solving the problem.

Alternative Pension Solutions

The solution described above could be called "pay up." Not every civic leader who understands the pension problem in Chicago is willing to accept this concept. In the recent past, various persons and organizations, including the city itself, have tried to advance proposals that could be described as "settle up" or "dry up." All these proposal seek to reduce the ultimate stream of payments to retirees from what is currently promised.

In 2014, the city attempted to modify the pension plan for municipal workers and laborers. A change enacted to the Ilinois Pension Code called for a reduction in certain terms of the benefits promised to active employees. In March 2016, the Illinois Supreme Court threw out the law, reaffirming what it had previously ruled on a similar attempt to modify state pensions. The city was trying to settle up by reducing benefits and enhancing funding for the plans. The Park District tried a similar reform that was likewise overruled in 2018.[19] The ruling confirmed, instead, that the constitutional guaranty of pensions without diminishment is inviolate. The case is closed for Chicago and Illinois.

Some civic groups nonetheless argued in amicus briefs that the public welfare of citizens is threatened when pension costs crowd out vital public services in municipal budgets. The court did not allow any parties to file these briefs, and so it would appear that these arguments might never receive a hearing. Any attempt to settle with a diminished pension benefit for either active or retired beneficiaries now faces the constraints of both the constitution and the precedent of the Illinois Supreme Court.

Discouraged by these developments some civic leaders have written about and advocated for some way for the US federal government to intervene in order to bring more balance between pension beneficiaries and taxpayers. One option would be municipal bankruptcy. This is not currently allowed by Illinois law and would require action by the state legislature. Were the legislature to allow municipal bankruptcy, then federal provisions would allow a court to break the pension contracts. Many leaders feel that bankruptcy is too risky for the city and that the reductions in benefits that a court might allow would not be material enough to make the undertaking worthwhile. Others have proposed a hybrid bankruptcy law that would apply only to public employee pensions. Still others, including one of the authors, have at times suggested that some other form of federal relief directed at troubled public employee pension plans be enacted.

Many uninformed persons feel that the solution is to minimize payments to the pension plans and "starve" them into a crisis where the pension plans dry up and default on their benefit obligations. There is no legal basis for this wishful thinking, but there is also no precedent for what happens when a city defaults on paying benefits for a pension plan that has run out of money. Cities in Illinois, notably Harvey and North Chicago, are in distress and already starving their pension plans, and it is not clear where those municipalities will end up. The fact that the funding levels of Chicago's pension plans will deteriorate for many years to come makes this alternative a real possibility.

While public officials have been paying lip service to solving the pension problem, the plans have in fact been drying up. As table 5.5 and the accompanying graph show, the unfunded pension balance will continue to grow for the next nineteen years. During this period, the city's pension funding will more closely resemble a pay-as-you-go scheme; and when the payment ramp reaches the level that the funding improves, the reality will be that someone must pay. Will taxpayers twenty years from now be willing to do so?

Without any legal basis or precedent, all of these proposals amount to serious but wishful thinking. If they prevail, these measures would go a long way toward balancing the interests of taxpayers and plan beneficiaries. They are not, however, a basis for sound policy and planning; to wait while the funds dissipate is not a prudent approach.

Apocalypse Now

One meaning of *apocalypse* is the revealing or uncovering of some secret. Another is the coming of a cataclysmic disaster. Both meanings apply to the pension problems in Chicago. As we have seen, when looking at the city's finances or the operation of CPS, pension costs are already gobbling up the budgets and crowding out current vital services. The relentless parade of new taxes and fees to fund the rising pension contributions over the next forty years will create uncertainty and unintended consequences. The schedule of increasing pension contributions in table 5.5 calls for an increase in taxes of $100 million every year for the next forty years. Even with such tax increases, it will be twenty years before the funding of the five plans begins to improve.

Avoiding the problem will not make it to go away. Some policy experts feel that bankruptcy might be a solution, but so far the insolvency of other cities in the United States have not brought significant pension relief. If bankruptcy ensued in Chicago and thereby provided a material reduction in the liability, it would be welcomed by taxpayers. But waiting for such speculative relief is in the same category of poor policy that got the city into this financial mess in the first place. Solving the problem needs a different level of thinking and will require several measures:

- discontinuing the offering of defined-benefit pensions for new employees in order to stop the liability from growing;
- changing the amortization schedule for catching up pension funding to twenty years or less; and
- increasing taxes now, with a new dedicated pension tax of $4.35 billion to fund the amortization. With this new tax, existing taxes of $2 billion that are funding current contributions should be eliminated.

CHAPTER 6

Overdue Oversight and the Reality of Corruption

Chicago is not the most corrupt American city. It's the most theatrically corrupt.
—STUDS TERKEL

〜

Bags of shredded paper, keyboards without monitors, and bare walls. That's what news crews found in a small office at 740 N. Sedgwick on the afternoon of November 12, 2015. FBI agents stood silently in the lobby of the city building, overseeing the transfer of computers and reams of documents, leaving the office in disarray.

An onlooker may have suspected wrongdoing from a public official. That would not have been a bad guess. Chicago streets have served as a backdrop to such a scene many times before. But that day was different. The FBI did not come to sting a shakedown from an alderman. They did not come to bust a city department hideout. They did not come to catch a crooked county commissioner. They came to assist Chicago City Council's first-ever watchdog, Faisal Khan, as he and his small staff disbanded an office that had been built to fail. In modern American history, Chicago appears to be the only major city that has shuttered an oversight body with no replacement waiting in the wings.

The Office of the Legislative Inspector General, or OLIG, was no more. The body had rejected the organ. "We felt like criminals," Khan said. "And that was the end of the Office of the Legislative Inspector General . . . there was almost a celebration of the return to status quo" (interview, August 2, 2017). Investigations and indictments made public in the months that followed revealed that as Khan and his team packed their personal belongings, handed over their investigations to the FBI, and headed home, misconduct continued unabated within Chicago City Council. That year, more than two-thirds of Chicago aldermen took in donations that appear to be in violation of the city's campaign finance rules.[1] Federal officials in 2016 indicted Alderman Willie Cochran for allegedly shaking down local business owners and credited Khan's work for initiating the investigation.[2]

Nearly six months after the OLIG's ignominious end, aldermen moved to transfer its oversight power to the Office of the Inspector General (OIG), the head of which is appointed by the mayor and approved by the city council. But city officials were sure to place blinders on that office, too. As of 2018, the OIG has no authority to investigate aldermen's largest source of discretionary funding—each receive $1.3 million per year in "menu money"—nor a secretive, $100 million a year workers' compensation program run by the city's longest-serving alderman out of a city council committee.[3]

Chicago government's reputation for corruption is far from a mere stereotype. It has earned that standing, and cultural echoes of machine politics reverberate through the city's oversight structure still today. But the city has taken material steps to prevent corruption; those steps have had real effects on city government, and the current oversight structure may need only a few simple changes to begin restoring trust in local leaders.

Corruption Capital?

Chicago is renowned worldwide for its culture of corruption. From 1920s speakeasies protected by Irish and Italian mobsters and aldermen with nicknames like "Hinky Dink" and "Bathhouse," to modern kickbacks worth millions for installing lucrative cameras at city intersections, the breadth, depth, and longevity of wrongdoing in Chicago government is unparalleled among major American cities.

The Windy City's reputation is not skin-deep. US Department of Justice data peg Illinois's northern judicial district, which encompasses the Chicago metropolitan region, as the nation's "corruption capital." From 1976 to 2013, the district saw 1,642 federal public corruption convictions, outpacing every major judicial district in the country.[4] However, although it is one of the most common data sets by which public corruption is analyzed in the United States, some researchers have called into question the use of DOJ data, which is composed of annual reports to Congress made by the Public

Integrity Section of the DOJ.[5] There are three main challenges regarding the DOJ data: First, federal judicial districts are too rough a proxy for cities, as they capture a number of counties outside the city proper and in some cases the entire state. Second, these data include indictments of federal and state officials as well as local officials, so they are not necessarily an indication of the level of corruption among city officials only. Third, public corruption cases tried by state and local prosecutors are not included in the data. Only looking at federal prosecutions introduces a number of questions regarding prosecutorial effort, resources, and partisan bias.

Still, there are some insights to be gained from reviewing these convictions. One is that when controlled for the population of each federal district, Illinois's northern judicial district does not top the list over the last decade. Table 6.1 shows that among the districts covering the fifteen largest cities, two Texas districts (western and northern, which cover San Antonio, Austin, and Dallas) and Pennsylvania's eastern district (covering Philadelphia) all rank higher for public corruption convictions from 2007 to 2016, in per capita terms.

Public corruption is inevitable, but Chicago corruption is notorious. Commentators across the political spectrum bemoan city government as a near kleptocracy. But a search of the *Chicago Tribune* archives and the University of Illinois at Chicago's anticorruption reports for city-level officials convicted of public corruption can provide a more realistic context. Table 6.2 displays city officials convicted of corruption in relation to their public duties over the last decade. Those convicted as part of a sweeping investigation, such as Hired Trucks or Crooked Code, are noted as such.

While the relative level of Chicago corruption compared with other major cities can be murky, what is not in dispute is the breathtaking frequency of wrongdoing among Chicago aldermen. Since 1972, more than thirty of some two hundred aldermen have been convicted of federal crimes related to their official duties, including bribery, extortion, embezzlement, and conspiracy.[6]

And of course, it is not just the aldermen. High-profile corruption cases in recent Chicago history include individuals operating in widely disparate areas of government. In October 2016, former Chicago Public Schools CEO Barbara Byrd-Bennett pleaded guilty to wire fraud after diverting $23 million in school district contracts to two consulting firms. She received more than $2 million from those firms in exchange for ensuring that they would fly through the bidding process unopposed.

TABLE 6.1   Top Fifteen US Cities Ranked by Federal Public
Corruption Convictions per 100,000 Population of Associated Federal
Judicial District

City	Associated federal district	Population of federal district, 2016	Convictions, 2007–2016	Convictions per 100,000
Philadelphia	Pennsylvania, Eastern	5,682,897	248	4.36
San Antonio	Texas, Western	6,803,524	291	4.28
Austin	Texas, Western	6,803,524	291	4.28
Dallas	Texas, Northern	7,055,730	297	4.21
Chicago	Illinois, Northern	8,356,697	339	4.06
Houston	Texas, Southern	9,275,996	342	3.69
San Diego	California, Southern	3,432,163	125	3.64
Phoenix	Arizona	6,728,577	234	3.48
New York City	New York, Southern	5,207,589	149	2.86
Indianapolis	Indiana, Southern	2,695,554	72	2.67
Jacksonville	Florida, Middle	11,391,896	261	2.29
Los Angeles	California, Central	19,181,197	404	2.11
New York City	New York, Eastern	8,245,118	137	1.66
Columbus	Ohio, Southern	5,837,397	72	1.23
San Jose	California, Northern	8,174,663	52	0.64
San Francisco	California, Northern	8,174,663	52	0.64
Average	—	7,653,471	215	2.96

Note: New York's eastern and southern federal judicial districts each cover portions of
New York City.
Sources: For population, 2012–2016 American Community Survey 5-Year Estimates,
US Census Bureau; for convictions, Department of Justice, "Report to Congress on the
Activities and Operations of the Public Integrity Section for 2016," https://www.justice
.gov/criminal/file/1015521/download.

In August 2016, former second-in-command at the Chicago Department
of Transportation, John Bills, was sentenced to ten years in prison for his
role in orchestrating Chicago's red-light camera program while taking bribes
from the company supplying the city with those cameras. Bills was convicted
of twenty counts of fraud, extortion, and other crimes for steering the lucrative
contract toward Redflex Traffic Systems, Inc. In return, he received $600,000
in cash, an Arizona condo, and other kickbacks from the company.

TABLE 6.2 Chicago City Officials Convicted of Corruption, 2007–2017

Name	Position	Crime	Sentence	Date sentenced
Lennie Perry	Driver, Streets and Sanitation	Bribery	9 years prison	December 2017
Barbara Byrd-Bennett	CEO, Chicago Public Schools	Wire fraud	4.5 years prison	April 2017
Roberto Uribe	Inspector, Department of Buildings	Attempted extortion	2 years probation, 6 months home confinement	October 2016
John Bills	Assistant Commissioner, Transportation Department	Tax fraud, mail fraud, extortion, conspiracy, and bribery	10 years prison	August 2016
Antionette Chenier	Clerk, Department of Transportation	Theft of government funds, tax evasion	2.5 years prison	September 2015
Curtis V. Thompson Jr.	Chief of Staff for Alderman Howard Brookins	Bribery	15 months prison	May 2015
Abd Ayesh	Supervisor, Department of Business Affairs and Consumer Protection	Official misconduct, theft	2 years probation	January 2015
Sandi Jackson	Alderman	Tax fraud	12 months prison	August 2013
Operation Crooked Code (sixteen employees)	Department of Buildings and Zoning	Bribery (primarily)	Various	Last employee sentenced March 2012
Al Sanchez (Hired Trucks)	Commissioner, Streets and Sanitation	Mail fraud	2.5 years prison	February 2011
Aaron Del Valle (Hired Trucks)	Aide, Streets and Sanitation	Perjury	12 months, 1 day prison	February 2011
Isaac Carothers	Alderman	Bribery, tax fraud	28 months prison	June 2010
Arenda Troutman	Alderman	Mail fraud, tax fraud	4 years prison	March 2009
Kurt Berger	Supervisor, Department of Buildings	Bribery	15 months prison	June 2008
John Sullivan	Managing Deputy, Streets and Sanitation	Perjury	Unknown	April 2008
Miguel Diaz	City Inspector	Bribery	3 months prison	February 2008
Valerie Jones (Hired Trucks)	Aide to Director Angelo Torres	Perjury	5 months probation	January 2008
John Resa	Engineer, Water Department	Perjury	15 months prison	November 2007
James Picardi	Operations Manager, Chicago Public Schools	Bribery	20 months prison	April 2007

Note: Data excludes the Chicago Police Department.

Corruption on such a grand scale is not limited to those as politically powerful as Byrd-Bennett or Bills. In 2014, an inspector general report found that a CPS technology coordinator stole $400,000 in school funds by creating fake vendors connected to his personal bank account. Left unnamed in the report, the individual fled to Mexico and was later found dead.[7]

Corruption has had a persistent, corrosive effect on the public's trust in local government. A 2016 survey of Chicago business leaders showed over 90 percent believed city government engages in some form of cronyism.[8] After being subjected to the deeds of nefarious public officials for decades, the average Chicagoan believes corruption is rampant. It is just a matter of finding out who, what, when, where, and why.

Beyond the social cost, corruption comes with financial and economic burdens. As detailed in chapter 8, a single three-month span in 2017 saw Chicago police misconduct alone cost the city more than $100 million.[9] Further, the role of aldermen as mini-mayors, as outlined in chapter 1, bottlenecks business development and invites corruption. Aldermanic staff serve as intake points for administrative tasks such as signage, awnings, sidewalk repair, and sidewalk café permits, to name only a few. That means the average small business owner depends on the good will, or at least ambivalence, of their local representative in order to succeed.

Have the city's solutions to the problem been commensurate with the scale of corruption? Recent events and stubborn blockades suggest they have not. City council still retains a few precious "black boxes." Inspectors general remain institutionally divided across branches of city government with varying degrees of independence from the bodies they are tasked with overseeing, and the city law department too often treats the mayor, rather than citizens, as its client. As one senior oversight official described the city in an off-the-record interview: "If you were to devise a system that had the appearance of oversight without it being truly effective, you would do this."

Further, Chicagoans must recognize that watchdogs are only one front in the battle of corruption; political institutions also affect the degree of misbehavior from public officials. Lack of partisan competition, a disempowered legislative branch, and a far-reaching executive branch all deserve examination for the roles they play in Chicago corruption. In Chicago, even the most tenacious, empowered, independent watchdog may not be enough to compensate for a political system ripe for abuse. Reformers would be wise to consider not just the "theatrical" corruption described by legendary Chicagoan Studs Terkel, which results in handcuffs and camera flashes outside the Federal Building, but the unfortunate reality of corruption *under the law.*

How Chicago Government Polices Itself

The City of Chicago opened its first official internal investigative offices in 1956, called the Department of Investigation. Rampant misconduct continued relatively unabated. The next major step toward honest government would not come until 1972 with the first in a series of court orders resulting from a lawsuit by Michael Shakman, an independent candidate for delegate to the 1970 Illinois Constitutional Convention. The 1972 consent decree prohibited politically motivated firings, demotions, transfers, or other punishment of government employees.[10]

In the late 1970s, the *Chicago Sun-Times* and Better Government Association performed an investigation of their own, sending reporters undercover to open a tavern called the Mirage. They found, among other things, numerous inspectors and other city employees taking bribes.[11] In the wake of their findings, the city's oversight office was rebranded as the Office of Professional Review. In 1981, that office was changed to the Office of Municipal Investigations. But regardless of its name, the commissioner or director of this office served at the pleasure of the mayor throughout its first few decades of existence. Its efficacy was also hampered by the fact that it did not wield subpoena power.

The 1980s brought Chicago, kicking and screaming, toward a new era of transparency. The city enacted its first freedom of information ordinance in 1983, which brought forth unprecedented public scrutiny of city documents.[12] And in 1987, the city adopted its first-ever ethics ordinance. A 1989 ordinance corrected some of the city's limitations on investigative independence and effectiveness in its establishment of the Office of the Inspector General (OIG), which exists to this day. The ordinance establishing the OIG called for an inspector general to be appointed by the mayor and subject to the approval of the city council. The inspector general is appointed to a four-year term and may only be removed "for cause," with a mandatory investigative hearing in the city council should the inspector general challenge such a removal.[13]

Additionally, the ordinance creating the OIG provided for investigative powers previously denied to the city's internal investigative agencies. The inspector general has the power to issue subpoenas to compel the attendance of witnesses for purposes of examination, as well as the production of documents and other items for inspection.[14] However, the Illinois Supreme Court ruled in 2013 that the OIG lacks independent enforcement authority over those subpoenas. That responsibility belongs to the city's law department, which operates in lockstep with the mayor's interests.[15]

The OIG's current investigatory powers and limitations, briefly summarized, enable it to do the following[16]:

- Initiate investigations
- Obtain access to premises, equipment, and records
- Request information from any officer, employee, agent, or licensee of the city
- Require employees, not officers, to report misconduct (under mayoral executive order, not ordinance)
- Issue subpoenas in investigations (without, however, the power to enforce them)
- Divulge investigatory files and reports to US attorney, Illinois attorney general, or state's attorney of Cook County

While the OIG is the city's standard-bearer in its fight against corruption, the office at times is hamstrung in its ability to carry out effective watchdog work. First, the rubber-stamp nature of the city council undermines the credibility of the office in terms of its independence from the mayor. Another restraint is a peculiar result of the OIG fulfilling the role of the ousted legislative inspector general. While the inspector general was granted jurisdiction over city council members and staffers months after Khan and his staff left their office, the OIG was not granted the authority to audit city council committees and other programs. This is widely known to be the result of heavy horse-trading by council member Ed Burke, chairman of the Finance Committee, out of which he controls the city's workers' compensation program without independent oversight. It is estimated to cost about $100 million per year.

"There's almost no one in city government outside of the [workers' compensation] program that knows how it works," claimed a 2016 TV news report on the oversight loophole. "No alderman we spoke to had any clue how it worked." The same report noted Chicago was the only major city to run its workers' compensation program out of a legislative committee. "The committee's function

[is] to manage the business of the council," said Alderman John Arena, "not to handle a program that deals with legal issues and medical issues."[17]

While the limitations of the OIG are of concern, they are only a part of what limits the efficacy of Chicago oversight as a whole, to the benefit of the one holding all the cards. Power is centralized in the mayor's office, but oversight of that power is diffused across different offices with different rules and funding sources. The mayor exercises a great deal of authority over sister governments, such as the parks, the schools, the housing authority, and more. But the city's oversight body does not enjoy a similar field of vision. The power is centralized, but oversight is not.

Chicago is home to five different inspectors general, including one for the city, one for Chicago Public Schools, one for the Chicago Housing Authority, one for the Chicago Park District, and one for the City Colleges of Chicago. The Chicago Transit Authority also had its own inspector general until 2011, when that authority was transferred to a state-level inspector general. There is also a Cook County inspector general. These watchdogs vary widely in power, rules, and funding, with decentralization having a number of deleterious effects on watchdog work.

Take contracting and procurement, for example. There is a great deal of overlap among individuals and businesses that do contract work for the city, the parks, the housing authority, and other sister governments. But the oversight of contract administration and management is broken up, meaning there is plenty of room to game the system. Getting drummed out of business with the city does not mean one cannot take a shot at the parks, for example. The same goes for employment.

While there has been steady progress in allowing for greater degrees of communication and flow of information between inspectors general, the city still lacks a holistic oversight body in line with how power is distributed. One must ask what more effective oversight is supposed to look like.

What Other Cities Do

The inspector general model is relatively fresh among the fifteen largest cities, with Houston, Jacksonville, and Chicago all adopting a city-level inspector general within the last thirty years (table 6.3). Among the fifteen largest cities, Chicago compares favorably in the power of its top watchdog. Few other inspectors general enjoy investigatory powers as broad as Chicago's. Further, in comparing the nature of appointment and removal of each city's top oversight official, Chicago does not stand out.

A review of the fifteen most populous cities reveals Chicago is one of six to entrust the mayor with the appointment of the city's top oversight official, and one of four to require legislative approval of that mayoral nominee. At one end of the spectrum of mayoral discretion are Houston and Philadelphia, where the mayor appoints the chief oversight official and can remove that individual with few institutional hurdles. At the other end is Los Angeles, home to an elected city controller who serves as the city watchdog. Another interesting model is Jacksonville's, where the inspector general is appointed by a seven-member committee, of which the mayor is only one member, and the inspector general may be removed only by a majority vote of that commission and city council approval. A deeper look at New York City, Los Angeles, Houston, Philadelphia, and Phoenix shows where Chicago compares favorably and where the city still has some room for improvement.

NEW YORK CITY

New York is home to one of the oldest and perhaps most widely respected anticorruption bodies in the country, the Department of Investigation, or DOI. In existence for more than 140 years, it is one of few if not the only major watchdog body in urban governance originally created by the state legislature, which established the office in 1873 and granted subpoena powers in 1884. The department now draws its authority from the city charter, in addition to a variety of executive orders from the mayor. Tasked with rooting out corruption, criminal activities, conflicts of interest, unethical conduct, waste, and abuse in the second-largest government in the nation (behind only the federal government), the DOI houses eight inspectors general. As one senior city oversight official put it, there is "one budget, one standard, one law, and one responsibility." All of those inspectors report to the DOI commissioner, who reports to city council and the mayor. Their powers for the most part align with those of Chicago's city inspector general, with the exception of that office's oversight limitations in the Chicago City Council.

New York's inspectors general were not always centralized. Similar to Chicago today, inspectors general once reported to the respective agencies they were tasked with overseeing—not the DOI—until the 1980s. But in the wake of a number of local corruption scandals, Mayor Ed Koch in 1986 signed an

TABLE 6.3   Top Oversight Official in Top Fifteen Cities

City	Chief oversight official	How position is filled	Removal provisions
New York	Department of Investigation Commissioner	Mayoral appointment, city council approval	Mayor may remove at will
Los Angeles	City Controller	Elected	Popular vote every four years
Chicago	Inspector General	Mayoral appointment, city council approval	Mayor may remove at will; requires council hearing if IG disputes
Houston	City Attorney	Mayoral appointment	City code does not outline removal process
Phoenix	City Auditor	Appointed by city manager	City manager may remove at will
Philadelphia	Inspector General	Mayoral appointment	Mayor may remove at will
San Antonio	Ethics Review Board	Mayor and each member of city council nominate one member, confirmed by city council	City council may remove for cause on majority vote
San Diego	City Auditor	Appointed by city manager and confirmed by city council	May be removed for cause by a two-thirds vote in city council after audit committee recommendation
Dallas	City Auditor	Appointed by city council	City council may remove for cause
San Jose	City Auditor	Appointed by city council	City council may remove for cause during term with 10–1 vote
Austin	City Auditor	Appointed by city council	City council may remove at conclusion of term (majority vote) or during term (three-quarters vote)
Jacksonville	Inspector General	Selection by Inspector General Selection and Retention Committee, confirmed by city council[a]	Removal proceedings may be initiated by committee for cause on a majority vote; must be confirmed by city council
San Francisco	City Controller	Mayoral appointment, board of supervisors approval	Mayor may remove for cause; requires two-thirds vote from board of supervisors
Indianapolis	Office of Audit and Performance Director	Mayoral appointment with city-county council approval	Mayor may remove at will
Columbus	City Auditor[b]	Elected	Popular vote every four years

[a] Committee includes the president of Jacksonville City Council, the state attorney of the Fourth Judicial Circuit, the chair of the Jacksonville Ethics Commission, the chair of the Jacksonville TRUE Commission, the public defender of the Fourth Judicial Circuit, the chief judge of the Fourth Judicial Circuit, and the mayor of Jacksonville, or their respective designees.

[b] The Columbus city auditor provides strictly financial oversight; there is not a city-level office with broad oversight of corruption generally.

executive order taking the IGs out of the agencies, making them employees of the DOI instead.[18]

Since 1990, New York had operated with an exception to this centralized system—the schools. The semiautonomous Special Commissioner of Investigation for the New York City School District was tasked with overseeing a school system serving more than one million students. In 2018, the DOI moved to bring the special commissioner under its wing as well.[19]

In addition to the inspectors general, New York employs a Conflict of Interest Board to assist members of city government in ethics training, ethics complaints, and ethics counsel, with the DOI serving as the board's investigative arm. Its leadership is appointed by the mayor, but the five board members serve staggered six-year terms, providing a check on total mayoral capture. No member may serve more than two consecutive six-year terms.[20]

New York's southern judicial district includes Manhattan, the Bronx, and six nearby counties. It saw 1,260 public corruption convictions from 1976 to 2013, nearly 400 fewer than Illinois's northern district. Keep in mind, however, that this district encompasses only 5 million residents. New York's eastern judicial district covers more than 8.2 million residents in Brooklyn, Queens, and Long Island but saw even fewer convictions than the southern district over that time period, with 789. In more recent history, from 2007 to 2016, New York's southern district saw 149 federal public corruption convictions and its eastern district saw 137. Over the same time, Illinois's northern district saw 339. In other words, despite being home to 60 percent more people, New York City's associated federal judicial districts combined saw 15 percent fewer corruption convictions than Chicago's.

LOS ANGELES

The City of Los Angeles has flown somewhat under the radar in its notoriety for corruption, given its size. It is even occasionally eclipsed by its smaller neighbors in Los Angeles County. A 2010 *Los Angeles Times* investigation led to a former city manager in nearby Bell, California, being found guilty on sixty-nine corruption charges, along with six other city officials and politicians. The Bell scheme had it all: inflated public salaries, personal loans to employees, illegal tax increases, shakedowns, and more. In recent memory, Los Angeles city government has not been racked by similar blatant transgressions, but the same cannot be said for its police department.

Los Angeles's most recent major corruption event is known as the Rampart scandal, which was one of the most widespread cases of police corruption in US history. The investigation implicated dozens of officers for wrongdoing ranging from unprovoked shootings and beatings to planting evidence and even a bank robbery in the late 1990s.[21] This resulted in courts overturning more than one hundred criminal convictions. In the wake of Rampart, as well as the infamous Rodney King beating, the city entered a consent decree with the Department of Justice that resulted in sweeping changes to police oversight, which are discussed in chapter 8. One lasting change spurred by these events was the establishment of an office of inspector general for the Los Angeles County Police Department. In addition to a local oversight, Los Angeles County created an inspector general's office via ordinance in 2014 to oversee the Los Angeles County Sheriff's Department.[22]

Oversight of other city government bodies is primarily handled out of the elected controller's office, which serves as both a taxpayer watchdog and the city's chief auditor and accountant. The office declares: "The Controller's job is to investigate and publicly report problems with city departments, increase governmental efficiency and save taxpayer money by improving operations, conduct financial and performance audits of all city departments, offices and programs, monitor and report on all matters relating to the City's fiscal health, keep the City's official financial records, and supervise all expenditures of the city."[23] Chicagoans will recognize some similar responsibilities in its own inspector general's office.

California's central district saw 1,360 public corruption convictions from 1976 to 2013, second only to Illinois's northern federal district, which was home to 1,642. However, the central district is by far the most populous judicial district in the nation, with more than 19 million residents. The northern district of Illinois has 8.3 million residents. In per capita terms, Illinois's northern district had nearly double the corruption convictions as California's central district from 2007 to 2016.

HOUSTON

The inspector general for the City of Houston is housed under the city's legal department, reporting to the city attorney. The city attorney is appointed by the mayor and confirmed by city council. Of the major cities, Houston's inspector general is one of the weakest and seems not to have yet found solid ground. That weakness stems in part from lack of independence from the mayor's office, lack of transparency, and lack of authority.

In 2010, the mayor of Houston moved the inspector general's office out of the police department and placed it under the purview of the city attorney's office. This lack of independence has been criticized by at least one former Houston inspector general. Additionally, the city keeps secret a large majority of the office's findings. "The public has a right to know what I've found," said former inspector general Bob Dogium.[24]

The federal judicial district that includes Houston was home to 342 federal corruption convictions from 2007 to 2016, giving it a per capita conviction rate on par with Illinois's northern district.

PHILADELPHIA

Among the federal judicial districts covering the fifteen largest cities, Pennsylvania's eastern district is home to the highest number of federal corruption convictions per capita over the last decade. But does this status reflect the efficacy of Philadelphia's chief watchdog?

Then mayor Wilson Goode appointed Philadelphia's first inspector general in 1985. Former US Treasury Department inspector general Leon Wigrizer stepped into the office with only a single other investigator under his control.[25] The mayor also established a system of "integrity officers" modeled after a practice in New York City, with one senior employee in each department and agency serving as an internal point person for waste and fraud. The office has expanded considerably since then, in addition to thirty-six integrity officers who currently report to the inspector general.

As it was at the time of the office's inception, the mayor still appoints the inspector general in Philadelphia. Along with Houston, it is one of only two of the fifteen major cities where the mayor appoints the inspector general without any additional hurdles. Its powers to investigate potential fraud, waste, abuse, corruption, and misconduct in city government are on par with inspectors general in other major cities. That said, it is the city's independently elected controller who takes the lead in auditing and other financial oversight.

The current inspector general's tenure stretches across two mayors, and she has declared something of a sea change in city government. In an op-ed column in the *Philadelphia Inquirer*, Amy Kurland drew a comparison between a 2003 case in which nearly the entire plumbing inspection department at the city's Department of Licenses and Inspections was convicted of extorting money from plumbers with a case in 2017 in which five employees of the same department reported to the inspector general's office that contractors had attempted to bribe them.[26] Despite such claims of progress, the office is still technically temporary, as it is not enshrined in the city charter and exists entirely at the executive's discretion.

PHOENIX

In Phoenix, watchdog work falls within the scope of the city manager, who is appointed by the mayor and approved by city council. The city manager then appoints a city auditor in the same way he or she would appoint any other department head. Members of city council are expressly prohibited in city code from interfering with the city manager's appointment or removal of any personnel, including the city auditor.[27] The council can, however, remove the city manager without cause with a two-thirds vote. If being removed for incompetence, malfeasance, misfeasance, or neglect of duty, the council may remove the manager on a simple majority vote.[28]

The city auditor does not just report to the city manager, but also the city's Audit Committee, which includes the following: three city council members appointed by the mayor, three members of the public appointed by the mayor, the city manager, the director of the Finance Department, and the director of the Budget and Research Department.

In recent history, Phoenix city government has not seen high-profile corruption scandals on par with other cities of its size. Phoenix ranks in the middle of the pack in terms of per capita public corruption convictions, but its associated federal judicial district covers the entire state.

Recommendations

While it may not seem like it to Chicagoans, city oversight has come a long way in the last few decades. But clear shortcomings stubbornly remain. First, the inspector general should enjoy access to all city documents in investigations, including those held by corporation counsel. The current abnormality—where the inspector general must seek enforcement authority from the city law department in order to acquire documents held by the city law department— is the primary avenue by which the mayor may still wield influence in the day-to-day operations of the office. Changing this means giving the inspector general the power to enforce its subpoenas.

An elected city attorney, discussed in chapter 1, could augment this reform by serving as a check on the mayor's power to interfere in the inspector general's operations. Further, the inspector general should have the authority to audit all city council programs, including the workers' compensation system and aldermanic funds. That the city council placed blinders on the inspector general with regard to these select items is an embarrassment that signals an unwillingness to reckon with history.

It is clear that expanding the city inspector general's reach to the city council was the correct choice, save for its limitations. Expanding its purview to the sister governments, which the mayor controls through appointment, is the logical next step. Chicago should consolidate its numerous inspectors general under one roof, akin to the Department of Investigation in New York City. The current city inspector general model, even with its flaws, is among the nation's strongest. Meanwhile, the remaining inspectors general are left struggling for basic measures to ensure independence, such as guaranteed minimum funding. Enabling cooperation in investigations and alignment in power and governance will improve oversight. One case against consolidating Chicago's OIG across sister governments is that it would offer an opportunity for the mayor to broaden his or her scope of influence even further. This is a valid concern that would be largely ameliorated by the other reforms outlined in this chapter and throughout the book.

Chicago could also take a cue from New York City's Conflict of Interest Board and operate a centralized ethics office, with a unified ethics code across city and sister governments. The city council should further amend the city ethics ordinance to cover aldermen and their staff, and the city's ethics training should be improved to at least the level of the State of Illinois.

Ultimately, the most powerful reforms toward making city government less prone to corruption are found in chapter 1. Eliminating the administrative authorities of city aldermen, aldermanic privilege, would go a long way toward blocking off one particularly attractive avenue for grift. When it comes to the present composition of city council, the words of New York City Police Department whistle-blower Frank Serpico regarding his fellow officers ring true: "Ten percent . . . are absolutely corrupt, 10 percent are absolutely honest, and the other 80 percent—they wish they were honest." The ombudsperson system incentivizes use of the office for personal benefit. Many are left wishing they were honest.

Fixing Chicago's corruption problem will require far more than just governance changes. Cultural shifts will need to occur. Tacit and even explicit approval of corrupt practices from Chicago voters has allowed the problem to fester for too long. If voters tolerate the shuttering of a major watchdog office or the hiding of certain programs from oversight, change will not be imminent. But at least to begin restoring Chicagoans' trust in local government, more concrete reforms cannot come quickly enough.

CHAPTER 7

Public Support for Private Enterprise at the Metropolitan Pier and Exposition Authority

A man is honorable in proportion to the personal risks he takes for his opinion.
—NASSIM NICHOLAS TALEB

⤚

The Black Box by the Lake

The rebirth of the nation's largest convention center began with a blaze. Built in 1960, a frigid night in 1967 saw the original McCormick Place turn to ash. The city dispatched two thousand firefighters to the lakefront, but two-thirds of the structure burned down within forty-five minutes. It was the largest conflagration Chicagoans had seen since the blaze that leveled the city.

"We will get to the immediate task of rebuilding McCormick Place," then mayor Richard J. Daley declared the morning after the fire.[1] Build he did. And the city has not stopped. The McCormick Place campus now includes 2.6 million square feet of exhibit space, two thousand hotel rooms across two publicly financed hotels, a 10,000-seat arena, and a 2.5-mile busway accessible only by conventioneers and political figures. None of these expansions, nor the tax hikes to fund them, have been subject to approval by voters.

Conventions do not hold the same place in the public consciousness as the city's schools, public safety, utilities, or transit. So why does the Metropolitan Pier and Exposition Authority (MPEA)—the body overseeing McCormick Place and Navy Pier—deserve special attention in a book about Chicago governance?

There are two reasons. First, the MPEA is unique among the bodies imposing a tax burden on Chicagoans. While most city entities are either disaggregated into their own taxing authority or support themselves from user fees, the MPEA is a mishmash—a creature of the city and the state that relies on taxing residents who by and large do not enjoy or desire to use convention facilities. The second reason is the scope of its burden. The MPEA holds more than $4 billion in debt, far more than bodies overseeing similar convention centers in other cities. To the tune of more than $150 million in local tax revenue in 2017, Chicagoans continue to subsidize a losing private enterprise. But this is not to say there are no winners.

McCormick Place's limited benefits flow disproportionately to select interests, both in business and politics. The mayor benefits from press conferences on tourism in bustling auditoriums, ribbon cuttings, and another political playing field upon which he can reward or punish various actors. A few hotel executives enjoy subsidized capital. The city does not treat the convention center business as it does most other industries, where costs are borne largely by the businesses themselves and the city enjoys tax revenue and other spillover benefits from their success. Instead, convention center costs have been socialized amid disappointing performance.

An observer of Chicago's financial struggles might wonder: Is this a game worth playing? Without reform, billions in tax dollars will continue to flow to an endeavor that has proven unable to turn a profit in a highly competitive industry, enriches a select few, and adds to residents' already enormous burden of municipal debt.

The Anatomy of the MPEA

The state created the Fair and Exposition Authority, later called the Metropolitan Fair and Exposition Authority, in 1955. It would oversee McCormick Place, which opened for business in November 1960. The bonds to build it were backed with racetrack revenues and anticipated revenues from conventions. In 1989, the Illinois General Assembly passed a law transforming the twelve-member Metropolitan Fair and Exposition Authority into the thirteen-member Metropolitan Pier and Exposition Authority, which was to oversee McCormick Place and a $150 million state-backed redevelopment of Navy Pier.[2]

Today, nine board members control the authority. Four members are appointed by the governor with consent of the state senate and four are appointed by the mayor. Those appointed board members then select a chairman. At least one board member must represent labor interests and at least one must represent convention industry interests. Unlike the schools or the parks, the mayor does not enjoy predominant control of the MPEA. Chicago voters are even further removed, despite shouldering the burden of MPEA taxes. Rather than being a creature of city politics, there is a sound argument to be made that McCormick Place came to exist only "by shifting the locus of both politics and public finance [of the development] to the state government."[3]

During the 1991 state budget debate, for instance, lawmakers authorized an expansion deal for McCormick Place along with support for downstate coal production and downstate infrastructure projects.[4] To fund the expansion, this plan imposed a suite of taxes on city and county residents from 1992 through the year 2025, including tax increases on restaurant meals, pickups from the airport, hotels, and rental cars.[5] In state house and senate testimony, multiple lawmakers touted the fact that while the entire state would benefit from McCormick Place's expansion, Chicago was more than willing to shoulder the entirety of the tax increases necessary to fund it.[6]

The state, city, and the MPEA board have enacted structural reforms in the face of disappointing convention performance. Changes include labor reforms after industry complaints of "poor customer service" and a "rigid and inflexible" bureaucracy, subsidies specifically directed at trade show clients to reduce the cost of their bookings, installing a state-appointed trustee to overhaul the authority, and outsourcing management services to a nonprofit entity (in the case of Navy Pier) as well as a private management company (McCormick Place).[7] But the MPEA's $4 billion in debt and the struggle to repay it, along with rising tax collections, still constitute an albatross for taxpayers.

The MPEA has seen its dominion extend far beyond just a convention center in the more than sixty years since its birth. The following is an overview of its assets.

MCCORMICK PLACE

The original McCormick Place and its successive expansions have often stood as the largest such spaces in the country. Its 2.6 million square feet of "prime exhibit space" made up more than 4.5 percent of all prime exhibit space in the United States in 2013, more than existed in all of Mexico.[8] Table 7.1 compares the ten largest convention centers in the United States.

McCormick Place spending has been justified for decades as a public investment that reaps rewards for residents. But the American convention

TABLE 7.1   Ten Largest Convention Centers in the United States

Rank	Convention center	Prime exhibit space (sq. ft.)
1	McCormick Place (Chicago)	2,600,000
2	Orange County Convention Center (Orlando)	2,100,000
3	Las Vegas Convention Center (Las Vegas)	1,940,631
4	Georgia World Congress Center (Atlanta)	1,400,000
5	Sands Expo and Convention Center / The Venetian (Las Vegas)	1,305,052
6	Kentucky Exposition Center (Louisville)	1,100,000
7	New Orleans Ernest N. Morial Convention Center (New Orleans)	1,100,000
8	Reliant Park (Houston)	1,056,213
9	International Exposition Center (Cleveland)	1,050,000
10	Kay Bailey Hutchinson Convention Center (Dallas)	1,018,942

Source: Carri Jensen and Hil Anderson, "Big Changes at Nation's Biggest Convention Centers," Trade Show Executive, September 2013.

center industry has not been the economic engine boosters have promised, with sustained growth failing to materialize.[9] McCormick Place has not been spared from this disappointment. As Heywood Sanders writes in his opus on the convention center industry, "over and over, Chicago and Illinois public officials and a roster of consultants promised that a bigger McCormick Place would yield hundreds of thousands of new convention attendees and billions in new spending and public revenues. Those repeated promises have proved to be false, the consultant projections unmet."[10]

Expansions in 1986 (600,000 additional sq. ft.), 1997 (one million sq. ft.), and 2007 (470,000 sq. ft., including one of the world's largest ballrooms) have not brought the McCormick Place gamble into the black. The convention center has yet to turn a profit when accounting for debt service, running consistent overall deficits.

Convention and trade show attendance at McCormick Place has slowly declined since 2001 and has remained relatively flat since 2007. Total attendance at McCormick Place from major events (including conventions and trade shows, as well as other public events) is down almost 18 percent since 2001. Despite flagging to flat attendance at McCormick Place, the MPEA has enjoyed a steady flow of tax collections and debt-financed investment. Table 7.2 illustrates the decline and its relationship to tax collections.

These struggles come in the face of significant natural advantages for Chicago as a convention hub. The combination of a central location, ease of access by air, and an abundance of world-class entertainment and restaurants is arguably unmatched. But McCormick Place has historically been unable to break even, much less pay down its debts. The MPEA has been more successful at attracting tax revenue than competing in the convention industry.

TABLE 7.2   McCormick Place Attendance and Authority Tax Collections

Year	Convention and trade show attendance (thousands)[a]	Total attendance (thousands)	MPEA tax collections (2017 dollars, millions)[b]	Tax collections per convention and trade show attendee	Tax collections per attendee
2001	1,334	3,038	$129	$97	$42
2002	1,160	2,853	$109	$94	$38
2003	1,557	3,042	$110	$71	$36
2004	1,119	2,503	$109	$97	$43
2005	876	2,220	$111	$127	$50
2006	1,190	2,241	$118	$99	$53
2007	812	2,271	$130	$160	$57
2008	960	2,389	$128	$133	$54
2009	893	2,041	$124	$139	$61
2010	850	2,013	$110	$130	$55
2011	769	2,055	$115	$149	$56
2012	883	2,213	$126	$143	$57
2013	864	2,316	$131	$152	$57
2014	882	2,340	$134	$152	$57
2015	938	2,443	$144	$154	$59
2016	888	2,458	$150	$169	$61
2017	852	2,502	$151	$177	$60

[a] Due to MPEA reporting, this category includes trade shows and meetings from 2001 to 2006 and trade shows only from 2007 to 2017.

[b] Includes food and beverage tax, auto rental tax, hotel tax, and airport departure tax.

Source: MPEA data as of January 31, 2018, acquired via Freedom of Information Act request.

The MPEA's dedicated revenue streams include a special sales tax, hotel tax, rental car tax, and airport pickup fees. Those four sources, which generated more than $2 billion from 2001 to 2017, are levied on a variety of activities and geographic areas, with convention center attendees making up a small fraction of those who pay.[11] Specifically, these taxes are a 1 percent food and beverage tax on restaurant bills, a 2.5 percent tax on hotels, a 6 percent tax on rental cars, and a variety of airport departure surcharges, ranging from $4 to $54, depending on the type of vehicle. Table 7.3 summarizes the data.

The restaurant food and beverage tax applies within official MPEA boundaries, which stretch far beyond the environs surrounding McCormick Place or Navy Pier, as far north as the southern border of the Lakeview neighborhood, as far south as the Stevenson Expressway, as far west as Ashland Avenue, and east to Lake Michigan.[12] These boundaries also include O'Hare and Midway Airports. The MPEA hotel tax applies to room rentals throughout the entire city. The car rental tax applies to rentals throughout Cook County, and the airport departure tax applies to all commercial vehicles operating at either airport.

The MPEA takes in more from taxpayers than from the convention center's customers each year. In 2017, the MPEA generated nearly $174 million in operating revenue from the use of exhibition facilities ($55 million), hospitality ($66 million), guest services ($29 million), parking ($12 million), and other sources ($12 million). But the authority took in more than $183 million in tax dollars: $151 million in authority taxes, and $32 million in state grants.[13]

The most troubling element of MPEA finances is not tax revenue outpacing operating revenue; it is the authority's debt accumulated through decades of expansion. The MPEA's interest and amortization payment on its debt in

TABLE 7.3   One-Year Snapshot of MPEA Tax Collections

MPEA tax	FY 2017 revenue collected	Total collected (%)
Hotel tax	$59,559,020	39
Food and beverage tax	$49,911,015	33
Automobile renting tax	$33,211,003	22
Airport departure tax	$8,403,725	6
Total	$151,084,763	100

2017 alone was more than $219 million. The authority's long-term debt obligations total more than $4 billion.[14] It is clear the MPEA can never pay off such a heavy burden on its own, given current industry trends. But that has not stopped talk of more expansions, all in the name of economic stimulus.

Since the birth of McCormick Place, economic impact studies and performance projections have been crucial tools in justifying further public subsidies. The first independent projection of the performance of the convention center, released in 1956, was authored by Booz Allen Hamilton consultants on behalf of the Fair and Exposition Authority. It found the convention center's revenues would be far too little to support the anticipated debt and concluded that "the convention center, alone, will not bring about a significant increase in the number of large conventions which choose Chicago as the site of their meetings. . . . Because of facilities being built or planned by other cities, the competition for the country's major conventions will increase markedly."[15] The authority then commissioned a new study from the Chicago Convention Bureau. The bureau's study pegged anticipated revenues at more than four times the revenues projected by the Booz Allen Hamilton study and proved sufficient to secure the bond sale.[16] Thus came McCormick Place.

With each new expansion, the MPEA has a study drawn up touting the potential increase in jobs, visitors, and local spending. But none of those expansions have ever resulted in the advertised boost. McCormick Place attendance has been largely flat since its inception despite vast expansion. Ultimately, performance projections and economic impact studies regarding McCormick Place have one or more of four shortcomings: they fail to account for development of new convention facilities in other cities, they fail to account for the impact of higher taxes necessary to fund expansion, they assume no effects on the private sector from public competition, and they offer little or no insight as to the relative magnitude of McCormick Place's economic activity.[17]

When painted against a backdrop of Chicago's tourism economy at large, McCormick Place's contributions begin to appear unworthy of the subsidies it has enjoyed for so many years. Take hotels, for instance. In return for millions of dollars in tax subsidies each year and billions in public debt, McCormick Place accounts for around two thousand publicly funded hotel rooms, and an additional nine hundred that are not publicly funded but rely on McCormick Place convention bookings for guests.[18] Consultant HVS predicted

McCormick Place–generated room nights could reach 1.5 million by 2020.[19] Meanwhile, Chicago is home to more than 41,000 hotel rooms in the central business district alone, accounting for nearly 11 million room nights in 2016.[20] Home-sharing service Airbnb reported 390,000 inbound guests in Chicago with an average stay of 3.3 nights—or an estimated 1.3 million room nights in 2016.[21] The company receives no taxpayer funding.

But what about the jobs generated? The vast majority of the jobs supported by McCormick Place, according to an MPEA-commissioned study released in 2017, are created as a result of related spending. Directly, McCormick Place employs seven hundred people, four hundred of whom live in the city of Chicago, according to the study. Enterprise Holdings, a car rental company forced to charge additional sales taxes on all rentals within the entire county in order to support the MPEA, employs two thousand people in its Chicago group.[22]

As the MPEA heralds studies regarding the impact of McCormick Place, the mayor, in turn, uses the McCormick Place campus as a symbol of well-considered investments in tourism at large. In 2014, Mayor Rahm Emanuel set a goal of attracting 55 million visitors to Chicago, a goal that the city claims to have reached ahead of schedule. Even a cursory look at third-party tourism estimates should invite some skepticism into these claims.[23] The city's tourism arm argues Chicago attracts some 50 million domestic visitors each year, an average of nearly 137,000 per day.[24] Under the person-trips model put forth by the US Travel Association, this would require the city to capture 2.3 percent of the nation's person-trips over one year.[25] Giving this claim the benefit of the doubt, what is the impact of McCormick Place? Under the most generous assumptions imaginable—that all visitors to all events at McCormick Place over an entire year came to Chicago from out of town and stayed overnight— McCormick visitors make up around 5 percent of the city's domestic tourism estimate. The billions of dollars directed toward this entity have not created an economic juggernaut, to say the least.

NAVY PIER

Reopened in 1995 after a redevelopment effort costing $187 million, some may think the MPEA's big-ticket spending on Navy Pier is a thing of the past. This perception is compounded by the fact that the pier, since 2011, has been operated by a nonprofit entity called Navy Pier, Inc., or NPI. But that perception would be inaccurate.

In 2013, Mayor Rahm Emanuel announced his Elevate Chicago tourism initiative, which pledged more than $1 billion in new spending toward McCormick Place and Navy Pier, including $55 million in tax increment financing, or TIF dollars, for the MPEA to buy land for a publicly financed hotel, the Marriot Marquis.[26] TIF funds are supposed to be used to redevelop blighted areas. But the MPEA transferred the money to Navy Pier instead. Despite misuse of a funding source meant for blighted neighborhoods, no political figure faced any serious consequences when this spending came to light in 2017. Beyond the TIF controversy, good government groups have taken issue with the NPI's refusal to respond to public information requests.[27] Given events since 2011, the pier's nonprofit status appears less like an effort to operate independently of taxpayer subsidies and more like a method by which to spend money in a more opaque manner.

Navy Pier enjoyed a record nine million visitors in 2016, according to city officials.[28] Historically, that total would have been enough to dwarf any competing attraction. But a new counting methodology based on tracking smartphones introduced in 2016 yielded an estimate of nearly 13 million visitors to Millennium Park in the second half of 2016 alone, making it the top attraction in the Midwest and one of the top ten most-visited sites in the country. These estimates have not been independently verified and should be taken with a grain of salt. Further, the counting methodologies for Navy Pier and Millennium Park do not exclude locals, making their rankings an inexact exercise in their value to the city's tourism industry.

Unlike McCormick Place, Navy Pier appears capable of turning a profit without direct subsidies. In 2016, NPI took in $55 million in operating revenue, with a net operating income of $4.6 million.[29] The entity saw a net operating profit of $2.5 million in the prior year. The entity is indirectly subsidized by taxpayers, however, in that NPI pays a mere dollar-a-year lease to the MPEA.

HOTELS

Chicago is home to the highest count of publicly financed hotel rooms in the nation, with more than two thousand rooms between two properties—one operated by Marriot and the other by Hyatt, both falling under the auspices of the MPEA.[30] The largest source of operating revenue for the MPEA is hotel stays.[31]

Despite claims since before McCormick Place's opening that the center would spur widespread private development in the surrounding area, the only significant private investment for decades was the McCormick Inn. The 625-room hotel opened a stone's throw from McCormick Place in 1973, with a majority of the funding coming from the controversial Teamsters Union pension fund. The Inn reportedly faced losses in its first few years of operating but eventually was able to earn a profit by serving conventioneers as the only major hotel in the area.[32]

Twenty years after it opened, the MPEA purchased and demolished the McCormick Inn to make room for a new six hundred thousand-square-foot exposition hall. The authors were unable to find out how much the authority paid the Teamsters for the hotel. Just a few years later in one of the first such deals in the country, the Metropolitan Pier and Exposition Authority in 1996 sold $127.4 million in revenue bonds to build an 800-room hotel adjacent to McCormick Place, which would be managed by Hyatt.

The Hyatt project heralded the arrival of the "headquarters hotel" trend nationwide, as cities tried to turn around poor convention center performance with large hotels that would draw conventions seeking a single site to house attendees. This development strategy was akin to "a version of the rat and cat farm," as one writer on urban politics described a publicly funded hotel as part of the expansion of New York City's Javits Center. "We use tax money to build a convention center that supposedly will stimulate the hotel industry, and then use tax dollars to build a hotel that supposedly will stimulate the convention industry."[33]

The December 1995 study supporting the hotel investment promised a big boost in convention center business, but those projections were not met and attendance continued to decline. Nevertheless, the MPEA financed a $180 million, 451-room expansion of the Hyatt, which was completed in 2013. Another major MPEA project—a 1,200-room Marriot hotel—opened in 2017 with $400 million in public financing.

While the MPEA enjoys a hotel revenue stream, there is no free lunch. Developing publicly funded hotels can have a negative effect on those in the private sector.[34] In 2005, a 977-room Hyatt hotel in downtown Houston was forced into foreclosure shortly after a thirty-seven-story publicly financed hotel opened its doors near the city's convention center.[35] In Chicago, Marriot and Hyatt continue to enjoy millions of dollars in revenue from conventions made possible by taxpayers, while absorbing a fraction of the risk (and none of the debt) held by the public.

THE ARENA

New MPEA developments continue to surface. Most recently, the authority funded the construction of a new basketball arena and associated hotel. In 2017, the MPEA opened the 10,000-seat Wintrust Arena and an adjacent 1,200-room hotel operated by Marriot. A pedestrian bridge connects the Marriot property directly to McCormick Place. Facing criticism for subsidizing a private university (the Wintrust Arena's home team is the DePaul University Blue Demons), Emanuel argued that the investment was not for DePaul, but rather the city was "subsidizing" another "event center" as part of the McCormick complex.[36] DePaul fronted less than half of the costs of construction. "If DePaul was not investing $70 million as a major anchor tenant, we would have to come up with the resources [to build the arena, and] I would not have the ability to transfer resources to Navy Pier and do the revitalization," the mayor said. The MPEA and the city contributed the remaining $103 million toward the $173 million project. A 2013 study commissioned by the MPEA found the arena would need to draw an average of 9,500 fans for each of DePaul's sixteen men's basketball games to break even on operating costs.[37] But in 2018, the inaugural men's basketball season drew an average of around 3,100 fans per game.[38]

THE MAYOR'S ROAD

Completed in 2002 at a cost of $43 million, the MPEA boasts a 2.5-mile, partially underground busway that shuttles conventioneers from McCormick Place to the Illinois Center hotels. Rather than wait in traffic for 20 to 30 minutes to reach Illinois Center from the convention center, a bus using the tunnel can travel the distance in around eight minutes. Known also as "the mayor's road," the "magic road," or the "bat cave," the tunnel was also reportedly used by Mayor Richard M. Daley to travel home quickly from city hall.[39]

"We are going to provide public access," the city's transportation commissioner said when touting the project in 1998.[40] But today, those who avail themselves of the road include only politicians such as the president of the Cook County board and the mayor, as well as some convention attendees. The taxpaying public that paid for the road does not have access, and neither do CTA buses, taxis, or rideshare vehicles.

What will they think of next?

What Do Other Cities Do?

As a public body pouring money into large convention spaces, Chicago is far from alone. Convention center exhibit space nationwide nearly doubled from 1989 to 2011, with state and local governments spending more than $13 billion on convention center building between 2002 and 2011.[41] Compared with similar convention centers, McCormick Place's financial performance is among the worst, with uniquely high debt among its peers. Unfortunately, while governance of publicly funded convention centers across the nation varies greatly, virtually all have made large investments with disappointing results. Table 7.4 shows the comparison.

An analysis of peer cities does not reveal potential solutions to the problem of overpaying and underperformance when it comes to convention centers. It does, however, show that Chicago's problems with the MPEA are not necessarily borne of uniquely poor management. Rather, Chicago is simply one among many cities engaged in a kind of futile arms race.

ORLANDO

Despite differing in governance compared with the MPEA, the Orange County Convention Center—the nation's second-largest convention complex, located in Orlando—has pursued similarly aggressive expansion with similar results. Its administrator reports to the county, so it enjoys slightly more elected accountability than Chicago. The 2.1-million-square-foot complex has expanded four times since 1983. The most recent expansion in the twenty-first century came at a cost of nearly $750 million. And officials are expected to pursue another $500 million expansion.[42]

In attracting trade shows and exhibitions, it has fared slightly better than the stagnant market at large. In 2016, the convention center hosted 122 trade shows and exhibitions; in 2005, the center had 114.[43] But its massive expansion since the turn of the century has seen only a modest return. Attendance figures in 2009 (781,000 attendees) were on par with attendance when the center was only half the size in 1997 and 1998. The year 2012 saw a high of 1.08 million visitors, which exceeded a peak of 921,200 visitors in 2000 before the expanded facilities had opened. But the center has not yet come close to the expected boost its expansion would yield. An Ernst and Young study projected attendance to double in the wake of the expansion.[44]

TABLE 7.4   Financial Comparison of the Four Largest Publicly Owned
Convention Centers

	McCormick Place (Chicago)	Orange County Convention Center (Orlando)	Las Vegas Convention Center (Las Vegas)	Georgia World Congress Center (Atlanta)
Operating revenue	$155[a]	$60	$60	$98
Operating expenses	$249	$68	$62	$96
Net operating income	–$94	–$8	–$2	$3
Tax revenue	$147	$240[b]	$265[c]	$87
Total debt	$3,993	$668	$846	$191[d]
Debt service	$244	$28	$33	$29

Note: dollars in millions, FY2016.
[a] Includes $60 million in hotel revenue.
[b] Includes all short-term hotel rentals; not all revenues collected are for the convention center.
[c] The authority is also the visitors bureau and spent $143 million on advertising and promotion.
[d] Estimated.

Financially, the center takes a loss each year, though not as severely as the MPEA. In fiscal year 2016, it experienced an operating loss of $8 million. However, the center is buoyed by a heavy flow of tax revenues. In 2016 alone, it received more than $230 million in revenue from the tourist development tax, which is levied on hotel bills in Orange County.

LAS VEGAS

Sin City is home to the third-largest convention center in the United States, as measured by exhibit space—the Las Vegas Convention Center. Built in 1955, the center is governed by a public-private entity called the Las Vegas Convention and Visitors Authority, or LVCVA, a fourteen-member board established by state law.

Eight members are elected: Clark County and the city of Las Vegas each elect two representatives; the cities of North Las Vegas, Henderson, Mesquite, and Boulder City each have one elected seat. The remaining members are from the private sector, nominated by the Las Vegas Chamber of Commerce and Nevada Resort Association.[45]

Like Orlando, Las Vegas has fueled its convention facilities largely via a tax levied on Clark County hotel rooms. But unlike many other cities, voters have had a role to play. County voters in 1956 approved a county bond issue to pay for the new convention center.[46] But subsequent expansions have met resistance from the voting public. Voters overwhelmingly struck down an $18 million bond proposal in 1964 and another in 1968. In 1970, however, after a marketing campaign backed by business interests noting that "not one cent" out of residents' property tax bills would flow to the center, voters relented, approving a $7.5 million bond issue.[47] The strategy proved successful again in 1974, and yet again in 1980.

But voter support was far from assured and indeed slowed expansion. This was a problem for boosters. Seeking refuge from the eye of the voting public, the LVCVA sought and received state approval to allow county commissioners to authorize expansion bonds backed by pledged revenue, such as the hotel tax, without need for a public vote. And eventually, the state authorized the LVCVA itself to issue bonds without the approval of county commissioners. By the late 1990s, the LVCVA had effectively freed itself from the constraints of county voters, and multiple large expansions followed.[48] But this has not brought about a sustainable business model.

The center sustained a net operating loss of about $2 million in 2016, depending on how one defines operating revenues and expenses, while enjoying over $261 million in room taxes and gaming fees.

ATLANTA

Atlanta's Georgia World Congress Center is one of the largest combined convention, sports, and entertainment complexes in the world. It includes not only a convention center, but Mercedes-Benz Stadium and a twenty-one-acre park. Those assets are governed by the Georgia World Congress Center Authority. The authority's board of governors is entrusted with the "management of the business and affairs of the authority." The board consists of fifteen members, all of whom are appointed by Georgia's governor.

The convention center's expansion has been relentless since its opening in 1976, fueled by the willingness of the governor and state lawmakers to approve new debt, with stated aims of keeping up with other convention hubs. Unfortunately, a familiar story of overpromising has emerged. Price Waterhouse consultants predicted annual attendance of more than 1.4 million after a more than 50 percent expansion of the convention space, which opened in 2002. Since then, the center has failed to attract more than 900,000 visitors in any one year. In recent years, total attendance has hovered around half a million.[49]

COMMONALITY

The most comprehensive work on the political history of American convention centers, Heywood Sanders's *Convention Center Follies*, points to a few primary reasons for the rise of convention center investment nationwide, and why one observes similar trends among the largest players:

- Convention center deals are forged by business interests and only seen by the public eye once completed.
- Public financing arrangements for convention centers are structured to avoid or limit public vote.
- Promises of economic impact—including increased attendance, hotel room stays, and new jobs—place convention centers in a privileged position in comparison with an array of other possible public investments.

All three points hold true in the Windy City. And, unfortunately, of a variety of governance structures, none seem particularly immune to the expansionist drive of the business interests that stand to benefit from the public dollar. Sanders writes:

> Business leaders thus have a broad array of options available to them in promoting convention centers. . . . They can outwait a reluctant mayor, as they did in Nashville and Atlanta, and deal with his or her successors. They can bypass the city government and work with a county government, as with Cleveland's Medical Mart and Convention Center, or they can seek the creation of an independent public authority such as the Greater Richmond Convention Center Authority or the Detroit Regional Convention Facility Authority that can involve suburban governments. And the state government is yet another potential vehicle, either directly, as in the case of Chicago's McCormick Place and Atlanta's Georgia World Congress Center, or by persuading a state legislature or governor to commit special grant funds, as Pennsylvania Governor Ed Rendell did for Erie and Lancaster, and the state of Arizona did for the Phoenix Convention Center.
> . . . The organized business community need succeed only once.[50]

This phenomenon begs for a solution: perhaps taxpayers should not be on the hook for the convention center business at all.

What to Do

The traditional role of American government has been to invest in public goods, which benefit most or all residents. It is difficult to argue that a convention center falls into the category of a traditional public good. Of course, proponents of public investment in convention centers cite positive spillover effects, such as additional jobs and investment. However, it would be tough to convince the average resident that the positive externality he or she enjoys from the billions in tax dollars that have flowed to the convention business is on par with what the same investment might yield in the city's schools, parks, public safety services, or transportation. There are public goods that almost everyone uses: public parks, roads, and policing, for example. Few Chicagoans enjoy or desire the use of McCormick Place.

Another way of viewing how Chicago might prioritize the provision of a convention center would be to ask the following questions: Would convention center services be underprovided in the absence of government intervention? If so, would the effects of under-provision be on par with the under-provision of other services funded by the government, such as schools, parks, and transportation? These questions can all be posed in similar terms with regard to Navy Pier. The honest answer is no.

One change the city could make in order to better situate tourism among an array of possible public investments is relatively simple. If the city is to properly analyze the impact of the tourism sector, a more robust city council should annually commission an independent study on the number of tourists the city attracts. The mayor's own tourism agency, Choose Chicago, is not an appropriate check on the mayor's claims of success in this area, which have been used to justify further subsidies to McCormick Place, among other policy choices.

A reality check is in order for McCormick Place. But what are the city and state to do? A frenzy of "convention center follies" across the nation means residents lack a case study in real reform. No major city has yet moved to divest from its convention center. Chicago is left to forge a new path.

First, officials should seek to do no harm through a process of progressive privatization. This would entail beginning a divestment of tax revenues from MPEA as quickly as possible through gradual repeal of authority taxes. Weaning the authority off of its largest source of revenue—taxpayers—is an essential step toward a successful venture. The city cannot afford to continue throwing money at a sinking enterprise.

Second, those profiting from hotels booking McCormick guests on MPEA property—not taxpayers at large—should assume greater responsibility in convention finances. Publicly funded hotel operators have been capturing a benefit stream from McCormick Place. They are able to sell more rooms at a greater average rate on dates when there is a convention. As such, the MPEA should seek to sell those hotels and oblige those profiting from them to assume greater fiscal responsibility over the convention complex. A useful comparison is the casino model. A casino is happy to pay for a room and buffet if the customer is gambling. At McCormick Place, the event space is the free room. The hotels are where the money is made.

There is also the question of the four main buildings that comprise McCormick Place. Only three of the nine convention halls in those buildings appear able to hit the magic 70 percent occupancy mark that experts believe indicates healthy attendance.[51] Six fell below the mark in 2016, including every hall in the Lakeside Center and the West Building.[52] The MPEA, with pressure from the city, should seek to repurpose the weakest-performing spaces as soon as possible. One possible use is a new police training facility. Reimagining parts of the McCormick Place campus for such a project might be more palatable to taxpayers and residents than a recent city council proposal to spend $95 million constructing the facility on Chicago's West Side, despite vocal opposition. If the MPEA cannot find an alternate, sustainable use without aid of tax revenue, those spaces should be packaged and sold.

However, the Lakeside Center would likely have difficulty attracting bidders because of the city's restrictions on lakefront development. This drastically limits its options for repurposing. In this case, the MPEA could be stuck between a rock and a hard place. One potential workaround involves a long-discussed casino. While a Chicago casino would require state action, McCormick Place's other spaces should be positioned as the city's prime candidates to be sold for such a purpose, with the Lakeside Center perhaps remaining as the sole convention space.

As an added safeguard against future follies, the MPEA should require majority approval from city voters via a referendum for any further bond issues, subsidies, or other revenue streams toward expansion of MPEA assets—such a barrier proved helpful (although fleeting) in Las Vegas, for example. In the long term, key governance changes may need to come via a new city charter. Public ownership or financing of hotels, convention centers, arenas, and retail spaces should be left out of the city's enumerated powers in such a charter. Divestment from McCormick Place would return the city to its roots in luring large events. Before business interests went to the public trough, the early to mid-twentieth century saw Chicago attract political and business conventions to privately owned and managed spaces, including the Chicago Coliseum, the Stadium, and the International Amphitheater. Today, Chicago is still home to many world-class venues, large and small, that are already competing for convention business without aid from taxpayers, not to mention untold newcomers who could take advantage of any gaps in supply resulting from the rightsizing of McCormick Place.

Convention center business is not the high-growth sector that boosters have made it out to be, as evidenced by the fact that Chicago is not alone in faring poorly at it. And there is little reason to think it will become a high-growth sector in the future—certainly not to the extent needed for McCormick Place to turn a profit without public assistance. Chicago cannot continue to divert more than $150 million a year to ventures that have not delivered on promised benefits for decades. And the MPEA's $4 billion in debt is a heavy weight for a city already awash in red ink.

With regard to Navy Pier, its financials indicate further taxpayer investment would be superfluous, especially given the city's other pressing financial matters. The MPEA should seek to turn operations over to the highest bidder, who would assume ownership of the land and be granted authority to run the attraction as it sees fit. The MPEA has proven unable to restrain an urge to funnel further public dollars to the pier.

The rise of Millennium Park as a premier destination perhaps signals a changing of the guard. While the park's development was by no means an exercise in good governance and fiscal restraint, it is an attractive, dynamic public space that does not require the city to enter a highly competitive industry, such as convention centers or large retail spaces. While impressive in scope and function, it is indeed just a park. Beautification projects such as Millennium Park and the Chicago Riverwalk benefit both tourists and residents, while playing on Chicago's inherent strengths. In those projects, city government leverages a core competency of managing the design of public spaces. Malls, trade shows, and their costs and risks, however, are best left in private hands.

CHAPTER 8

Policing in Chicago

Every society gets the kind of criminal it deserves. What is equally true is
that every community gets the kind of law enforcement it insists on.
—ROBERT KENNEDY

〜

Laquan McDonald fell dead on Pulaski Road on October 20, 2014. The seventeen-year-old high school student was shot sixteen times by police officer Jason Van Dyke. McDonald was black. Van Dyke is white. Although the initial police report on the shooting claimed McDonald lunged at police officers with a knife, dashcam video footage would later reveal that McDonald was walking past Van Dyke as the officer began firing at close range.

In the weeks that followed, city hall's fifth floor began spinning. Top mayoral staff and the city law department quickly became aware of the political implications of McDonald's death. After all, protests of police misconduct three hundred miles south in Ferguson, Missouri, had been gripping the national psyche for months. On December 8, 2014, the head of the inaptly named Independent Police Review Authority sent an email to Mayor Rahm Emanuel's deputy chief of staff for public safety.[1] The email contained a link to a press release describing suggestions from two local watchdogs that video evidence might contradict claims from the Fraternal Order of Police that Van Dyke's life was in danger. In an email to Emanuel's chief of staff and others the following morning, the head of the city law department, Stephen Patton, wrote that he expected a lawsuit from McDonald's family.[2] That lawsuit, however, was never filed.

Emanuel was in the thick of a contentious campaign season, with voters heading to the polls on February 24, 2015. On February 10, journalist Jamie Kalven published a copy of McDonald's autopsy mapping the sixteen shots, which flew in the face of police claims that the teenager had died of a single gunshot wound. "The decision of whether or not to release the video ultimately rests with Mayor Rahm Emanuel," Kalven wrote.[3] It would be nearly three hundred days until the public would see it. On election night, Emanuel failed to reach the 50 percent threshold necessary to win outright, meaning he would face a run-off election April 7 against his opponent, Jesús "Chuy" Garcia.

Mere weeks prior to the run-off election, lawyers representing McDonald's mother began official discussions with the city law department regarding a financial settlement.[4] After discussing city settlements paid for other victims of police shootings, attorneys for the family noted that "none of the cases discussed involve a graphic video which depicts, in vivid detail, a 17-year-old being shot multiple times as he lay helpless on the street."[5] While both sides began offering settlement proposals, Patton and the city law department continued to press for the arrangement to include an assurance that the video would be kept confidential until criminal charges were concluded. On April 8—the day after Rahm Emanuel won his run-off election—the law department softened its confidentiality demand, allowing for the video's release if a court ordered it to be made public before the conclusion of the investigation. The two parties ultimately came to an agreement.[6] Less than a week later, Patton testified to the city council's Finance Committee that the settlement should be approved. After questioning from just two of the seventeen alderman in attendance, the committee approved the settlement on a unanimous voice vote.[7] Presiding over his first city council meeting after his reelection, Emanuel banged the gavel after a 47–0 approval of a $5 million settlement for the shooting of Laquan McDonald. There was no debate. And not a single alderman had seen the video.

Journalist Brandon Smith, unsuccessful in efforts to acquire the video via a Freedom of Information Act request, sued the city in August. A Cook County judge ruled in Smith's favor in November, and the city released the video just hours after Van Dyke was charged with murder. In the wake of the judge's ruling, Patton directly edited the mayor's remarks, talking points, and letters about the McDonald shooting.[8]

The thirteen-second clip of Van Dyke killing McDonald provoked enormous backlash, including allegations that Emanuel's administration had kept this footage from the public for electoral purposes. Activists and political opponents called for Emanuel's resignation. But all they would get was the dismissal of the city's police superintendent—a vacancy later filled by the mayor. Motivated voters were also able to oust the Cook County state's attorney, who waited thirteen months to prosecute Van Dyke despite the fact that her office received the video two weeks after the shooting.[9] Few if any critics questioned the role of the city law department. And there was no serious reform of the process by which the city council approves settlements.

But there was more scrutiny than ever on Chicago's history of poor police governance. For some, a dark history was brought into a new, disturbing light. Of particular concern was the lax environment surrounding police discipline. Though citizens had filed at least twenty complaints against Van Dyke since 2001, none resulted in disciplinary action. That number placed Van Dyke among the most frequent subjects of complaints in the entire department, as approximately 80 percent of Chicago police officers are the subject of zero to four complaints throughout their careers.[10] Van Dyke would have rarely seen anyone punished for a complaint—even those who get many of them. Of the more than 28,000 complaints filed against Chicago Police Department officers from 2011 to 2015, less than 2 percent resulted in discipline, typically in the form of a reprimand or a suspension of less than one week.[11] A Reuters analysis found that in 2016, 1,000 citizen complaints sent to Internal Affairs resulted in just one disciplinary action.[12]

Journalists fought for a decade to gain access to data about those complaints from citizens. In the wake of the McDonald shooting, these and other journalists offered especially valuable insight. *Chicago Tribune* writers noted that the city's collective bargaining agreement with police unions made it especially difficult to enact any serious discipline. For decades of contract negotiations, union officials with city officials on the other side of the bargaining table had swapped money-saving measures for increased protection from scrutiny.[13]

Indeed, the unions stepped in to destroy the complaint data that brought this phenomenon to light. In October 2014, the union representing rank-and-file Chicago police officers sued the city to prevent the release of records more than five years old. The suit by the Fraternal Order of Police argued that officers would face "public humiliation and loss of prestige in their employment" were those older records made public.[14] The Illinois Police Benevolent and Protective Association, which represents higher-ranking officers, filed a separate, similar lawsuit. Both suits cited a provision in their collective bargaining agreements that mandated the destruction of most complaint records after five years.[15]

But those records were crucial not just in providing context for officers such as Van Dyke but also for unraveling another dark corner of Chicago's police history: the reign of Jon Burge.

This Chicago police commander's methods allegedly included electric shocking, suffocation with plastic bags, and beatings. Lawyers have claimed Burge's "midnight crew" of officers and detectives tortured as many as 120 men between 1972 and 1991, mostly African American, to elicit confessions. The Chicago Police Department fired Burge in 1993 after an internal review board determined he tortured a murder suspect. In 2010, Burge was convicted in federal court of perjury and obstruction of justice for lying under oath in a deposition for a civil suit—he denied witnessing torture or abusing suspects. Burge was not charged with torture outright. But prosecutors did have to prove allegations of abuse to support the other counts. He spent four and a half years in prison and on home confinement.

So what has changed in the wake of the Burge scandal? The most significant result came in the form of recompense to Burge's victims. While undoubtedly necessary, it has done little to protect victims of future misconduct. In 2015, after years of back and forth, the city council initially approved a $5.5 million reparations fund for Burge's victims. Lawyers involved in the case believed it was the first time a municipality had paid reparations for such misconduct.[16] As recently as January 2018, the city was paying out additional multimillion-dollar wrongful conviction settlements tied to Burge's actions.[17] Overall, the city has paid alleged victims of Burge detectives more than $111 million.[18] Chicago Public School students in eighth and tenth grades are required to learn about the Burge legacy each year. The man himself now lives in Florida and has continued to collect a police pension of about $4,000 a month.[19] Efforts to depose former mayor Richard M. Daley regarding what he knew about Burge's conduct have been unsuccessful (Daley served as the Cook County state's attorney during Burge's tenure). In two cases the city reached a settlement with the victims before Daley took the stand; in a third, Daley's lawyers cited an undisclosed medical issue with Daley.[20] None of this aftermath could be considered reform.

Whether in discrete actions, such as attempting to hide the evidence of a young man's death or turning a blind eye to torture, or in larger governance failures, such as collective bargaining rules that produce upsettingly little discipline, Chicago's status quo seems to prioritize the interests of political actors and inept police officers. The losers are the victims of misconduct, the well-meaning officers who must bear witness to eroding trust in their profession, and the taxpayers who pay for these mistakes.

Crime, Public Safety, and Policing in Chicago

These stories paint a distressing picture of policing in Chicago. They are supported by facts. Crime, public safety, and policing are complex concepts. The public feels safer if crime is reduced. Taxpayers are willing to spend money on policing to reduce crime. For a variety of reasons, though, reported crime is only a fraction of what actually occurs, and so public safety may not result from policing. Reported crime statistics can be misleading. Nevertheless, the public and the media simplify these issues with one measure: the homicide rate.

Table 8.1 shows the conspicuous fact that homicides in Chicago exceed both the first and second most populous US cities and have done so for over a decade.[21] This table shows that in 2006, Chicago had a homicide rate of approximately 17.3 per 100,000 residents, while New York and Los Angeles

TABLE 8.1   Comparative Homicide Rates, Three Largest US Cities

		New York City	Los Angeles	LA and NYC combined	Chicago
Population (2010)		8,175,133	3,792,621	11,967,754	2,695,598
2006	Total homicides	596	480	1,076	467
	Per 100,000 population	7.3	12.7	9	17.3
2016	Total homicides	335	294	629	762
	Per 100,000 population	4.1	7.8	5.3	28.3

Source: For population: U.S. Census https://www.census.gov/2010census/popmap / Homicides; for city data: http://www.city-data.com/crime/crime-Chicago-Illinois.html ; https://www1.nyc.gov/site/nypd/stats/crime-statistics/historical.page; http://www.city -data.com/crime/crime-Los-Angeles-California.html.

had a combined rate of 9 per 100,000. But ten years later, the combined rate of those two cities had fallen to 5.3, while Chicago's had risen to 28.3. Chicago had more than five times as many homicides per capita as the largest two cities combined.

If Chicago had become so lawless, would it be safe to assume that the rate of other violent crimes would likewise be elevated? A look at FBI crime statistics for a single year, 2015, tells a far different story. Table 8.2 shows those numbers for four categories of violent crime, and Chicago looks more favorable in this context.

Looking at the numbers again in table 8.3 for the same time period, but now for nonviolent crime and arson, a different story unfolds. The per capita rate reported by Chicago was lower than the total for ten other cities.

TABLE 8.2   FBI Violent Crime Statistics, Top Fifteen US Cities

		Violent crime per 100,000				
	Population (2015)	Total	Murder	Rape	Robbery	Aggravated assault
New York	8,537,673	585.8	3.4	14	198.2	357.2
Los Angeles	3,962,726	634.8	7.1	55.7	225.9	346
Chicago	2,728,695	903.8	23.8	52.5	353.6	480.2
Houston	2,275,221	966.7	13.3	43.3	451.7	458.3
Philadelphia	1,567,810	1,029.0	17.9	84.3	431.5	495.3
Phoenix	1,559,744	593.8	7.2	65.1	193.6	327.8
San Antonio	1,463,586	587.2	6.4	71.7	135.7	373.4
San Diego	1,400,467	398.6	2.6	40.4	98.4	257.1
Dallas	1,301,977	694.2	10.4	60.1	320.8	302.8
San Jose	1,031,458	329.6	2.9	36.4	110.5	179.8
Austin	938,728	372.5	2.5	51.9	99	219.2
Jacksonville	867,258	648.3	11.2	54.3	161.2	421.6
San Francisco	863,782	776.8	6.1	39.8	417.9	312.9
Indianapolis	863,675	1,288.0	17.1	78.4	440.2	752.3
Columbus	847,745	546.3	9.1	95.1	264.2	177.9

Source: https://ucr.fbi.gov/crime-in-the-u.s/2015/crime-in-the-u.s.-2015/offenses-known -to-law-enforcement/violent-crime

TABLE 8.3   FBI Nonviolent Crime Statistics, Top Fifteen US Cities

	Population, 2015	Nonviolent crime per 100,000				
		Total	Burglary	Larceny	Motor vehicle theft	Arson
New York	8,537,673	1,518.7	164.9	1,267.4	86.4	N/A
Los Angeles	3,962,726	2,359.6	407.8	1,544.2	407.6	28.5
Chicago	2,728,695	2,946.3	482	2,089.7	374.6	19.6
Houston	2,275,221	4,397.5	872.8	2,928.7	596	29.5
Philadelphia	1,567,810	3,147.4	515.6	2,310.7	321.1	21
Phoenix	1,559,744	3,491.3	820.5	2,198.3	472.5	N/A
San Antonio	1,463,586	5,029.5	794.8	3,812.8	422	17.8
San Diego	1,400,467	2,082.0	366.2	1,351.9	363.9	12.4
Dallas	1,301,977	3,440.2	854.2	2,002.8	583.3	26.8
San Jose	1,031,458	2,427.1	474.7	1,273.7	678.7	9
Austin	938,728	3,771.0	532.6	2,990	248.3	9.7
Jacksonville	867,258	3,673.0	701.3	2,704.6	267	8.2
San Francisco	863,782	6,138.0	600.4	4,737.1	800.5	31.5
Indianapolis	863,675	4,790.8	1,283.5	2,929.5	577.9	N/A
Columbus	847,745	3,934.3	851.6	2,715.6	367.2	47.8

Source: https://ucr.fbi.gov/crime-in-the-u.s/2015/crime-in-the-u.s.-2015/offenses-known -to-law-enforcement/violent-crime.

Overall crime statistics are not a reliable measure of public safety or the efficacy of policing. In 2008, the American Society of Criminologists (ASC) issued a statement cautioning the use of the FBI numbers.[22] The FBI offers its own caution.[23] Paul Wormeli, a member of the ASC, has written about misreporting of crime statistics.[24] In an interview with Wormeli, he indicated that there are several reasons to disregard the comparison of statistics from one city to the next (telephone interview, January 25, 2018). First, there is wide variation in the extent to which victims report crime to the police. In recent years the reported "clearance rate," or the percentage of crimes where the perpetrator is apprehended, has hovered below 30 percent in Chicago for homicides and often below 10 percent for shootings.[25] In 2017, the homicide clearance rate was a mere 17 percent. This is much lower than in other big cities.[26] It can be assumed that most homicides are being reported, but it would appear that in a city with low clearance rates, citizens are reluctant to report rape, robbery, and aggravated assault.

Another distortion that especially plagues the nonviolent crime statistics is a particular police force's policy in responding to crimes against property. Some police departments do not have the resources to respond to every crime, and so they cut back on crimes against property. Many have policies whereby crimes against businesses are not reported. Wormeli noted that San Jose, California, had a policy of nonresponse if the issue was a matter of the victim's getting insurance reimbursement, stating that the police were not in the business of helping insurance companies. Looking at Chicago's relatively low reported rate of nonviolent crime set against the outlying homicide rate, the only logical conclusion is that a high rate of lawlessness is not being reported or even policed. For these and other reasons it is difficult to use any measure of comparative lawlessness other than the homicide rate per capita; based upon that rate lawlessness in Chicago is an outlier. Figure 8.1 shows the history of Chicago's homicides for the past fifteen years.

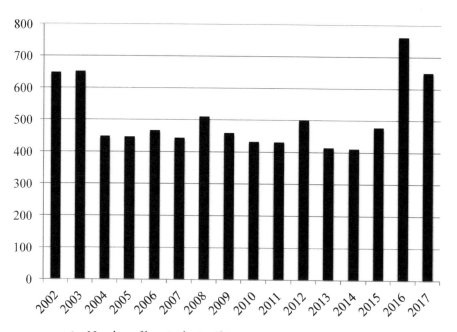

FIGURE 8.1. Number of homicides in Chicago, 2002 to 2017.

In recent years, as the Chicago homicide rate has become a top news story, the response of police and city officials has become rote; the reason for so many shootings and homicides is the presence of guns and the lack of economic opportunity. The phrase "a job can stop a bullet" has entered common usage, and several public policy forums have been so titled. In 2008, the US Supreme Court in the case of *District of Columbia v. Heller* ruled that the Washington, DC, ban on the possession of handguns was unconstitutional. Prior to *Heller*, the possession of a gun in Chicago was a felony. In 2010, the US Supreme Court ruled that Chicago could no longer ban handguns.[27] Although the handgun prohibition was nullified by these court rulings, from 2009 to 2014 the homicide rate steadily decreased with the exception of a bump in 2012. During this same period the US economy was recovering from the Great Recession. If the improving economy was providing jobs, then the prosperity that continued during 2015, 2016, and 2017 should have resulted in the downward trend in homicides continuing. It did not.

For decades, the homicide rate in Chicago has been one of the highest in the country. There was, however, one inflection point in late 2015 that caused the city to pull away from the pack of large US cities and become much worse: it was the release of the Laquan McDonald shooting video. As the US Department of Justice (DOJ) noted, "the reasons for this spike are broadly debated. . . . [But] there is little debate . . . that trust has been broken between the CPD and the people it serves."[28]

At the same time that the homicide was soaring, Chicago policing was being investigated. In the aftermath of the court order to release the McDonald shooting video, the DOJ opened an investigation of the Chicago Police Department. Even in advance of that formal announcement, the mayor appointed a special Police Accountability Task Force. The DOJ investigation began on December 7, 2015, and issued its report on January 13, 2017. The task force worked much more quickly and issued its report in April 2016. There is a significant overlap between the two reports, and they both paint a picture of a police force that has lost the trust of the public, especially the trust of those in areas where crime is high and citizens need the most protection.

The task force report highlighted five specific problem areas:

- Community-police relations
- Legal oversight and accountability

- Early intervention and personnel concerns
- De-escalation
- Video release policy

The DOJ report was more legalistic, but it covered similar topics, including the following:

- Unconstitutional use of force
- Insufficient accountability systems
- Insufficient personnel policies and practices
- Insufficient community policing

Both reports reveal a different narrative than the guns-and-jobs story. They conclude that the CPD has lost the trust of citizens in high-crime neighborhoods through the unconstitutional use of force, by abusing residents and suspects, and subsequently failing to connect with the community. When a homicide occurred, the victims could not count on the police to protect them. Fellow gang members and relatives would take the law into their own hands and revenge the killings with tit-for-tat shootings that only escalated the violence. Innocent bystanders who might know those involved did not trust the police to listen to them; indeed, they feared that they would not be protected if gang members found that they had snitched. No wonder the clearance rate, which has been declining for years, became so low. The poor reputation of the police department may have been caused by a small number of "bad apples," but the flagrant impunity and failure of accountability sent a strong message to the community that some officers were more likely to prey on them than help them. That is why the McDonald story resonated so powerfully in high-crime neighborhoods, and why it marks an inflection point in the homicide rate.

Since the reports were issued, the city has taken some steps to remedy the deficiencies the reports highlighted. The Independent Police Review Authority, discredited by the DOJ report, was replaced by the Civilian Office of Police Accountability (COPA) on October 5, 2016. While the mandate in the legislation making the change promised more accountability, some felt that this action was more rebranding than substantive reform.[29] Both entities were charged with receiving complaints about policing, investigating, and making recommendations to the CPD and the Chicago Police Board (CPB).

The CPB likewise came in for criticism by the DOJ report. The board is charged with adjudicating complaints against police. In the reports, it was accused of siding with police in the vast majority of cases and of acting more like a civil service commission protecting the rights of police officers rather than providing justifiable accountability. The police chief at the time of the McDonald shooting, Garry McCarthy, complained that disciplinary efforts he sought for police officers were often overturned by the CPB. In recent years, the mayor has replaced most of the CPB members in an effort to enhance effectiveness and overcome its bias against discipline. The board is also charged with recommending candidates for the position of police chief to the mayor. In the middle of all the DOJ and task force investigations, the mayor fired McCarthy. The board conducted a nationwide search for his replacement and recommended three candidates to the mayor. Instead of choosing among them, the mayor approached a police department veteran who had not applied for the job and offered it to him. This required action by the city council to suspend its CPB ordinance for one day so that the law could be circumvented. The mayor has been criticized for retaining such a heavy hand in policing.[30]

Of course, Chicago is not the only city plagued by these problems. And in those cases where the DOJ has investigated, the result was often federal oversight that succeeded in turning around troubled police departments. If the DOJ found that a city had violated the US Constitution, it might enter into a consent decree whereby the DOJ oversees the city's police department until specified deficiencies have been cured. Such oversight can last for many years. There is a long list of cities where the DOJ has intervened. In the case of Los Angeles, oversight lasted from 2001 to 2013 and has been credited for the remarkable turnaround of that police department, which was plagued by corruption and the graphic Rodney King beating. Many community leaders in Chicago, including some who served on the task force, had hoped that the city would enter into such a consent decree. Unfortunately, the incoming administration of President Donald Trump, through his attorney general Jeff Sessions, decided not to proceed with a consent decree.

In the wake of the DOJ's refusal to push for a consent decree, the attorney general for the State of Illinois filed suit to appoint a federal judge to provide the oversight that would have ensued from a federal consent decree.[31] As of this writing the city and the attorney general have negotiated the terms of this consent decree and are requesting public comments before finalizing it on September 1, 2018. The Fraternal Order of Police has objected to the agreement and has filed suit to block it. The proposed settlement is modeled on consent decrees entered into in other cities and addresses the specific shortcomings uncovered in the DOJ report. Some leaders are hopeful that, should this oversight be undertaken, there could finally be a check on the old way of doing business. Nevertheless, the proposed decree does not change the governance of policing, nor does it prohibit changes in such governance.

If these reforms are to work at all, it will take years for trust to be restored. Meanwhile, the city suffers from lawlessness, heartbreak, insecurity, and the cost of poor policing. In a February 2018 address to the Economic Club of Chicago, former Chicago and federal education official Arne Duncan estimated that the normal homicide rate for the city of Chicago should be 92 per year. If that is the case, then the past decades have seen thousands of lives lost because the Chicago police have not provided the level of public safety that citizens deserve and expect, and which taxpayers pay for. As noted earlier, when the homicide rate is such an outlier, then the presumption is that lawlessness reaches over into other areas of public safety. The full range of insecurity, heartbreak, and misery on the streets of Chicago is evident when speaking to longtime residents of neighborhoods directly affected by gang violence. The failure of providing public safety to those families is plain to see.

What about Other Cities?

While any policing oversight, whether from the DOJ or initiated by the Illinois attorney general, will focus on policing practices, it will not address the structure of city government. What can we learn from the major US cities in that regard? The problems plaguing Chicago are not unique, and other cities from time to time have experienced surges in all manner of criminal activity. Those cities have also struggled and found a way out of their troubles.

Table 8.4 provides information on police staffing and homicide rates in the fifteen largest US cities for 2016. These per capita statistics show that the major cities are divided into two groups. The top five cities account for 70 percent of homicides and 63 percent of the population of the fifteen cities. It will be those cities whose policing we will explore. The remaining ten cities are smaller and have not struggled with policing problems to the same degree Chicago has.

TABLE 8.4   Police Officers and Homicides for the Top Fifteen US Cities in 2016

	Total number of officers	Officers per 10,000	Murder rate per 100,000
New York	36,228	42.3	3.4
Los Angeles	9,850	24.6	7.1
Chicago	11,954	43.9	23.8
Houston	5,182	22.2	13.3
Philadelphia	6,313	40.2	17.9
Phoenix	2,762	17.4	7.2
San Antonio	2,152	14.4	6.4
San Diego	1,815	12.8	2.6
Dallas	3,279	24.8	10.4
San Jose	939	9	2.9
Austin	1,807	18.9	2.5
Jacksonville	1,758	20	11.2
San Francisco	2,296	26.4	6.1
Indianapolis	1,612	18.6	17.1
Columbus	1,848	22.1	9.1

Source: Officers count, Governing, http://www.governing.com/gov-data/safety-justice /police-officers-per-capita-rates-employment-for-city-departments.html; murder rate, FBI Uniform Crime Reports, https://ucr.fbi.gov/ucr-publications#cius; City of Columbus, OH, https://www.columbus.gov/police-annualreports/.

NEW YORK

New York City's breathtaking charter revision of 1989 affected practically every area of city government—except policing. In broad strokes, the mayor has more uncontested control of policing in New York than in Chicago. The mayor appoints the police commissioner without the need for any city council ratification. The police department is run by a group of commissioners who are not sworn officers, a group that can include civilians as well as law enforcement professionals. Within the department itself, there is a chain of command for the sworn officers. In interviews with those familiar with this arrange-ment, it appears the parallel commissioner structure allows the top police commissioner to oversee a variety of crucial efforts without a cumbersome chain of command. This also allows the commissioner to bring in experts on areas outside of standard policing, especially counterterrorism. While the city council does not ratify the appointment of the commissioner, that body conducts regular hearings on police affairs and is active in legislating not only local law but police conduct ordinances as well. The city council president is the city ombudsperson, but it appears that the city council president's duties rarely involve police matters. Instead, the Civilian Complaint Review Board, as well as the Human Rights Commission, deal with individual complaints against the police. Unlike the Chicago Police Board, these agencies cannot discipline but must refer cases to the department's internal affairs division.

This reluctance to tie the hands of the mayor is a result of two relatively recent events that have caused New Yorkers to put their faith in the strong mayor. The first is the series of terrorism acts that began with the 1993 bomb-ing of the World Trade Center and ended with its destruction in 2001. The second is the protracted but ultimately successful effort of the city to rid itself of the evils of Cosa Nostra control of vital public services and unions. The prosecutions pursued by then US Attorney Rudolph Giuliani carried over into a campaign to rid the waste-hauling function of Mafia influence. Giuliani is also known for implementing the "broken windows" approach to crime fighting that some, but certainly not all, have credited with a dramatic reduction of crimes of all kinds. Giuliani presided over all these crises, and it is understandable why New Yorkers have been reluctant to meddle with this governance structure.

LOS ANGELES

Unlike New York, Los Angeles has the most widely distributed police power structure of any other major city. The mayor has the least to do with policing. Los Angeles runs a police department with fewer police officers than Chicago and a similar budget, even though it contains 50 percent more residents. The Los Angeles Police Department (LAPD) is run by a commission consisting of five commissioners. The commissioners are appointed by the mayor with staggered terms, are confirmed by the city council, and can be removed by the mayor; a commissioner who is removed, however, can appeal to the city council. No commissioner has ever been removed in the normal course of city operations, but it is customary for a new incoming mayor to remove and replace four of the five members at the beginning of his or her term. Three positions report to the commission: the police chief, the police inspector general, and the executive director of the commission. The commission runs the police department, the mayor does not. The commissioners are civilians, and they meet all day once a week. A final piece of the power puzzle is the city attorney, who is elected and owes no duty to the mayor.

Policing in Los Angeles has come a long way since its nadir in the 1990s. The reputation of the LAPD took a severe blow in the aftermath of the Rodney King beating and ensuing riots. About the same time, a scandal in the Rampart Division uncovered widespread police misconduct not unlike what Chicago has experienced. In 2001, the LAPD entered into a consent decree with the DOJ with federal oversight that lasted until 2013. The consent decree was resisted at first by both the police department and city officials, but now both believe that the city could not have reformed its police department without the force of the federal government (interview with LAPD Executive Director Richard Tefank, August 16, 2018).

While the governance structure of policing was developed by the city a century ago, some practices that have evolved under the consent decree have been quite beneficial. The commission oversees police conduct and investigations of misconduct. This oversight was significantly enhanced by the requirements of the consent decree. It is also helped by the robust office of the inspector general. Whenever there is the use of deadly force by a patrolman, a representative of the inspector general as well as from the district attorney's office show up on the scene. The inspector general's department is present for all interviews with officers who have used deadly force, and such interviews take place as soon as practical after the incident. There is no "hands off" period as in Chicago. Relations between the department and patrolmen are governed by state law, the Peace Officers Bill of Rights. A collective bargaining agreement is negotiated with the mayor and approved by the city council, but primarily deals with compensation matters.

Los Angeles is an inspiring example of turnaround in a major city police department. It would be impossible to determine whether the governance structure or the consent decree was the greater influence, but these two factors combined to make Los Angeles the envy of cities like Chicago.

The City of Brotherly Love resembles Chicago in many ways. The police chief is appointed by the mayor directly and serves at will. The mayor, likewise, appoints the law department. There is no separate inspector general for public safety. The Philadelphia Police Advisory Commission may make recommendations to the police department but has no real authority.

The results for Philadelphia likewise resemble Chicago's. The homicide rate for 2015 at 17.9 per 100,000 of population was second highest among the largest fifteen cities, and the number of patrolmen per 10,000 is third highest behind New York City and Chicago. The resemblance of both governance structure and results for these three cities compared to their peers is certainly a correlation. It may not prove causality, but it does make governance a prime suspect.

HOUSTON

Houston is closest in size to Chicago, and its police governance is also quite similar. The police chief is appointed by the mayor and approved by the city council. The city attorney is likewise the mayor's pick and controls the inspector general. The city auditor's office concentrates more on financial and management matters. The civilian review board meets in secret and only reports on disciplinary actions, not cases where no action is taken. To oversee the police department city officials must rely on the broader municipal governance structure with an independent city council and term limits that keep a long-term mayor from being co-opted by the police department and its unions. This oversight took action in 2009 when the mayor recommended that forensics be removed from the troubled Houston Police Department crime lab. The removal was finalized in 2014. The collective bargaining agreement with patrol officers contains many of the provisions present in Chicago, and this has led to the same protections in cases of misconduct.[32]

A NOTE ON DALLAS

Dallas is not among the largest five US cities, but its efforts at reform are worth noting. Dallas does not have a high homicide rate now but that was not always the case. Several years ago, the city's murder rate was higher than New York, Los Angeles, and Chicago. Then the police chief, David O. Brown, undertook wholesale reform. Central to this was regaining the people's trust with transparency and a vigorous effort to reduce the lethality of interactions between the police and the community. There were some critics of his effort, and the department has experienced an increase in resignations. But with the crime rate plunging, the department needs fewer patrol officers.[33] Dallas may provide one example for Chicago. The 2016 fatal shooting of five police officers in Dallas should not be taken as an indictment of its reformed policing culture.

Settlements

In addition to the horrible toll that police misconduct takes on victims, families, the community at large, and a city's reputation, there is also a dollar cost associated with lawsuits, judgments, and settlements. Police misconduct lawsuits are among many claims that are made on city governments. Claims for damages can arise from a wide variety of incidents, from minor auto damage from potholes to employment practices, human rights violations, and major catastrophes. If the city runs a hospital, it could be responsible for malpractice claims. In some cities police misconduct represents a large proportion of payouts, and in others the share is smaller. In New York City, for instance, total payouts for fiscal year 2017 were over $1 billion and $308 million, or 30 percent, were against the New York Police Department.[34] In Chicago for the years 2006 to 2012, claims against police averaged 67 percent of payouts and ranged from a low in some years of 52 percent to a high of 84 percent.[35] Table 8.5 shows the amounts of payouts and litigation costs from data that could be found for the largest US cities. New York and Chicago stand out as having the highest per capita payout costs; and the per capita cost of police department claims is higher in Chicago than New York.

Lawsuit payouts attributed to the Chicago Police Department come from a variety of claims. In one of the best studies of the subject Mark Iris divided claims into the five categories using detailed source data (table 8.6). Federal civil rights lawsuits are actions taken for complaints of general police misconduct, including excessive force, illegal searches, and false arrests. Wrongful convictions are self-explanatory, but Iris's data includes only the claims that are brought against the CPD and not other elements of the justice system. Torts are minor damages like auto accidents and other minor damage to property that, while numerous, are not particularly costly. Pursuit cases are a separate category of tort damages resulting from auto chases by police. They

TABLE 8.5   Average Payouts and Litigation Expenses, Top Fifteen
US Cities

	Population (2010)	Total payouts[a]	Payouts per capita	Total litigation expense[a]	Fiscal years
New York	8,491,079	$710,608,667	$83.70	N/A	2014–16
Los Angeles	3,928,864	$75,323,990	$19.20	$37,251,312	2014–16
Chicago	2,722,389	$153,133,333	$56.20	N/A	2013–15
Houston	2,239,558	$4,461,832	$2.00	$9,077,651	2014–16
Philadelphia	1,560,297	$46,171,124	$29.60	N/A	2014–16
Phoenix	1,537,058	$5,594,253	$3.60	$5,614,326	2014–16
San Antonio	1,436,697	n/a	n/a	n/a	n/a
San Diego	1,381,069	$41,415,548	$30.00	$5,780,134	2014–16
Dallas	1,281,047	$6,052,267	$4.70	$3,523,328	2014–16
San Jose	1,015,785	$3,781,852	$3.70	$7,104,989	2014–16
Austin	912,791	$1,110,287	$1.20	$3,412,764	2013–15
Jacksonville	853,382	$5,404,889	$6.30	$950,602	2014–16
San Francisco	852,469	$36,925,061	$43.30	$19,146,597	2014–16
Indianapolis	848,788	$3,483,312	$4.10	$1,145,204	2013–15
Columbus	835,957	$1,398,968	$1.07	$986,667	2014–16

[a] Averaged over three fiscal years.
Source: http://www.governing.com/gov-data/City-lawsuit-legal-costs-financial-data
.html.

are rare but quite costly. Other cases are those that do not fit into these categories and consist primarily of employer-employee claims. In addition to these direct payouts, Iris reports that there were many millions of dollars of costs both internally and for outside counsel to either litigate or settle these suits.

Payouts have increased dramatically since 2012. In 2013, payments for lawsuits and costs soared to $96 million and were $67 million in 2014, $44 million in 2015, and $52 million in 2016.[36] In 2017, payouts totaled $100 million in just the last two months of the year.[37] In all these years, the amount of the payouts exceeded what the city had budgeted for them.

The handling of lawsuits against the CPD has been a major blow to the reputation of the city law department. The city has been sanctioned by judges

TABLE 8.6   Chicago Police Department Lawsuit Payouts by Type, 2006 to 2012

Year	Federal civil rights lawsuits	Wrongful convictions	Torts	Pursuit cases	Other cases	Total
2006	$14,216	$8,035	$883	$6,100	$4,319	$33,553
2007	$23,917	$9,975	$1,154	$4,312	$169	$39,527
2008	$23,302	$22,849	$1,550	$28,218	$5,857	$81,776
2009	$27,508	$4,400	$4,500	$50	$3,197	$39,655
2010	$32,558	$7,895	$4,383	$3,000	$2,442	$50,278
2011	$28,116	$1,660	$1,716	$6,580	$417	$38,489
2012	$27,085	$15,125	$1,073	$1,385	$403	$45,071
Total	$176,702	$69,939	$15,259	$49,645	$16,804	$328,349

Source: Mark Iris, "Your Tax Dollars at Work! Chicago Police Lawsuit Payments: How Much, and For What?," *Virginia Journal of Criminal Law* 2, no. 25 (2014): 38, 41, 44, 46, 48, and 49, http://virginiajournalofcriminallaw.com/wp-content/uploads/2014/08/2.1 -Iris-SMW-3.31.14.pdf.
Note: Dollars in thousands.

eight times since Emanuel became mayor, and discovery-related penalties have exceeded $1 million over the past six years.[38] Federal judges have publicly criticized the law department.[39] The head of the Chicago Law Department's Federal Civil Rights Litigation Division has resigned for failing to turn over evidence.[40]

The accounting and budgeting for lawsuit payouts understates costs and aggravates the legacy cost problem for city residents. The city records the cost of lawsuits when judgments are entered or settlements reached. When these costs are recorded they often exceed budgeted amounts. In 2016 the city budgeted $19,844,350 for the payment of police judgments but paid out $81,287,651.[41] The closest parallel in the private commercial sector would be accounting for product liability costs. Whether it is the commercial firm or its insurer, the anticipated costs are reserved.[42] If a loss has been identified, its cost is estimated and it is included in a loss reserve. If no loss has been identified, some estimate is still included in a separate unearned reserve. A city that struggles with a structural deficit and annually needs to invent ways to balance its budget is reluctant to tackle the issue of estimated lawsuit costs, especially given that potential payouts are related to events that are decades old. Since the city did not establish a financial reserve for these costs when the underlying incidents occurred, this burden is being shifted onto future generations.

Chicago's Governance Structure and Public Safety

Earlier chapters of this book looked generally at the governance structure of the city and cited examples of poor decisions or chronic problems that could be prevented or mitigated by changes. As critical as the problems of policing are for the city, they are in a sense just another one of the areas that would benefit from general changes to government. These changes include the elimination of the aldermanic system and its replacement with a smaller independent city council. They also include making the city attorney an elected office. But there are also special actions that would be required to address policing shortcomings. These include changes to the collective bargaining agreements, a special accommodation of lawsuit payout liability, and the consideration of a Los Angeles–style police commission.

Currently the city council is not equipped to provide meaningful, deliberate police governance. In an interview, Garry McCarthy, the police chief fired by Emanuel in the wake of the McDonald shooting, recounted the story of courtesy calls he made with aldermen when he first arrived in Chicago. He was stunned that they felt free to make recommendations to him for district commanders within their wards. McCarthy also observed that at the city council hearing wherein aldermen approved the appointment of his successor, Eddie Johnson, there were many who sang Johnson's praises, but none who asked him about his strategy for reducing the homicide rate.

The elimination of the aldermanic structure and the creation of a smaller, more legislative city council concerned with citywide problems have the potential to provide critical oversight to policing. A clearly independent city council with a robust public safety committee would be a key component of police oversight. After all, it is the council that must legislate many of the other changes city governance requires.

Although not many cities have one, an elected city attorney in Chicago would considerably strengthen the capacity of city government to deal with public safety. In addition to the police code of silence, city government has its own. The city law department fiercely fought efforts to release the McDonald video. McCarthy has stated that in four and a half years with the CPD, he met with the city attorney only once. McCarthy is not the only one to claim that a city attorney serving at the pleasure of a highly political mayor has an inherent conflict of interest. Does the city attorney serve the people or the mayor? The city attorney is the one official charged with representing the city when lawsuits are filed. If independent, the city attorney can more capably balance the interests of taxpayers, plaintiffs, and city officials, and voters can hold the city attorney accountable at the next election.

If the city were to make these two changes, would they give sufficient heft to police oversight and create enough independence from the ebbs and flows of mayoral political capital? In other words, should Chicago consider something like the Los Angeles police commission? Clearly the current operation of the Los Angeles Police Department is superior to that of Chicago. The homicide rate is a fraction of Chicago's and, as we saw in table 8.1, Los Angeles has fewer patrol officers and operates at about the same cost as Chicago for a much larger city. The LAPD has recovered from a national reputation every bit as poor as Chicago's.

A police commission has many advantages. First and foremost it would bring even more distance between the mayor and the police. For decades it has been too difficult for police superintendents to discipline errant patrolmen, as their efforts have been stymied by a Chicago Police Board beholden to the mayor and hamstrung by a collective bargaining agreement that some say has institutionalized the code of silence and lack of accountability. Further, the mayor has been able to dismiss police superintendents practically at will. With a police commission, where the police chief reports to the commission and not to the mayor, steps for handling discipline would be more measured. Such a commission also brings civilian oversight into the chain of command over the police. And finally, installing a police inspector general's office that reports to the commission and works with a staff large enough to keep an eye on policing adds significant investigatory oversight. The recent Chicago effort to create one position assigned to policing within the city's inspector general's office has been insufficient.

With Los Angeles's superior experience, it is hard to see disadvantages to the commission model. Of course, there is the usual Chicago lament that too many independent city officials will give rise to political mischief and unnecessary fiefdoms. This is the same logic that has kept the city mired in a mayor-centric structure for over one hundred years. A commission with multiple members appointed by the mayor but insulated from the mayor's wrath does not give anyone the grandstand that critics worry about. Adopting term limits for the mayor, which would result in most of the police commission members turning over with the mayor, is a strong check on the growth of fiefdoms.

In March 2018, the Chicago Grassroots Alliance for Police Accountability (GAPA), a consortium of community organizations, published a report of its study of policing and called for the creation of a police commission.[43] The GAPA proposal is the closest thing to copying the Los Angeles model that has surfaced in Chicago in recent years. It goes a step further by electing local neighborhood councils that in turn would elect the citywide police commission. Another community group, the Chicago Alliance Against Racist and Political Repression, has introduced a plan similar to GAPA's but goes further by giving a Civilian Police Accountability Commission (CPAC) the ability to investigate and fire police officers.[44] It is the authors' opinion that the Los Angeles model with the citywide commission appointed by the mayor contains sufficient safeguards for the community without the disruption of the elections called for by GAPA. Nevertheless, the GAPA and CPAC proposals should be given serious consideration and debate. Thus far, both have been dismissed out of hand by the city's political leadership.

Regardless of the changes discussed here, the structure of the collective bargaining agreement with the patrolmen must be addressed. The compensation component of the agreement should be overseen by a combined effort of the city council, the mayor, and an independently elected city controller. Either the rules surrounding civil service protection of patrol officers must be stripped from the agreement and administered by a police commission or the State of Illinois should enact a law protecting both the public and the rights of police officers, as did the State of California.

With a robust and independent council committee on public safety and an independently elected city controller, the city can also address what appears to be excessive police staffing. While the various police investigations were under way, the city announced plans to add hundreds of new officers.[45] As table 8.4 indicates, most large cities operate with roughly half of the per capita police force that Chicago deploys. If the expenditures for the police and fire departments were proportionate to comparable spending in Los Angeles, the city would save about $648 million a year just on compensation. When the pension multiplier is considered, the savings are much greater. Recently, the Chicago inspector general has criticized unchecked overtime in the police department, which is costing over $100 million a year.[46] In 2015, it was reported that the CPD had undertaken some internal staffing studies, but it has refused to make them public.[47] If the civil protections elements for the police and fire departments can be removed from council oversight, it can focus on making the department economically efficient.

Chicago continues to prove that it is slow to take the necessary actions without outside oversight, whether imposed by the DOJ or the Illinois attorney general. As of this writing, the steps taken by the city have languished. The new position of deputy inspector general for public safety, reporting to the city's inspector general, was created. In April 2017, the position was filled but was vacant again in January 2018 when the first occupant left. Finally in July 2018 a new candidate was selected. COPA, which was created as a more capable successor to IPRA, was headed by Sharon Fairley. In September 2017 Fairley announced that she was leaving to run for attorney general of the State of Illinois. COPA appointed an interim chief administrator, Patricia Banks, and found another permanent head in April 2018.[48] It is now almost four years since Laquan McDonald was killed, and little has changed. Strong federal oversight of the CPD for many years will be an essential component of any turnaround. The proposed consent decree has strict deadlines for actions to be taken by the CPD, so it is hoped that the urgency contained in that document will lead to swift staffing and enhancement of the Office of Inspector General and COPA.

Addressing policing problems would be incomplete without a plan to better manage and control lawsuit payouts. In order to ultimately bend the curve of soaring payouts, the shortcomings of policing must be addressed. This will require adopting all of the human resource efforts described in the reports of the two investigations and the resulting consent decree, with special focus on an effective early intervention system for errant patrolmen. Until that curve is bent, the city can take steps to mitigate the costs. As noted above, it is a conflict of interest to expect a city attorney appointed by a mayor to conserve both the city's political and financial capital. An independent city attorney who is evaluated on keeping payout costs to a minimum has a better chance of doing so than under the current arrangement. Mark Iris noted in his study that in 2009, the city law department toughened its stance to deter frivolous lawsuits, and as a result, the number of suits began to drop sharply as this became known among the plaintiffs' bar. Unfortunately, this drop intersected with rising claims attributed to the Burge affair. In other jurisdictions, state law has put limits on the amount that can be paid out for automobile accidents. Texas has such a limit of $250,000 per person and $500,000 per incident. Iris has calculated that if Illinois had had such a limit, payouts would have been reduced by $46 million.[49]

Separate from the effort to better manage payout costs is the accounting and budgeting issue. If nothing is done to estimate and address mounting payout costs, the lag in budgeting and recording them will join deficits, city debt and pension obligations, and deferred maintenance as the financial burden left to future generations. Sound city management would get ahead of this problem. The city should hire independent professional consultants who can analyze payouts and report publicly on expected losses. The study might follow the private sector and estimate the known anticipated losses in order to provide a credible estimate of future claims which cannot be currently estimated. An independent city council would commission this study or ask the inspector general to do so. Then, with the study in hand, the council, the mayor, and the independent controller would have to craft a financial plan to provide for the costs without deferring them to future generations. This prudent behavior would be new to Chicago, but it is long overdue.

Among the public goods that only government can provide, public safety reigns supreme. All citizens desire, deserve, and demand a police function that protects bystanders, the innocent, and the accused. Policing comes at a cost, but taxpayers cannot be expected to absorb the unnecessary costs of abuse and mismanagement. Citizens and taxpayers alike know it is time for Chicago to learn how to recover from both long-standing and recent failures by listening to other cities that have gone before it.

CHAPTER 9

Creations of the State

*And that government of the people, by the people, for the
people, shall not perish from the earth.*
—ABRAHAM LINCOLN, *GETTYSBURG ADDRESS*

∽

New York, Los Angeles, and Chicago take different approaches when it comes
to writing the rules that govern a city.

On November 7, 1989, the voters of the City of New York approved, by a vote of
fifty-five percent to forty-five percent, the broadest and most radical changes to
their Charter since 1901. These changes abolished the City's historic Board of Estimate, while preserving a borough voice in government, expanding and increasing
the powers of the City Council, retooling almost all of the City's significant deci-
sion-making processes, and adding a myriad of other changes. These changes were
the product of a revision process that started in mid-1987 with the first hearings
of an initial Charter revision commission, and moved to an intense and dramatic
pace after March 23, 1989, when the Supreme Court declared the voting system in
the Board of Estimate unconstitutional in *Board of Estimate v. Morris*.[1]

On December 6, 1998, residents of the San Fernando Valley submitted more than
200,000 signatures on a petition to require the study of the feasibility of seceding
from the City of Los Angeles. . . . By the turn of the twenty-first century, Los
Angeles was closer than any modern American city to actual breakup by democratic vote.

On June 8, 1999, the voters of Los Angeles chose by a 60 percent majority to adopt the new city charter, the city's first comprehensive charter revision in seventy-five years. Secession generated reform that had eluded Los Angeles civic activists for generations. . . .

On November 5, 2002, Los Angeles voters turned down Valley secession by a two-to-one majority, although the measure narrowly passed in the Valley. Hollywood secession failed by a larger margin, not only citywide but within Hollywood itself.[2]

On June 27, 1990, the Chicago City Council met. The meeting was recorded in 973 pages of the *Journal of the Proceedings of the City Council of the City of Chicago, Illinois*.[3] In the meeting, the appointment of Arenda Troutman and Lorraine Dixon as aldermen by the mayor was approved by the council. The council also acknowledged the heroism of Ms. Wanda Smith in aiding the apprehension of a mugger, supported the boycott of California table grapes by the United Farm Workers, and devoted thirteen pages to an ordinance to prohibit the city from doing business with South Africa. On page 701 of the *Proceedings*, the council approved the complete revision of the city code, the ordinance that spells out how the city is governed. This matter took up five pages of the document.

The contrast of democratic self-government among New York, Los Angeles, and Chicago could not be greater. Both New York and Los Angeles undertook a very thorough and public process of deliberating over a new charter, and their charter commissions were made up of community leaders with experience and knowledge of government. Those charter commissions worked diligently to come up with sound governance structures, and both encountered intense and intelligent opposition. In the case of Los Angeles, there were two competing commissions, one established by the mayor and elected by voters, and another appointed by the city council. The commissions interacted with the public in open and transparent meetings, sold their ideas, and then put the charter revisions up to a public vote. In Chicago, by contrast, the revision of the city code appears as a mere afterthought by a city council of insiders that was too busy with more trivial matters.

If Chicago is to make the changes described and recommended in this study, it would be best served by adopting a charter and a legitimate charter revision process. Unfortunately, Chicago and the State of Illinois have created a legal environment that currently does not allow for a charter.

The Legal Foundation for City Law

The legal environment for municipal law throughout the United States is a fairly simple hierarchical cascade. It begins with the US Constitution. The writers of the Constitution dealt mostly with the formation of the federal government. However, in article 4, section 4, it states: "The United States shall guarantee to every State in this Union a Republican Form of Government." As a result, every state has a government that with minor differences resembles a miniature federal government. It is primarily in the Tenth Amendment that the Constitution talks about the powers of lower levels of government. It says: "The powers not delegated to the United States by the Constitution, nor prohibited by it to the States, are reserved to the States respectively, or to the people." States are sovereign, and it is up to those state governments to create and govern municipalities and other forms of local government.

Over the years, state law governing cities has evolved. Initially, the states passed specific laws that allowed or prohibited any lesser level of government action. When specific laws are required, this environment is called "general law" or "statutory law," also known informally as following Dillon's Rule. A city under general law acts like the child's game Simon Says. The state says the city can do X and cannot do Y. If the city wishes to do Z, the state must pass a law to authorize it. Throughout the nineteenth century, as cities grew in size and complexity, local governments sought a more streamlined way to create and oversee local law. When the US Supreme Court ruled that states still held sway over local law, some states started to develop the theory of "home rule." Under home rule, a lesser level of government can take broader action without specific state legislation, subject to any restrictions the state might impose on municipal government. In other words, "home rule" flips the default. Without it, a municipality may exercise only those powers specifically granted by the state. With it, a municipality may exercise any powers not specifically restricted by the state.

Today home rule is widespread, but each state seems to have a different way of granting it. One of the principal ways that local levels of government— counties and cities—can embrace home rule is to adopt a charter. Another is through specific legislation, such as the Illinois Municipal Code. Many cities large and small across the country have adopted a city charter and have regular procedures for revising that charter. As discussed here in other chapters, some of the charter revision efforts in cities like New York and Los Angeles have been quite dramatic and consequential. These charters are thorough in approaching most of the matters of concern to voters, taxpayers, and citizens. The laws of Illinois are not as conducive to municipal governance as elsewhere, and whereas other states specifically provide for charter creation, Illinois law is moot on the subject. Illinois was late to the home rule game, adopting the concept in 1970 when the state constitution was rewritten for the first time in one hundred years. Although Illinois is now a home rule state, the laws surrounding these home rule rights can be difficult for a layperson to understand. The following are the relevant sections of the 1970 Illinois State Constitution dealing with local government.

ARTICLE VII
LOCAL GOVERNMENT

SECTION 1. MUNICIPALITIES AND UNITS OF LOCAL GOVERNMENT

"Municipalities" means cities, villages and incorporated towns. "Units of local government" means counties, municipalities, townships, special districts, and units, designated as units of local government by law, which exercise limited governmental powers or powers in respect to limited governmental subjects, but does not include school districts.

SECTION 6. POWERS OF HOME RULE UNITS

(a) A County which has a chief executive officer elected by the electors of the county and any municipality which has a population of more than 25,000 are home rule units. Except as limited by this Section, a home rule unit may exercise any power and perform any function pertaining to its government and affairs including, but not limited to, the power to regulate for the protection of the public health, safety, morals and welfare; to license; to tax; and to incur debt.

(f) A home rule unit shall have the power subject to approval by referendum to adopt, alter or repeal a form of government provided by law, except that the form of government of Cook County shall be subject to the provisions of Section 3 of this Article. A home rule municipality shall have the power to provide for its officers, their manner of selection and terms of office only as approved by referendum or as otherwise authorized by law.

(m) Powers and functions of home rule units shall be construed liberally.

SECTION 8. POWERS AND OFFICERS OF SCHOOL DISTRICTS AND UNITS OF LOCAL GOVERNMENT OTHER THAN COUNTIES AND MUNICIPALITIES

Townships, school districts, special districts and units, designated by law as units of local government, which exercise limited governmental powers or powers in respect to limited governmental subjects shall have only powers granted by law.

SECTION 11. INITIATIVE AND REFERENDUM

(a) Proposals for actions which are authorized by this Article or by law and which require approval by referendum may be initiated and submitted to the electors by resolution of the governing board of a unit of local government or by petition of electors in the manner provided by law.

(b) Referenda required by this Article shall be held at general elections, except as otherwise provided by law. Questions submitted to referendum shall be adopted if approved by a majority of those voting on the question unless a different requirement is specified in this Article.

Two things stand out in the constitution's wording that make city charters rare or nonexistent. First, nowhere is there a mention of a charter. The most recent city charter for Chicago is from 1863.[4] That charter, granted decades before home rule emerged, looks more like corporate articles of incorporation than a self-governing document. Instead of using charters, home rule municipalities in Illinois govern themselves through the adoption of municipal ordinances, like those codified in the Municipal Code of Chicago, subject only to specific restrictions enacted from time to time by the state legislature. Municipalities not under home rule are governed by state law codified as the Illinois Municipal Code, or Chapter 65 of the Illinois Compiled Statues. In New York the Home Rule Law governs city charter creation and revision and allows a charter by government appointment of petition by voters.[5] In California, the charter powers are incorporated directly in that state's constitution.[6]

Second, it is unclear how a city would pass laws to govern itself. The Illinois Constitution states that "a home rule unit shall have the power subject to approval by referendum to adopt, alter or repeal a form of government provided by law." Such wording allows a city like Chicago to adopt a city code. It would appear that such wording would also allow a city to create a charter and an ordinance governing the revision of a charter if it wished to do so.

The wording, however, says that the city has the power subject to approval by referendum provided by law. If the change is less significant, can the council just make it by ordinance without referendum? In the case of the complete revision of June 27, 1990, there was no referendum. On November 16, 2011, the city council added the power for the mayor to appoint a chief sustainability officer. The wording of this provision takes up nearly half of all the mayor's powers, and yet it was enacted by the council without a referendum. Was it an adoption or alteration of a form of government? If neither, what would constitute such a change? From the foregoing discussion it would appear that a switch to a charter system would be so significant that, if not previously incorporated in a change to the constitution, it would require action by the Illinois General Assembly.

A further question is whether citizens may petition the city to adopt or alter its form of government. To reiterate, the Illinois Constitution says: "Proposals for actions which are authorized by this Article or by law and which require approval by referendum may be initiated and submitted to the electors by resolution of the governing board of a unit of local government or by petition of electors in the manner provided by law." It would appear that the voters ("electors" in the constitution's wording) can petition for a charter or change of form of government but only in a manner provided by law. But where is the law that governs such a petition and what does it say? The authors could not find such a provision. Both New York and Los Angeles explicitly confer such power to voters.

Is state law in Illinois friendly to voter initiatives? It is the spirit and letter of the Illinois Constitution that the right to petition is severely restricted. In that portion of the Illinois Constitution which deals with amending it, section 2, any initiative by voters to amend the constitution for a specific issue, other than narrowly defined legislative matters, is not allowed. Citizens' initiatives can only change the legislative provisions of the constitution, and such efforts have failed many more times than they have succeeded. Here is the wording:

SECTION 2. AMENDMENTS BY GENERAL ASSEMBLY

(a) Amendments to this Constitution may be initiated in either house of the General Assembly. Amendments shall be read in full on three different days in each house and reproduced before the vote is taken on final passage. Amendments approved by the vote of three-fifths of the members elected to each house shall be submitted to the electors at the general election next occurring at least six months after such legislative approval, unless withdrawn by a vote of a majority of the members elected to each house.

SECTION 3. CONSTITUTIONAL INITIATIVE FOR LEGISLATIVE ARTICLE

Amendments to Article IV of this Constitution may be proposed by a petition signed by a number of electors equal in number to at least eight percent of the total votes cast for candidates for Governor in the preceding gubernatorial election. Amendments shall be limited to structural and procedural subjects contained in Article IV.

In the Illinois Municipal Code, the only area where citizen initiative is mentioned is when citizens of a previously unincorporated area petition for incorporation. For the remainder of the laws governing the operation of the city, it falls to the city itself to make its own laws, and there is no provision that requires a city to seek the approval of voters. Thus it is questionable whether a home rule municipality could even allow such initiatives to change municipal law.

When it is unclear what the law requires, it is up to the courts to decide. In the case of changes to the form of government in Illinois, there are a handful of cases whereby decisions by local government have been challenged because they did not put the measure up for voter approval. In one case, the change made by a governing board was considered so minor as to not require a referendum.[7] In other cases, the change was considered a change in the form of government and was ultimately reversed because there had been no referendum.[8] It would appear that the minor changes undertaken by the City of Chicago in the city code were not a change of form, but the changes recommended elsewhere in this book would certainly require approval by referendum.

In summary, under current Illinois state law it appears that a municipality may change its form of government either by ordinance or by adopting a charter process, but not easily. Either way, the change would be so significant that it would require voter approval and would likely need to be allowed by state legislation. Voters must approve the changes but cannot petition for them. The question of whether the government of Chicago would ever entertain such changes is one for political speculation.

City Charters

Among the fifteen largest cities in the United States, only Chicago and Indianapolis do not have a city charter. In the states where the other thirteen cities reside, charter governance is considered superior to other statutory accommodations. Charters and charter revision are the normal way that cities form their governments. The National Civic League agrees and has produced an excellent *Guide for Charter Commissions.*[9]

The *Guide* spells out those matters which are of concern to charters and those which are not. A typical charter covers the following areas:

- Powers of the city
- City council
- City manager
- Departments, offices, and agencies
- Financial management
- Elections
- General provisions: transparency, ethics, etc.
- Charter amendment
- Transition and severability

The *Guide* also sets expectations about what a change to a charter can and cannot do. A charter may do the following:

- Alter a form of government so that the new form is better aligned with the preferences of citizens
- Restrict or increase options available to government leaders
- Redistribute powers among elected officials, appointed officials, and governing bodies, as well as between city officials and citizens
- Convert elected governmental positions to appointed positions and vice versa

But a charter cannot be expected to accomplish the following objectives:

- Automatically increase the quality of governmental products and services
- Eliminate political infighting
- Jumpstart the local economy
- Decrease local crime

- Improve the school system
- Stop a controversial project
- Change or eliminate state-mandated activities

The *Guide* contains sound advice learned from numerous municipal charter revisions on how to conduct the charter adoption and revision process. Although the charter process must be allowed by government actions, the *Guide* speaks about the role of officials:

> While in many cases the mayor and/or council plays a role in the appointment of the commission members, the involvement of elected officials should end at that point. The charter process functions best when it is rooted in citizen involvement rather than one influenced by political officials directly serving as members. . . . the commission should do its work independently and give the council and the voters its best thinking about charter change. Commission membership should be diverse in every respect so that it fairly represents the community. Commission members must be prepared to work hard; membership is not honorary. The most effective charter commissions are not dominated by lawyers, scholars, and accountants, but made up of civic-minded intelligent lay people with a common-sense approach to things.[10]

Chicago could learn much from the *Guide*, as well as from the experience of other major cities. The examples of New York City and Los Angeles are worth noting. The New York City charter revision effort of 1989 is perhaps the best example of thoughtful governance revision in modern American history. The areas addressed included the following:

- City council powers and status
- Council size and terms in office
- Districting
- Council rules of procedure
- Citywide elected officials (mayor, comptroller, and council president)
- The process for budgets, land use, franchise and licensing, and procurement
- The role of the Independent Budget Office
- The requirement of openness and substantive information
- A ban on elected and high-ranking officials from being political party leaders

The Los Angeles charter revision of 1999 is slightly less thorough than New York's because it was a more voluntary effort. New York's revision was forced by a finding by the US Supreme Court that the existing governance structure was unconstitutional. Los Angeles undertook charter revision when areas of the city threatened secession. Nevertheless, Los Angeles addressed many key areas of city government:

- Powers and duties of elected officials (mayor, city council, controller, and city attorney)
- Elections
- Ethics commission
- City planning
- Police department
- Proprietary departments (airports, harbor, water, and power)
- Public works, recreation, and parks
- Neighborhood councils
- The budget process
- Contracting

In Los Angeles, the June 8, 1999, vote was split into separate measures, one for the charter and a second measure to increase the size of the council from fifteen to twenty-one or twenty-five members. The new charter passed with 60 percent of the vote, but the measures to increase the size of the council failed. Those opposing a larger city council made the argument that increasing the size of the council would bring to Los Angeles Chicago-style politics. As noted in chapter 1, they derided this as ludicrous.[11]

Two Choices for Illinois and Chicago

If the people of Chicago wish to enact the changes described in this book, there appear to be two routes to pursue.

A cleaner and more thorough way to address the deficiencies in Illinois law would be to amend the constitution. At a minimum this would require that the article on local government be changed to allow home rule cities to adopt city charters. Such a revision should preserve the current requirement that significant change requires a referendum. Allowing citizens to initiate charter adoption or revision should be given serious consideration as the law is debated. Addressing charter revision in these ways is nothing new, and there are many examples from major cities. In fact, the 1954 Home Rule Commission suggested as much. It recommended that the state legislature enact specific powers "permitting the Chicago City Council, or the Chicago electorate by the initiative process, to propose changes in the form and structure of city government, subject to referendum approval, but without the necessity of prior state legislative approval."[12] Illinois and Chicago leaders should study constitutional provisions in other cases and can see what effect certain provisions have had on municipal governance. Providing for city charters and the right of citizens to initiate and approve them is the norm, and political leaders should not fear these reforms.

If a constitutional amendment is not possible, for whatever reason, the second way to implement changes for the benefit of the city of Chicago would be to make changes by city ordinance, including changes to the Illinois Municipal Code, relating specifically to city governance. Under current law, such changes are not possible by citizen initiative. The political leaders would have to decide on their own to adopt a charter or change laws in a manner that resembles a charter. Such a change in the form of government would require a referendum. This manner of implementing change is less robust but might be more politically feasible than wholesale change of the Illinois Constitution.

In our discussion of governance reform we refer frequently to the involvement of voters, either in approving changes or initiating them. This preoccupation can be attributed to the fact that voter involvement is at once so pervasive throughout the United States and so absent in Illinois. Critics of voter initiatives can find examples, often in California, that are not to their liking and that make for popular examples of overreach. In particular, referenda are criticized as being overly influenced by moneyed interests. But James H. Svara and Douglas J. Watson, in their book *More than Mayor or Manager: Campaigns to Change Form of Government in America's Large Cities*, find the criticism of referenda fueled by money and simplistic arguments to be "overblown."[13] They go on to posit that the referendum process is a valuable medium for educating voters, who may be just as likely to reaffirm their current form of government as change it. A city without voter involvement leaves the citizen with only two choices: to accept the status quo or to leave.

Entities Not Subject to Home Rule

The discussion of home rule and charter adoption, even if adopted, would only affect the City of Chicago, not the schools, parks, or any other sister units of government. Those entities are not home rule entities and are subject to other specific state legislation. Changes to school governance would still have to come about by state legislation, changes to election law would require revision of the state election code, and changes to pensions would fall under the state pension code. These codes are archaic and reflect an agglomeration of laws passed over the past century that have been cut and pasted into one long string of provisions. Average Chicagoans reading these codes would likely be overwhelmed by their mind-numbing wording, confusion, and irrationality. There are provisions that seem to call for government action that has never occurred. For instance, the pension code contains a chapter that governs the Chicago Teachers' Pension Fund. Section 17–127 of that chapter deals with state financing for the fund. Note the requirement in subparagraph (b):

> b) The General Assembly finds that for many years the State has contributed to the Fund an annual amount that is between 20% and 30% of the amount of the annual State contribution to the Article 16 retirement system, and the General Assembly declares that it is its goal and intention to continue this level of contribution to the Fund in the future.

Despite being written into law, the state instead made a flat annual contribution to these pensions of $60 million. Some might argue that a separate block grant to CPS was intended to discharge this obligation, but a voter might ask why the money did not go into the pension fund as the legislation directs. The point here illustrates how cumbersome and ineffective specific legislation can be for entities not under home rule.

To implement the changes recommended in this book will require changes to several state laws. The question for lawmakers and those seeking change is whether it would be better to rewrite the entire code to more accurately reflect reality and be more accessible to citizens or to let sleeping dogs lie and make yet one more amendment to be inserted as an additional paragraph. As noted above, the Chicago City Council decided to completely rewrite its city code. Good governance would call for the rewrite, but good politics might overrule that objective.

Political Obstacles

Any reader with even passing familiarity with Illinois and Chicago politics will immediately realize that both routes to charter adoption are fraught with seemingly impossible political obstacles. The same politicians who have led the current governments—in some cases for decades—will not readily yield such powers. We would be asking for the fox to reform the hen house.

While the political obstacles in Chicago currently seem immovable, it must be noted that the city only accounts for 20 percent of the state's population. In recent decades, the legislature has created state legislative districts that encompass areas in the city of Chicago together with nearby suburbs; the reach of Chicago-rooted legislators, therefore, exceeds 20 percent. Theoretically, a movement by lawmakers representing 80 percent of Illinois voters who reside outside Chicago city limits could force changes that would benefit their communities as well as Chicago. This assumes that they act independently. Reality must acknowledge, however, that the current Speaker of the Illinois House of Representatives has been in that office for decades, is the chair of the state Democratic Party, and resides in the city of Chicago.

The Possibility of Change

Change from outside the ruling class could come in two forms: change the rulers or petition for a change in the rules. Changing rulers in Illinois and Chicago does not come easily. Both the State General Assembly and the Chicago City Council have leading members who have served for decades. The wife of the longest-serving alderman sits on the Illinois Supreme Court, which interprets state and local law. One family has occupied the mayor's office in Chicago for the majority of voters' lifetimes. However, nothing lasts forever, and rulers do die, age out, or are voted out of office. What is critical for Chicago's citizens and the future of the city itself is to know what one would like new leaders to do. Civic leaders who desire governance reform are better prepared for the future than those who have not given the subject any thought.

In the early twentieth century, there were several attempts to amend the old Illinois Constitution to provide for home rule. Then in 1954, a blue-ribbon Chicago Home Rule Commission tackled the same issues and came to many of the conclusions echoed in this book.[14] As outdated as the one-hundred-year-old Illinois Constitution was, it still allowed for citizens to attempt a change. The drafters of the 1970 constitution wittingly or unwittingly erected barriers much more formidable to reform.

More than in most other states, the law in Illinois is closed and impervious to change by concerned citizens. If ever there were a rigged political and legal environment, this is one. Other cities and states, however, have faced archaic political and legal regimes and have nonetheless found a way to reform. Often this comes about as the result of an irresistible legal challenge or from a civic crisis that is so fundamental that to carry on with "business as usual" becomes unacceptable. It is the premise of this book that if nothing changes, the probability of such a civic crisis increases daily. If there is any reason for hope, it lies in the fact that examples of good governance and good government reform abound across the country.

The changes called for include three main components:

- the adoption of a new local government section of the Illinois Constitution that allows for a city charter and a charter process;
- the inclusion of the right of citizens to petition the city for charter revision; and
- the rewriting of other Illinois codes for non–home rule entities that incorporate the changes suggested in other chapters of this study.

CHAPTER 10

The Audacity of Hope?

Only a crisis—actual or perceived—produces real change. When that crisis occurs,
the actions that are taken depend on the ideas that are lying around. That, I believe,
is our basic function: to develop alternatives to existing policies, to keep them alive
and available until the politically impossible becomes the politically inevitable.
—MILTON FRIEDMAN

〜

About This Book Again

Longtime Chicago journalists, politicians, and academics might find that this book covers well-plowed ground and offers nothing new. Somewhere, however, in a high-rise office building in the Loop, a thirty-year-old professional will look out the window at Northerly Island and never know that there was an airport there. If they are from Chicago, they were thirteen when it was torn up. If they moved to Chicago after college, they will find many of the stories in this book new and surprising. The underlying events and circumstances described here will continue to become more distant over time. The history of bad decisions will become increasingly hidden from future Chicagoans. That is why this book exists.

This book is reportage. It tells stories about Chicago, presents statistics, talks about what happens in other cities, and draws conclusions. All of what is presented is public knowledge and has been reported piecemeal in newspapers, blogs, and magazines. There is no scientific analysis undertaken. There is no way to prove that one form of urban governance is superior to or works better than another, although countless leaders across the United States have grappled with the issues and found other models. There is no way to determine just how much fiscal load will sink a government, although it is widely acknowledged that sound finances are essential to sound governance.

The authors have selected certain areas and aspects of Chicago government to examine and excluded others. Perhaps the obvious exclusion is the government of Cook County, and it is at the county level that critical tax matters small and large have unfolded as this book was written. The Cook County Board of Commissioners backtracked on a controversial soda tax amid widespread citizen backlash. On a larger scale, the inequity of the property tax assessment process has been exposed yet again, costing the assessor his job. This latter matter, when rectified, will have an enormous impact on the tax bill for high-priced residences and commercial property. In 2003, the Civic Federation sponsored a study of Cook County governance that was not unlike this book. That work, known as *The Quigley Report*, was widely hailed and then ignored. It mentioned the assessor's office but was mute on the assessment scandal.

Other entities appearing on Chicagoans' tax bills were excluded. Although this book examines the Chicago Board of Education, it does not look at the Chicago Park District, the Metropolitan Water Reclamation District, or the community college district. Also excluded are divisions of the city government, including the airports. There were several factors that went into the decision not to examine the governance of these entities. While many of these entities have governance control similar to the areas that were examined, in most cases the fiscal problems are not as distressed or the obligations are adequately covered by those using the public goods. In other cases, it was expected that the entity would be included in a city charter revision. There are certainly governance and fiscal concerns for all these units of government, but they do not rise to a level the authors felt needed addressing in a full-length book. Our intent here is to stimulate broader thinking on the handful of matters that are critical to the city, with the hope that by bringing change to them the reform will spill over into these other entities.

This book is not a fire bell. Granted, the problems described in these chapters tell of serious trouble. Nevertheless, the city is not on fire, it is not bankrupt, and its economy and population are not in free fall. The word *crisis* is perhaps the most overused word in political discourse, and the authors use it sparingly. The point of view of this book is that problems are better addressed when the gun is not at our heads. The time to undertake charter revision or a reconsideration of governance is not when events force hasty and unstudied compromises with too little deliberation; the time to address financial problems is now, when we are not yet at a brink.

This is also not a history book. There are dozens of fascinating books that tell the story of Chicago's past. The authors only included enough of the recent past to illustrate governance failure and to give context. In Chicago's case, the past is not a guide to the future. We cannot retrace our steps and reestablish every person and business who made up the city at its demographic and economic peak in 1950. Like Moses at the Red Sea, the past has caved in behind the city, and now the city must face the future.

What this book does seek to do is collect in one volume information and analysis about the key issues with which Chicago is grappling. For those who have not followed some of these issues, it attempts to explain them as simply and succinctly as possible. It seeks to open eyes to the ways that other cities have organized themselves to govern and solve problems. And finally, it seeks to recommend those changes that seem to be most obvious.

This book is unique in its singular focus on the governance structure of the City of Chicago. One book that, on the surface, comes closest to a similar approach is *Fixing Illinois: Politics and Policy in the Prairie State.*[1] It looks at state-level problems in Illinois and presents ninety-eight different recommendations in the areas of finances, education, human services, health care, economic development, transportation, government, and corruption. Where that book talks about specific policies and laws, this book looks at the underlying structure of governance. Our approach has been nonpartisan, and we do not have specific solutions to problems to recommend. Instead we trust that, with rational governance, distributed power, checks and balances, and sufficient deliberation, Chicago government will make better decisions. While many of the recommendations in *Fixing Illinois* are attractive, it conspicuously omits the critical shortcomings of the Illinois Constitution and how those flaws have led to poor decisions and resulted in the problems the authors' recommendations seek to fix. Even a title that promises to fix Illinois is more ambitious than merely offering a new Chicago way of operating.

This book does not promise to "fix Chicago," a critical distinction that cannot be emphasized enough. In dealing with governance, we lay out specific proposals that, if adopted, would make for better decision making on the part of the city government. But just changing the way government works, though necessary, is hardly sufficient for the city to improve. For that to happen, the leaders over the next decades will need to take specific actions to improve conditions, and if the problems cannot be directly solved, they must at least allow the city to outgrow them. It is a possibility that an independent city council could go rogue and take actions that, in hindsight, would be considered as egregious as some of those described in this book. An elected city controller could grandstand and fail to improve finances, an elected city attorney could continue to serve the mayor and not the city, and an elected school board could derail any improvement that the current appointed board may have achieved. There are risks in changing governance. The only thing the people of Chicago can to rely on in calling for change is the experience of those in other big cities who have gone before them.

Readers and leaders will take issue with some of the ideas presented here. They may have different ideas, and they might be right. If this book can stimulate dialogue and further study that leads to constructive change, it will have succeeded. If it goes the way of the Quigley study of Cook County or the 1954 study of home rule in Chicago and collects only dust, while the particulars of Chicago governance remain unchanged and the structure archaic and inadequate, such inaction would be disappointing, but at least it would not be uninformed. That is why this book exists.

About Chicago

For many, Chicago has never been a better place to live. On a cool day in April 2018, fifteen construction cranes could be counted from the sky deck at the top of the John Hancock building. Some projects are residential high-end rentals and condos, and some are new offices, either in the Loop or the rapidly growing West Loop. The construction boom is a sign of expansion and confidence. From the depths of the financial crisis in March 2010 to March 2017, the city added over 168,000 jobs, an increase of 16.6 percent.[2] The following year, growth stalled, and only 510 new private sector jobs were added.[3] Driving the boom are sectors with their own patterns of spending and consumption. These big drivers are service, baby boomer in-migration, government, leisure, and hospitality.

As manufacturing has declined nationwide, including Chicago, services of all kinds make up a growing segment of employment. Although trade, transportation, and utilities remains the largest segment of employment in the Chicago area, the next four categories in terms of number of people employed include professional and business services, education and health services, government, and financial activities.[4] This vast service sector includes lawyers, bankers, nurses, consultants, and those who work at tech and design companies. As the sector expands, it drives the demand for new office and commercial space.

As the baby boomers age, they are moving into the city and consuming all it has to offer. The percentage of the Chicago metropolitan area population that is over fifty-five years of age increased from 18 percent in 1970 to 24 percent in 2016.[5] Those who have the money are fueling the boom in high-end rentals and condos in the city.[6] With 24 percent of the population, this demographic accounts disproportionately for more business in key sectors. These are the people who spend on health care, housing, the performing arts, and upscale dining.

With more than 500,000 jobs in the metropolitan area, government is the fifth largest segment of the workforce. In every *Crain's* list of Chicago's top employers, some unit of government occupies four of the top five spots.[7] With the exception of federal employees, these other employers are paid with state and local taxes.

Right behind government are the 456,700 people working in the leisure and hospitality industry. The same Bureau of Labor Statistics summary that counts these workers also states that the average hourly wage in this segment is between $10 and $13 per hour, compared to $60 per hour for lawyers and financial consultants and $30 per hour for accountants, nurses, and government workers. The products of leisure and hospitality work are consumed by Chicago residents, suburban commuters, and visitors from around the United States and the world. A small portion of the city's construction boom includes this sector's hotels and restaurants.

Here, then, are the engines of the economic boom in Chicago. Other types of jobs, such as corporate headquarters workers and tech start-ups, are included in the above statistics, but their numbers are relatively small. Some call Chicago an emerging global city, but much of the growth involves Chicagoans serving Chicagoans. The big private-sector growth engines are creating the construction jobs and expanding employment. The city's population is level or declining, and public property that includes schools, roads, sewers and the like are already built out, with not much public money being spent for their renewal. The manufacturing sector has declined, and the locations where factories once hummed are now empty lots awaiting gentrification by the service sector. Chicago's hope rests with these leading sectors: services, baby boomers, government, and hospitality, all of which are growing. The cranes do not lie.

This growth, however, is uneven. Chicago has been described as two cities so often that the term has become almost a cliché. The idea originated with the National Advisory Commission on Civil Disorders, known as the Kerner Commission, when it stated in its report that "our nation is moving toward two societies, one black, one white—separate and unequal." This is certainly true of Chicago. Numerous reports on the crime problem identify inequality, lack of jobs, and poor neighborhoods as root causes. In 1970, 17 percent of Chicagoans were classified as low income and 3 percent were of very high income. By 2010, 46 percent were low income and 15 percent were very high income. The middle-income population declined from 45 percent to 16 percent.[8] A drive through the city or a bus ride from the city's core to outlying poor neighborhoods tells the story in real time. This divide between the haves and have-nots is real and highly unjust.

There is another, altogether different divide that exists in Chicago, that between a city with growing successes and one with growing problems. The successes noted above are real, are visible, and are being enjoyed by individuals, businesses, and ultimately city government. The problems that this book is concerned with are also real; they do or will hurt individuals, businesses and organizations, and ultimately city government. Those problems are a growing fiscal deficit and an accompanying governance deficit. Can the successes outrace the problems? Can we grow our way out of trouble?

Chicago's leaders are counting on this growth to solve its fiscal problems. A significant portion of this book has described the debt and legacy costs Chicago has racked up. The City of Chicago has $9 billion of general obligation debt, Chicago Public Schools owes $7.7 billion of similar general obligation debt, the Metropolitan Pier and Exhibition Authority owes over $4 billion in debt that is supported by Chicago taxes; the city will continue to budget for $50 million in lawsuits, and the annual contributions for public employee pensions will be near $2 billion for the five largest city plans in 2018. This is all municipal credit card debt, empty calories of government expenditures for past mistakes that contribute nothing toward public services for citizens today. If the city is to make any headway with its structural deficits and debt, it will need billions more in revenue. To pay off these debts rather than dump them on future generations who will have had nothing to do with incurring them—and who will receive no benefit from paying them—will require very significant funding.

The increased taxes required annually to extinguish the city's legacy costs can be itemized as follows:

Pay off CPS general obligation debt in ten years	$500,000,000
Pay off the city's general obligation debt in twenty years	$325,000,000
Increase pension plan contributions for twenty years	$2,350,000,000
Increase budgeting for policing lawsuit costs	$50,000,000
Total	$3,225,000,000

Other problems such as schools and policing will also require money, but progress in those areas will have more to do with governance and demographic trends than mere finances. If the recent success indicated by the improvement in some measures of school performance is due to the growth of charter schools, then the cap on charter school growth might challenge that improvement. The homicide rate is already falling from its peak in 2016, but will it continue until Chicago reaches parity with other cities? Will the city be able to genuinely embrace community policing and satisfactory accountability with the negligible changes in governance that have been undertaken so far? Critics of the ideas proposed here may point out that the big governance mistakes are all in the past, but events unfold and then they come to light. The public has no way of knowing whether decisions made recently will have a negative impact in the near or distant future. Are the city and its affiliates capable of avoiding poor decisions under the same aldermanic system and secretive mayor's office that brought about the current state of affairs? Citizens are justified when they say they never know what is being cooked up.

The race between the two cities—the race between the growth of success and the growth of problems—will be the central drama in Chicago for the next few decades. Success has grown unevenly in the past, and the 2020 census will be but one measure of the city's vitality. From the current perspective it does not appear that success is growing fast enough to outpace trouble. The final reality is that success often stumbles but problems seldom do.

About Government

The idea of considering the structure of governance has a long philosophical tradition. The most notable ancient was Aristotle, who talked about "the right distribution of offices, their number, their nature, [and] their duties."[9] Of all the wisdom in his work one minor point applies today as much as it did in ancient Athens: "since many . . . of these offices handle the public money, there must of necessity be another office which examines and audits them, and has no other functions. Such officers are called by various names—Scrutineers, Auditors, Accountants, Controllers."[10] Was he the inventor of the inspector general? Centuries later the Western philosophers who laid the foundation for modern thinking also spoke to the point of separated powers. This group included Thomas Hobbes, John Locke, Jean-Jacques Rousseau, Montesquieu, Immanuel Kant, and Hegel. Montesquieu noted, "When the legislative and executive powers are united in the same person . . . there can be no liberty."[11] Kant agreed, saying "the legislative authority ought not at the same time to be the Executive or Governor."[12] A century later, Hegel observed that "the state as a political entity is cleft into three substantive divisions . . . the Legislature . . . the Executive . . . [and] the Crown."[13] This comment by Hegel concerned itself with constitutional monarchy, but it could also be applied to large cities where the mayor is the political sovereign and the city manager is the executive official.

The great American tradition of separated powers was drawn from these Europeans. James Madison, who is credited with the thinking behind our Constitution, made sure that document clearly created three coequal and separate branches of government. He joined with Hamilton and Jay to sell the states on ratification, penning Federalist No. 47, devoted solely to the separation of powers. In this essay he reiterated the philosophers' conclusion that "the accumulation of all powers . . . in the same hands . . . [is] the very definition of tyranny."[14] The republican form of government which the Constitution requires of each state also imitates the three separate federal branches of government. At the local level, most cities separate powers among the mayor, the city council, and the local courts. In this manner checks and balances prevent tyranny and make for better decision making.

The great twentieth-century political scientist Samuel P. Huntington elaborated on these ideas in his analysis of political maturity in the developing world. The concepts explained in his book *Political Order in Changing Societies* offer a profound framework for looking at Chicago's governance. The book looks at the process whereby traditional or tribal societies change as they grow economically and seek to modernize. He debunks the automatic assumption that economic growth will lead to better political systems. For that to happen the society must develop strong political institutions with qualities that can transcend individual leaders.[15]

The essence of Huntington's argument is that political systems benefit from the functional distribution of power.

> To cope successfully with modernization, a political system must be able, first, to innovate policy, that is, to promote social and economic reform by state action. Reform in this context usually means the changing of traditional values and behavior patterns . . . the rationalization of authority structures, the promotion of functionally specific organizations, the substitution of achievement criteria for ascriptive ones, and the furthering of a more equitable distribution of material and symbolic resources.[16]

This understanding is not limited to political scientists. Nassim Nicholas Taleb, who gained fame coining the term *Black Swan* and writing a book about the phenomenon of the 2008 financial crisis, has recently written about fragile and antifragile organizations. He identifies five factors that are sources of fragility: "a centralized governing system, an undiversified economy, excessive debt and leverage, a lack of political variability, and no history of surviving past shocks."[17] Fragile organizations and governments are vulnerable to shocks and do not survive them well.

By Taleb's standards Chicago is quite fragile. In April 2016 the city received a grant from the Rockefeller Foundation to hire a chief resilience officer and to develop a resilience plan. The website for the foundation lists all manner of shocks that the resilience plan is intended to anticipate and provide for. The officer hired came from the city water department. He left a year later, and the post remains empty.[18]

Yet another way of looking at government is through the lens of management theory. Peter F. Drucker, the prominent management consultant and educator, has written about the role of disagreement in decision making. "Decisions of the kind the executive has to make are not made well by acclamation. They are made well only if based on the clash of conflicting views, the dialogue between different points of view, the choice between different judgments."[19] In the same work he quotes General Motors CEO Alfred P. Sloan: "Gentlemen, I take it we are all in complete agreement on the decision here. Then, I propose we postpone further discussion of this matter until our next meeting to give ourselves time to develop disagreement and perhaps gain some understanding of what the decision is all about."[20]

Psychologists likewise look at the dynamics of decision making. Daniel Kahneman, a pioneer of decision science, lamented in the early 1970s that "crucial decisions are made, today as thousands of years ago, in terms of the intuitive guesses and preferences of a few men in positions of authority."[21] Michael Lewis writes of Kahneman that "the failure of decision makers to grapple with the inner workings of their own minds, and their desire to indulge their gut feelings, made it [according to Kahneman] 'quite likely that the fate of entire societies may be sealed by a series of avoidable mistakes committed by their leaders.'"[22]

Applying all these perspectives, the conclusion points in one direction: the city of Chicago would make better decisions if power were distributed, if different governmental functions were more accountable to voters and citizens, if the democratic process were more robust, and if the city were not hobbled by crushing legacy costs. The stories told in this book are a testament to this thinking. The closed political system, whereby the mayor appoints and controls the city council and elections discourage democracy, leads to decision making by gut feelings without disagreement. Power and influence are concentrated on the few interests that maintain access to or constrain the mayor: vendors, public employee unions, and real estate concerns. The rest of the populace would be better represented if power resided in a robust, independent city council and in elected financial and legal officials.

Poor governance has cost Chicagoans billions. The bill for poor decision making includes legacy costs of structural deficits, debt, unsettled lawsuits, and deferred maintenance—all of which are crowding out core services. It is hard to predict when, but everyone acknowledges that eventually the bill will come due. If the theory of fragility holds any water, Chicago is primed for a shock it will struggle to overcome.

About Change

The self-help speaker Jim Rohn is best known for saying, "Your life does not get better by chance, it gets better by change." And yet even the idea of change in Chicago seems foreign.

In researching this book and speaking to scores of everyday Chicagoans, the authors have met universal skepticism. The skeptic's lament comes in many forms: you cannot fight city hall; those in power will never give it up; the corruption is so endemic that the situation is hopeless; the elite only care about themselves and not everybody else; it is a one-party town, what do you expect; the unions control the city; the city has never given black Chicagoans a fair shake and never will.

Speaking with elites has sometimes revealed a different form of reluctance. They fear putting governance of the city in the hands of voters. They retain negative memories of the contentious "council wars" of the Harold Washington era. Some feel Chicago's problems are not unique and that other cities are currently or have recently dealt with the same issues. Others see no trouble that the current boom cannot outgrow. They ask, why change? Or, why change now? Even if they wish to see selected changes, they think such changes should come only as a result of crisis. What would it take to change and where will the impetus come from? Raphael Sonenshein, in his report on the Los Angeles charter revision effort, captured the spirit well. "The good-government argument for reform sat off the coast, awaiting a political storm to carry it to shore."[23]

Huntington addresses the gap between our ideals and our institutions in his 1981 book, *American Politics: The Promise of Disharmony*.[24] Better than any other frame of reference, his analysis, illustrated in table 10.1, shows the different responses that Chicagoans have to the gap between the way they think city government should work and the way that it does. The skeptics and leaders can locate themselves in one of the four quadrants of the table.

Huntington's book, while a valid look at American politics, does not give much guidance for the future of Chicago. Relevant for Chicago, however, are the two axes that make up the quadrants of table 10.1: the perception of a gap between the ideal governance for Chicago and its existing institutions, and how intensely an individual feels about those ideals.

The ideals presented in this book may be boiled down to two simple concepts: rationalizing governance through the judicious distribution of power, and the prudent improvement of the finances in every element of Chicago government. Who could argue with these ideals? It turns out that many of Chicago's leaders both in and out of government either maintain mental

TABLE 10.1 American Responses to the Gap between Their Ideals and
Their Institutions

| | | Perception of the gap | |
		Clear	Unclear
Intensity	High	Moralism	Hypocrisy
of beliefs		(eliminate the gap)	(deny the gap)
in ideals	Low	Cynicism	Complacency
		(tolerate the gap)	(ignore the gap)

Source: table 2, "American responses to the Ivl gap," in Samuel P. Huntington, *American Politics: The Promise of Disharmony* (Cambridge, MA: Belknap Press of Harvard University Press, 1981, copyright © 1981 by Samuel P. Huntington), 64.

models that undermine their perception of a gap between ideals and institutions, or they do not feel that strongly about the gap—or both.

The idea of mental models developed in the twentieth century and the first line in a book about them provide a succinct definition: "People's views of the world, of themselves, of their own capabilities, and of the tasks that they are asked to perform, or topics they are asked to learn, depend heavily on the conceptualizations that they bring to the task."[25] Those who think about Chicago or make decisions based upon its future do so with the mental models they bring to the task.

It would be beyond the scope of this book to exhaustively analyze the prevailing mental models of Chicago's leaders. Nevertheless, the stories and conclusions in this study provide a basis for proposing a few mental models that have prevailed.

The paradox of accountability. The more concentrated the power, the more accountability the system provides. If we do not like how things are run, we only have one person to throw out of power, the mayor. Typical of this attitude is a quote from former Cook County State's Attorney Richard Devine: "What's often forgotten is that civilian control already exists. How that control is exercised may not be to the liking of some, but it is there. Both the mayor and the city council have a large say in how the department is run. The mayor is elected to serve as chief executive, and the police department reports to the mayor, a civilian."[26] This belief in false accountability is antithetical to the American tradition of the distribution of political power. The illogic of this paradox of accountability would be laid bare if the people of Chicago were to take it to the extreme and, instead of electing the mayor, ask that he be appointed by the president of the United States. This is the practice in other countries but would hardly be considered the American way.

Make it free. If government can minimize or make invisible the cost of a project, then there is no trade-off. The use of long payoff periods, deferring expenses well into the future, devising new borrowing entities, and unconstrained borrowing make it possible to enjoy things currently without paying for them. In a recent example, the city estimates it will take until 2048 for it to receive a return on its $99 million investment in the Riverwalk sufficient to retire the debt.[27] No business would make an investment with a thirty-year payoff, but the Riverwalk project was never questioned; it was free. In economics, every choice has a trade-off; in strategy, every move leads to a countermove by an opponent. But in Chicago, every decision the government wishes to make seems completely unconstrained. The only limitation is the intensity with which the government desires to make the decision.

Any investment in development will yield a benefit. This belief posits that it is a central role of government to invest in the city's future and that any such investment will yield some benefit. There need not be any rational criteria for government investment decisions; rather, quoting Daniel Burnham's directive to "make no small plans" is sufficient justification for a project with decades-long implications. There is no consideration that, should there be a market opportunity, the private sector would fill the need.

The mayor gets the benefit of the doubt. With every government decision and action, the mayor gets the benefit of the doubt. The US president, the governor of Illinois, and the president of the Cook County Board are rarely afforded the same leniency. But in the city of Chicago, whatever the mayor does is rubber stamped by his city council and executed by his appointees and boards. In a city with so many smart people, leaders believe that surely the mayor has thought things through. Our simple political system with a strong mayor suits our collective psychology.

Any step in the right direction will eventually solve the problem. A step, no matter how minimal or inconsequential it may be, if it is in the right direction, if it will help solve the problem, is equated with actually solving the problem. Without regard to its national ranking, the city is making progress with all its problems, and any such progress is considered satisfactory.

There are two flaws in this mental model. First, it allows for ignoring the magnitude of problems. When discussing pensions, for instance, few have any comprehension of the concept of billions. (Here is a little case study using two questions: How much time is equal to one million seconds? How much time is equal to one billion seconds? The answer to the first question is 11.57 days. See the end of this paragraph for the second answer.) The second flaw of this mental model is the difference between the ethics of intent and the ethics of results. Adherents to the former feel that so long as one's heart is in the right place, the action is justified, even if it will yield an adverse result or none at all. The opposite is the ethics of results, which judges a policy solely by the result and not the intent. Steps taken in the right direction are motivated by the ethics of intent. One billion seconds is thirty-two years.

Chicago is exceptional. Chicago is a great, global city with a proud history, many natural advantages that helped it thrive, and a promising future. It has risen from its ashes to become the City of the Century. As a result, there is no need to look elsewhere for ideas or practices that can make it better. Instead, it expects others to visit and learn why we call it "the city that works." Why is it that some leaders in other major cities would consider it ludicrous to emulate Chicago?

⌒

Chicago is capable of mobilizing when it wants to. It can turn out multitudes when sports teams become national champions. Its business leaders mobilized tens of millions of dollars to lure the Olympics. Its US senator became the president of the United States. There is a civil society in Chicago that provides thinking and leadership. There are bright business leaders, community and union activists, newspapers and newscasters, think tanks, heads of nonprofit organizations and major foundations, world-class universities, and professionals of all stripes. Where do they place themselves in Huntington's quadrants? What would change in their idealism or perception of the gap between the ideal and city's institutions if they rejected the six mental models described above as false?

While everyone in the city of Chicago and the state of Illinois can find this book to be of use, this book is aimed directly at these leaders of civil society. It must be obvious to all concerned that Chicago governmental officials will not voluntary change and will likely resist change. Civil society, the leaders enumerated above, currently support the political class, and so it is up to them to initiate change. They are the ones who should read this book, debate its arguments, form ad hoc associations to advocate for change, and use their public and private capacities to advance reform. If they abdicate their responsibility, they leave change up to the mob on the street or the bankers in court.

Some say that it will take a crisis to bring about change in Chicago. A few look at the financial challenge and think bankruptcy might be inevitable and not necessarily a bad thing. They too seek freedom from responsibility. A crisis could come in some other form, either as the ultimate conclusion of an unfolding drama or as a complete surprise, a shock. When the crisis comes, will the leaders in government take the time to think through long-term solutions to problems, or will they lurch from one impulse to another? Will anyone question his or her mental model? Will leaders of civil society muster the will to mobilize for change, or will they continue in their acquiescence?

The Audacity of Hope

Chicagoans surely recognize the title of President Obama's pre-election book based upon a sermon he heard from his minister, Jeremiah Wright. It acknowledged many of the country's problems and prepared readers to tackle them. The leader's job is to define reality and give hope.

Hope is a feeling that something good will happen or be true. Audacity can be a willingness to take bold risks, but it may also entail rude, disrespectful behavior. Now we ask the reader to contemplate Chicago's fate. Is it audacious to hope that without any changes in governance the city and its leaders will overcome the formidable problems it faces and improve decision making? Or is it audacious to hope that, short of a crisis, city and civic leaders will take the risk to undertake changes in governance as peers across the country have done?

APPENDIXES

NOTES

BIBLIOGRAPHY

INDEX

Proposed Governance Changes, Policies, and Actions

Chapter 1

The city should establish a charter-making process and create an initial charter that effectuates the other changes in this chapter.

The aldermanic ward structure should be eliminated and replaced by council members and council districts.

The city council should be reduced in size to twenty members, each elected from districts.

A specific ordinance should prohibit council members from exercising aldermanic privilege and any executive functions within their districts. Council menu funds should be eliminated.

Term limits should be enacted for council members and the mayor. Two four-year terms appears to be an appropriate norm.

The city council should elect a president, who would preside over meetings, make assignments to committees, and assign committee chairs.

Vacancies on the council should be filled either by a vote of the full council or remain vacant until the next regularly scheduled elections.

The establishment of city council legislative districts should be conducted by an independent commission of private citizens who have not held elective office.

The city council should allocate to itself sufficient funds to establish professional staff for its standing and special committees.

The city should establish the elected position of city attorney to head the city law department.

The city should establish the elected position of chief financial officer.

Chapter 2

The state legislature should change the date of Chicago municipal elections to November in even years, preferably the presidential election years.

The state legislature should reinstate partisan municipal elections for Chicago. The city charter should prohibit office holders from governing party organizations.

Chapter 3

CPS must free itself from pension debt by either turning the liability over to the state or raising taxes and amortizing the debt over a twenty-year period.

CPS must raise taxes to pay off its general obligation debt over a ten-year period.

CPS must establish the annual practice of preparing, publishing, and approving a balanced, ten-year, forward-looking financial plan.

Once the fiscal actions listed above have been implemented, CPS should lobby for state legislation giving voters authority to approve tax increases and borrowing.

Illinois should join most other states in outlawing teachers' strikes.

Once the above changes, as well as the city governance changes in chapter 1, have been implemented, the city should consider electing either a school board or a single school overseer.

The state should transfer chartering authority for charter schools to an entity other than CPS.

Eventually, the city might consider creating the position of city school chancellor to oversee the management of a portfolio of all schools within the city, including public, charter, and private schools.

Chapter 4

The changes recommended in chapter 1 should assure that the budget and finance committees in the city council have sufficient power and capability to provide independent oversight of city finances.

As recommended in chapter 1, the city should elect the chief financial officer.

The city should make a plan to amortize its general obligation debt over a fifteen-year period and raise taxes to fund the pay down.

Once the plan to amortize the general obligation debt has been implemented, the city charter should require voter approval of all taxes and borrowing for the city.

The city should prepare all financial statements and budgets using generally accepted accounting principles.

The city should implement practices to make financial information easily accessible and understandable by laypersons and citizens.

All financial decisions should be independently scored and analyzed by the elected chief financial officer.

The elected chief financial officer should regularly audit the performance of all city departments.

The chief financial officer should annually prepare a forward-looking, ten-year, balanced financial plan for the city and all its departments.

The city should form a group including the mayor, the chief financial officer, and members of the budget committee to review and revise all city collective bargaining agreements to protect taxpayers and citizens.

Chapter 5

The city should freeze and discontinue offering defined benefit plans to new employees. Any retirement benefit offered to new employees after the discontinuation should be a defined contribution type and should be approved by the mayor, independent city council, and elected chief financial officer. It should be affordable and incorporated into the ten-year balanced financial plan.

The city should modify the schedules to amortize the pension debt for all city pension plans over twenty years. To do so it must contribute a combined $4.35 billion every year to all the plans.

The city charter should prevent the city from offering a defined benefit retirement plan in the future.

Chapter 6

The city should grant the inspector general's office the power to enforce its subpoenas.

The city should grant the inspector general authority to audit all city council programs, including the city's workers' compensation system and all aldermanic funds if the aldermanic system is not eliminated.

The city should consolidate its numerous inspectors general under one roof. The city inspector general would oversee this office.

The city should operate a centralized ethics office in partnership with a consolidated inspector general's office, with a unified ethics code across city and sister governments.

City council should amend the city ethics ordinance to cover aldermen/council members and their staff.

The city's ethics training should be improved to at least the level of the state of Illinois.

Chapter 7

The city should privatize as many of the Metropolitan Pier and Exposition Authority's (MPEA) investments as legally possible, taking the following steps:

The MPEA should sell its hotels and oblige those profiting from them to assume greater fiscal responsibility over McCormick Place and Wintrust Arena.

The MPEA should repurpose underperforming McCormick Place convention halls. If the authority cannot find an alternate, sustainable use without aid of tax revenue, those spaces should be packaged and sold, perhaps for a casino. Lakeside Center should be retained as the only convention facility.

MPEA should transfer Navy Pier operations from the nonprofit to the highest bidder, who would assume ownership of the land and be granted authority to run the attraction as it sees fit.

As MPEA investments are sold, officials should initiate a proportional repeal of MPEA taxes.

The MPEA should require majority approval from city voters via a referendum for any further bond issues, subsidies, or other revenue streams toward expansion of MPEA assets.

Public ownership or financing of hotels, convention centers, arenas, and retail spaces should be left out of the city's enumerated powers in a city charter.

City council should annually commission and publish an independent study on the number of tourists the city attracts and related spending.

Chapter 8

The city should establish a police commission that is appointed by the mayor. This commission would oversee the police department and the police inspector general.

All police oversight provisions in the police collective bargaining agreements should be replaced by a state law that spells out how the civil rights of citizens and police officers would be protected.

The mayor and the city council should jointly commission an independent company to study the legacy cost of police lawsuits and settlements and make a plan to avoid dumping this burden on future generations. This will involve a tax increase to provide sufficient current reserves for liabilities paid out in the future.

Chapter 9

The state should adopt a new local government section of the Illinois Constitution that allows for a city charter and spells out a charter revision process.

The charter process should include the right of citizens to petition the city for charter revision.

The state legislature should rewrite the codes for non–home rule entities to incorporate any of the changes suggested in this book that would not specifically relate to the City of Chicago and that would not be incorporated in any potential charter creation, and make them easier for laypersons to read and understand.

Chapter 10

The increased taxes required to extinguish the city's legacy costs are:

Pay off CPS general obligation debt in 10 years	$500,000,000
Pay off the city's general obligation debt in 20 years	$325,000,000
Increase pension plan contributions for 20 years	$2,350,000,000
Increased budgeting for policing lawsuit costs	$50,000,000
Total	$3,225,000,000

APPENDIX B

Survey of Governance Characteristics of the Fifteen Largest US Cities by Population

In researching this book the authors studied the governance documents and practices of the country's fifteen largest cities by population. In addition they interviewed office holders, academics, or civic leaders in all of the cities. In chapter 1 the results of this research are provided for Chicago and the two cities that are larger than Chicago: New York and Los Angeles. The results of the research for the other twelve cities is presented in this appendix in narrative form.

Houston

Chicagoans keep a close eye on Houston as the population figure of that Texas city closes in on Chicago's and it threatens to become the third most populous American city. Houston has a lot going for it, with jobs in energy, aerospace, and medicine, and it is in a state that itself has been gaining on California in terms of population.

Houston also has the outdated reputation of being an unregulated and chaotic city with no zoning rules. Houstonians would claim that they have zoning and land use regulation, but those regulations are not codified. Nonetheless, the city of Houston has some admirable governance structures. Although Houston's mayor holds significant control, his power is still less than in other major American cities. The city council consists of sixteen members, eleven from districts and five from the city at large. All city officials are limited to two four-year terms. None of these council members have executive powers or responsibilities within their districts, and since there is no zoning code, none can make individual zoning decisions. The council members do have access to a small "pothole" fund to benefit citizens within their districts, but this is not substantial enough to be controversial. The mayor sits on the city council and holds a vote. Redistricting is undertaken by the city council with technical support from several area universities. Vacancies on the city council are filled by appointment or by a special election, if feasible.

Houston has an elected city controller, whose responsibilities include certifying or approving the budget. The controller has often had an opposing relationship with the mayor, which ultimately provides healthy oversight of the chief executive. Unfortunately, as with other cities across the United States, the controller's position did not help Houston avoid accumulating what citizens feel is crippling pension debt.

Philadelphia

Philadelphia is the birthplace of American democracy, but it is also an old northeastern city whose urban problems have piled up over the centuries. From time to time, though, the city has had an active reform element that has successfully kept governance updated. The current city charter dates from 1951. In the 1990s, under Mayor Wilson Goode, excessive spending led to a shutdown of borrowing, so the state stepped in and formed the Pennsylvania Intergovernmental Cooperation Authority (PICA). This state control, along with the requirement that borrowing and tax increases be authorized by referendums, has led to a healthier financial condition for this early American city.

Another city with a strong mayoral form of government, Philadelphia nevertheless has an independent city council. The council is composed of ten members from districts and seven who are elected at large. These at-large members are elected using limited voting, which assures that two minority party candidates are elected.[1] Vacancies are filled by special elections called by the council president. There is both a strong committee structure and a strong meeting process in the city, assuring the city council will be informed on policy background as it faces legislation. The ten district council members control real estate development in their own districts. As in many other cities, gerrymandering can occur; a recent finding of corrupt redistricting was corrected in 2015.[2] Council members have no term limits, but the mayor is limited to two consecutive four-year terms.

The voters of Philadelphia elect the mayor and council members. They also elect a city controller, who has significant powers to audit and report on city finances. In 2016, the controller reported to PICA on projected city budgets from 2017 through 2021.[3]

Phoenix

The Phoenix City Charter, which is found on the city's website, spells out the provisions of government.[4] Eight council members are elected from city districts for no more than three four-year terms, with vacancies to be filled by a special election. Redistricting is a very public process that includes several rounds of community meetings, approval by the US Justice Department, and finally passage by the city council. Phoenix is a council-manager city, so council members have no executive authority or responsibilities within their respective districts. A political scientist who taught at Arizona State University and who is an expert on city governance finds that Phoenix government is quite effective and free of upheaval and crisis; he gives credit to the long-serving city manager Frank Fairbanks, who retired in 2009 (James Svara, telephone interview, June 6, 2017).

San Antonio

The council-manager structure of government is widespread in Texas and prevails in San Antonio as well. This necessarily means that the mayor is weak, and it can lead to a weak city council. San Antonio is a relatively young, rapidly growing city like many in the Southwest, and it scores well in measures of fiscal health.[5] The San Antonio City Council consists of eleven members, ten elected from districts together with the mayor, who is elected citywide. No other city officials are elected. Both council members and the mayor are limited to four two-year terms.[6] Council members have no formal executive responsibilities or powers within their districts, but they do engage in informal logrolling at budget time. Vacancies are filled by special election. The committee function is quite weak because most deliberation is undertaken by the city manager's staff. In fact, the mayor and council members often do not attend committee meetings.

San Diego

The last twenty years have not been kind to municipal government in San Diego. In the mid-1990s, the city began falling behind in payments to its municipal pensions, leading to a full-blown fiscal crisis. With trust in local government declining, voters refused to authorize higher taxes, so the city began skimping on city services, particularly fire protection and waste water treatment. Critics claimed that the damage from wild fires in 2003 was substantially aggravated by inadequate firefighting resources.[7] While the city has struggled to mend its ways, it suffered again when a recent mayor resigned over charges of sexual harassment.

A new city charter for San Diego was approved in November 2004, converting it from a council-manager form to a strong mayoral form of government. The charter, like many, is easy to find and read.[8] It calls for the election of nine council members from districts, who are limited to two four-year terms. Vacancies are generally filled by special election, except if there is less than one year left in the vacated term. Districts are determined by a rather elaborate redistricting commission. The public retains the right to petition to reject the commission's plan, and if supported by a referendum, it can require the commission to draft an entirely new plan. San Diego has reasonable governance provisions, but the authors of *Paradise Plundered*, a definitive narrative of the city's woes, claim that governance is not sufficient without strong civic engagement and political culture.[9]

Dallas

Dallas is another relatively new city of the South and vies with Phoenix for being the largest city governed by a council-manager form of government. In the past, Dallas briefly held the title of having the highest rate of violent crime per capita of any major city, but now it is one of the safest. Recently, it gained notoriety for having had a run on its policemen's pension fund. Unlike Chicago and Illinois, Texas allows changes to its pension plans, and recent legislation has provided needed relief. As a large city, Dallas's problems are unremarkable when compared to others. This does not, however, keep the elite from arguing and advocating for a change in governance structure; for decades there have been active and public debates about the benefits of the city manager form of government.[10] Currently, some feel the balance of power has shifted to a stronger mayor who is usurping the powers of a more professional city manager.

Whether or not the city would do better abandoning its current form, there is much to be learned from its unique structure. Unlike many other cities, Dallas has an updated city charter that clearly describes its governance.[11] The city council is elected from fourteen districts, and the mayor, a voting member of the council, is elected at large. It is this council that has the power to hire and fire the city manager. Vacancies are filled by special election and terms are limited: four consecutive two-year terms for council members, and two consecutive four-year terms for the mayor. While council members do not have formal executive powers or authority over developments within their districts, they are given broad informal deference from other council members.

Committees of the council are robust, and membership as well as chairmanship is assigned by the mayor, this being another form of domination by reward and punishment. Council districts are set every ten years by an independent commission appointed for the purpose by the mayor. The city attorney and city auditor are appointed by the council.

San Jose

San Jose is still another newer western city that enjoys the benefit of the council-manager form of government. As a result, the council and its committees are not as strong as in other cities. The council committees meet once a month and are staffed by the city manager's office. Unlike Chicago, though, the city council meets weekly. Council members have no executive authority, and their only fiscal allocation is an $800,000 stipend for running their offices and the exercise of authority over spending for parks in their districts. The San Jose city charter calls for the election of ten city council members from their respective districts.[12] As is everywhere the case in California, officials are limited to two four-year terms. Vacancies are filled by a more complicated process that gives the council the power to appoint in certain circumstances until a special election can be held. The council also holds ultimate power of redistricting after reviewing the work of an independent advisory commission.

Austin

With just under one million people, Austin has cultivated a reputation as a big small town that seems immune to big-city problems. It is the home of hip cultural institutions and Whole Foods. That reputation notwithstanding, the city seems to harbor a political culture of secrecy and opacity. Learning about the governance structure of the city is a formidable undertaking. The city's website shows a link to a copy of its charter, but the charter is not there.[13] Another page shows a link to the 2012 Charter Committee's report, but clicking that link results only in being informed that "access is not authorized."[14] In researching Austin city government, a briefing from former city councilman Don Zimmerman proved most illuminating. According to Zimmerman, city government has been so thoroughly captured by the city manager that political control of government barely functions. This seems in marked contrast to Dallas, where the same form of government prevails. A retired professor of public policy from the Lyndon B. Johnson School of Public Affairs at the University of Texas–Austin gives a more balanced appraisal of city governance, but he agrees that the former city manager had some detractors and left significant structural problems associated with the cost of public safety salaries and city pensions. The current mayor is popular and the city council asserts its independence, but unless there is an effective city manager, problems will not be tackled.

Some features of Austin government are admirable but others need improvement. The city council consists of ten members from ten districts, with an eleventh being the mayor, who is elected at large. Council members and the mayor are limited to two consecutive four-year terms; vacancies are filled by special election. The council members and mayor have no formal or informal executive powers other than to hire or fire the city manager. Zimmerman reports that council committees are worthless, since all information is hoarded by the city bureaucracy and the council's policy direction is often ignored. For example, the council must vote on the city budget by October 1, but members are not given the proposed budget until mid-September.

Jacksonville

Jacksonville, Florida, has a unique city government. It is one of those rare instances where a major city and its surrounding county combined their governments. Undertaken in 1968, this combination allegedly was originally intended to allow whites to govern the city, which had become majority black. If this was the intention, it has been frustrated by the result. Approximately 30 percent of the city council is black, reflecting a similar percentage of the general population, and the most recent ex-mayor is black as well. Jacksonville, like most other cities, has its problems, but compared with other major cities it has less than its share.

The city's governance structure is defined by Florida's limited home rule statutory environment. Jacksonville's city charter is easily found and read on the government's website.[15] The charter may be amended by the government without voter approval. Within its strong mayoral form of government, both the mayor and council members are elected for a four-year term and are limited to two consecutive terms. There are nineteen council members, fourteen from specific districts and five elected at large from special super-districts. Vacancies are filled by special election, and seats remain vacant until then. Council members have no powers or authority for executive functions within their districts, and both land use and zoning have become quasi-judicial under Florida law. The council has six standing committees, and their participation in government is robust. The budget and finance committee alone has an auditor and a staff of eighteen certified public accountants.

San Francisco

San Francisco city government also has a reputation for being chaotic, but it might embody more order than it seems at first glance. Thinking of this city, we might be reminded first of the 1978 assassinations of Mayor George Moscone and Supervisor Harvey Milk by fellow Supervisor Dan White. The turmoil of this event masks the quite constructive fact that Milk had been elected as a gay city official, the first in public office in the nation, an achievement which represented a significant gain for a social movement that had been concentrated in San Francisco. Here was the evolution of representative democracy and the accommodation of changing social norms in action.

The city's government has some limited virtues. The current charter became effective with the voters' approval in July 1996, after twenty years of work. It strengthened the form of government by doing away with the position of chief administrative officer, and it consolidated that power with the mayor. Other functions were streamlined and rationalized, and the entire charter was rewritten to be easier to understand.[16] Although the resulting governance structure is more like Chicago's than most other cities, it still retains many safeguards. The charter is readily found, recently updated, and easy to read.[17] It clearly spells out a strong mayoral form of government. The board of supervisors consists of eleven members elected from districts, and it in turn elects a powerful board president. Both the mayor and the supervisors serve four-year terms, and all are limited to two consecutive terms. Vacancies on the board are filled by mayoral appointment to fill out the remaining term until the next scheduled election. The committee process of the board is not very robust, however. Committees have no staff, and they rely on either legislative aides or the mayor's own staff. The budget committee does solicit advice, as well as an annual audit, from an outside independent CPA firm. Supervisors have no executive authority or powers within their districts; zoning is vetted by the mayor's planning department. Although the city controller is appointed by the mayor, the city attorney is elected.

Indianapolis

The recent history of Indianapolis city government reads like events that happened a hundred years ago somewhere else. Indianapolis, like Jacksonville, combined the city and county into a unified government called Unigov. With state laws that allowed cities to annex unincorporated lands without the consent of the annexed, Indiana enjoyed a favorable climate for such a combination.[18] The growth of Indianapolis and the formation of Unigov took place in 1970, overseen by the Government Reorganization Task Force appointed by Mayor Richard Lugar. The driving force was for the financially strained city to tax those who lived outside its borders but used its services, a tactic often discussed in Chicago. It was also a way to expand Republican power as Democratic affinities grew in the inner city.[19]

The state of Indiana offers very limited home rule powers, so governance provisions reside in state law more than in a city charter or municipal code. There is little for Chicago to learn about governance structure from "the Circle City." When the city took over the county, it combined the city council and county board. The new city council of twenty-nine members is very large, with twenty-five members elected from districts and four elected at large. That is why Indianapolis, along with recently expanded Jacksonville, are the only major cities with fewer constituents per council district than Chicago. There are no term limits; indeed, one of the council members has served for decades. Vacancies are filled until the next general election by the precinct committee of the party whose candidate vacated the seat. The council does not have a particularly robust committee structure, and it relies heavily on the mayor's staff. The council is relatively weak, and the mayor has been allowed to push through some risky deals: Mayor William Hudnut built a sports dome without first securing a major sports franchise, and Mayor Greg Ballard sold a parking concession, following the example of Chicago, albeit for a smaller number of spaces and a much better deal.[20]

Columbus

Columbus, Ohio, is like several other of the new breed of top cities. It grew in size years ago by annexation, and in recent years the growth of new industries and businesses, state government, and the giant Ohio State University continues that trend. By contrast, the formerly large Ohio cities of Cleveland and Cincinnati have shrunk in both size and importance by missing out on these growth trends. It was not until the new millennium that the demographic trends of increasing black and Hispanic populations rose to anywhere near national proportions. Rapid growth is also a dynamic that minimizes legacy costs and unfavorable political traditions. Like a new broom, Columbus sweeps clean.

The city's leaders have kept up by improving governance. The most recent charter was created in 1916, when Columbus was a small town. But it has been regularly revised and amended and is easily found on the city's website.[21] The city council consists of seven members elected at large; vacancies are filled by a vote of the remaining council members. There are no limits to terms on the council. As council members are elected at large, there is no concern about whether they hold executive or administrative powers within their districts and there is no conflict of redistricting. The downside of such an arrangement, however, can be disproportionate representation from some neighborhoods at the expense of others. A local political scientist reports that a different divide has emerged, one between the left-leaning liberal Democrats and the downtown financial and real estate interests. At-large elections carry a different fundraising challenge for candidates. Also elected are various perfunctory offices, along with the important city auditor and city attorney positions. Although the auditor does not have voting rights or formal budgetary control, recent experience with a popular and long-serving officeholder shows that both the council and mayor show great deference to the auditor's judgments, and her reports help shape public dialogue.

Survey of the Fiscal History and Characteristics of the Fifteen Largest US Cities, Excluding Chicago

New York

"Ford to City: Drop Dead." This famous headline from the *New York Daily News* on October 30, 1975, describing President Ford's decision not to aid New York City, punctuated the long and painful process leaders of New York had been working on to correct for decades of fiscal irresponsibility. The city "was facing several kinds of acute financial problems. The first problem was the underlying fact that the city's recurring expenses exceeded its actual recurring revenues. The second problem was . . . the banks were becoming reluctant to lend money against city revenues that were merely aspirational. The third problem was a crisis of political culture: none of the people with power to manage the city's affairs was willing to face the first two crises and change the behavior that produced them."[1] Commenting on city borrowing, Dick Ravitch, the man who led New York through the crisis, wrote: "cities need access to the credit markets for two reasons that are respectable and one that is not."[2] The first respectable reason is that it will need to borrow in the short term to balance mismatches of revenue and expenditures during a year. The second is to borrow in the long term to fund capital projects. The dubious reason is to cover operating deficits. The banks had had enough of this dubious reason.

The solution to the problem was a series of actions taken in stages to provide funds and to impose control. The control would not come from the federal government, as the newspaper headline implied, but from the State of New York in the form of a Financial Control Board, which now, forty years later, is still overseeing the city's budget. It was the end of unlimited home rule. Onerous new taxes were imposed, some even on financial transactions, just as the stock market and the New York–based financial industry were nearing the depths of the grinding bear market of the mid-1970s. The bottom of the business cycle is not the best time for a city to go broke, but that is what tends to happen.

The city charter, which was adopted in 1989, further strengthened the capability to control finances within the city. Now the budget is managed by the coordinated oversight of several robust functions. Central to these efforts are the city council's Finance Committee, the mayor's Office of Management and Budget, the city comptroller's office, and the Independent Budget Office, which was created to provide analysis and information not tainted by the mayor's office. These powerful offices, now redesigned, along with the state's Financial Control Board, all kept—and continue to keep—an eye on New York City's finances. Not stopping there, the 1989 charter also spelled out proper budget and management practices so that city officials could not take short cuts. The charter prescribed how revenues were to be estimated, how funds might be impounded, how budgets could be modified midyear, the process of capital budgeting, how off-budget spending was to be authorized, and several other key provisions.

Others might feel that New York has gone overboard in addressing the governance of its finances, but when the state took over city spending and taxation and then, in a separate move, the governance structure was found unconstitutional, the city took these matters quite seriously. By comparison, other cities have adopted less comprehensive measures, but ones still sufficient to manage effectively.

Los Angeles

Los Angeles prides itself on being a "good government" city, and that includes its finances. Late in the last century Los Angeles underwent a tumultuous charter revision effort. It is surprising, then, that in his book telling this story, Raphael Sonenshein devotes only two pages to financial management.[3] The city already had an effective structure in place. In addition to the office of the mayor and the council, the city elects a city controller and a city attorney. The controller is the CFO of the city and is responsible for reviewing the budget, audits, and bookkeeping. The city attorney advises the city on matters of law but also weighs in on budget concerns. The work of council committees is energetic and is supported by the office and staff of the chief legislative analyst. Both city borrowing and tax increases require voter approval. A tax increase specifically requires a minimum two-thirds vote.

Houston

For as large a city as Houston is, the debt load on citizens is one of the lightest of the major US cities. It is another city that elects a controller who holds fairly broad budgetary powers. An adversarial relationship between the mayor and controller is not unusual. The city council is charged with setting the tax levy each year, and if they wish to increase the levy more than five percent, they must hold at least three public hearings and post notices in the newspapers. Borrowing and bond issues over $100,000 require voter approval.[4] It is no wonder that Houston's finances seem so favorable. Houstonians, however, feel their pensions are woefully underfunded, a topic discussed in chapter 5.

Philadelphia

Philadelphia, like New York, experienced a period of uncontrolled spending and borrowing in the 1980s, primarily under the administration of Mayor Wilson Goode. As he left office, the city was virtually bankrupt and the State of Pennsylvania stepped in with the Pennsylvania Intergovernmental Cooperation Authority (PICA). Under PICA oversight, the succeeding mayor cleaned up the financial mess. Like New York, PICA still oversees Philadelphia, which now boasts much more stable finances. The city has a capable and independently elected city controller. General obligation borrowing is limited to a multiple of available revenue, and any borrowing above that cap requires the approval of voters. Philadelphia schools, although independent of the city, are controlled by a board appointed by the mayor and governor. The Philadelphia School Reform Commission is similar to PICA in that it arose out of fiscal mismanagement. Good fiscal habits can be as contagious as bad ones.

Phoenix

Phoenix is the largest US city that operates under the council-manager form of government. Under this organization, the council hires a city manager, who in turn hires all those officials who operate the city: the police chief, fire chief, controller, and city attorney, among many. For smaller cities this form works well. What is surprising is that, as these cities grow, the form continues to deliver high-quality government. Any city needs a manager who can run things while the mayor is busy with the political enterprise of the city.

As noted in chapter 1, Phoenix was blessed to have the longtime services of an outstanding city manager, Frank Fairbanks. He and the people of Phoenix were in turn blessed by the rare competency of the city's chief financial officer, Jeffrey S. DeWitt, who maintained stability of finances when home values and tax revenues declined 25 percent after the 2008 financial crisis. In 2013, the government of Washington, DC, hired DeWitt away from Phoenix, and he has repeated his performance in the nation's capital.[5]

While Phoenix is lucky to have had such fine managers, the structure of its government does not necessarily assure good financial management. The council is independent from the mayor, but both are also independent from the city manager. There is the possibility for council oversight of finances, but information inevitably comes from the city manager's office. The council can raise taxes and borrow money without voter approval.

San Antonio

San Antonio's structure is similar to Phoenix's, but lacks the good fortune of having competent city management. The council committees are not robust, and they rely too heavily on management. The council can raise taxes no more than 10 percent without voter approval. Voters likewise must approve bond issues, but the city can borrow on short-term certificates of obligation and tax notes without voters' approval.[6] Although the city is keeping up with pension funding, pensions are taking a toll on municipal finances, and the city's overall debt is high relative to comparable cities.

San Diego

Fiscal trouble in San Diego gained national attention in 2006 when five pension officials were indicted by a federal grand jury for fraud and conspiracy.[7] The charges related to a 2002 pension crisis that in turn unmasked and triggered severe fiscal difficulties. The charges against the indicted officials were eventually dismissed, but government leaders took the matters seriously and mounted a reform and improvement effort that has turned San Diego's financial picture into one of the healthiest among the major US cities. A notable element of this financial turnaround was a five-year freeze for pensionable compensation for all city employees. This measure was favored by 65 percent of voters when adopted in 2012. Although the freeze was gamed by some high-ranking officials, it had the effect of contributing to the healthy recovery of the city's finances.[8] That said, as of 2018, the ballot initiative that brought about the pension overhaul is still being fought in the courts.[9] In the midst of the fiscal crisis, San Diego underwent a charter revision whereby the city abandoned the council-manager form of government in favor of the weak mayor-strong council form. Currently, the city controller is hired by the mayor. All tax and bond matters still require the approval of voters.

Dallas

The power dynamic between elected officials and the city manager in Dallas seems to favor the officials. Some allege that the mayor usurps the power of the city manager and his staff, just as antagonists on the city council criticize the mayor. The result is a deteriorating financial situation and a pension problem that has attracted significant nationwide attention. Nevertheless, the general obligation debt portion of total bonded debt ($5.3 billion) is a little more than $1.5 billion, modest when compared to other major cities.[10] The city cannot incur indebtedness that exceeds 105 percent of the assessed valuation of property, and any bond with maturities exceeding ten years requires voter approval. Tax increases are limited by state government provisions, but otherwise the approval of voters is not required.

San Jose

San Jose city government is of the council-manager form. Like the other managed cities, its finances are in comparatively good condition. The budget function is a city department run by the manager, but the city council approves the budget and voters approve taxes and borrowing. Of note is the thorough, forward-looking five-year forecast of the city budget.[11] This document includes a detailed forecast of local economic conditions and then goes on to prepare optimistic, pessimistic, and base-case projections of city revenues and expenditures. This report is easy to read and understand and is surely of great value to voters and council members.

Austin

Although Austin is the eleventh largest city in the United States, its finances are more like a midsized city. It, too, is organized with a council-manager government. Most of the bonded indebtedness is in the form of revenue bonds, and general obligation debt is less than $1.4 billion.[12] Locals in government are concerned about pensions, but they are in satisfactory condition compared to other big cities. All borrowing requires voter approval, but the city council may tax without it.[13] Former councilman Don Zimmerman said that council members find it hard to get timely and sufficient information from the city manager to make sound financial decisions.

Jacksonville

The City of Jacksonville has a large number of revenue-producing, city-owned enterprises that have issued revenue bonds. Nevertheless, the city has also issued over $2.2 billion of general obligation bonds, a rather sizable amount.[14] The mayor proposes a city budget, but the council has a staff with eighteen certified public accountants and plays a key role in budgeting and financial decisions. The city council can set tax rates as prescribed by Florida law, but special taxes and extensions of the sales tax require a referendum. A referendum on borrowing is only required if financed by sales taxes, but that is the principal form of general revenue, so there are regular tax referenda. Finances are strictly governed by state law; budgets must be balanced and in accordance with the Governmental Accounting Standards Board, and spending is accordingly controlled. Despite these controls, the complicated issue of pensions has been neglected, and the city's plans are significantly underfunded.

San Francisco

The City of San Francisco constitutes a fairly small population center within one of the nation's largest and most vibrant metropolitan areas. It is responsible for core city services and leaves education and other functions to their respective entities. Within its narrowly prescribed domain, the city has managed its finances well. San Francisco appears to have a high level of debt at $13 billion for a modest big-city population, but digging into the 2016 comprehensive annual financial report shows a mere $3 billion of general obligation debt. Much of the remainder of the debt is for business-type activities such as the San Francisco International Airport, water department, hospital, and port activities. This debt is secured by the revenues of those entities and is not a general obligation of the city.[15] The structure of San Francisco's government and financial management is more mayor-dominated than most other cities. The city controller is appointed by the mayor, and the mayor's office is responsible for preparing and presenting a budget to the Board of Supervisors. Nevertheless, borrowing and taxation require the approval of voters.[16]

Indianapolis

For a city of nearly 900,000 people, the finances of Indianapolis are remarkable. In 2016, it had a general fund surplus exceeding $200 million. Its debt is almost entirely in the form of revenue bonds and TIF funds. It is hard to find any general obligation debt.[17] The finances are under the control of the mayor and his appointed city controller. A county auditor, a rather minor player, is elected. There are significant caps imposed by the state legislature on the city's ability to raise taxes, and so Indianapolis lives within its means.

Columbus

From a financial point of view, Columbus is another remarkable Midwest city. It runs budget surpluses and has less than $2 billion of general obligation debt. The secret for Columbus was its elected auditor, Hugh Dorrian, who served thirteen terms, more than fifty years.[18] Dorrian acted more like a chief financial officer than a mere auditor, and his tenure and stature elevated financial management above any mayor's spending conceits. In addition to this healthy governance structure, Columbus city government seeks voter approval for all borrowing for both general obligation and enterprise debt.[19]

NOTES

Introduction: The Cost of One-Man Rule

1. Kelly Tarrant, "Patronage Play: Chicago Mayors Have Appointed 28 Aldermen in the Past 28 Years," Project Six, May 31, 2017, https://thesecretsix.com/2017/05/31/patronage-play-chicago-mayors-have-appointed-28-aldermen-in-the-past-28-years/.
2. Chicago City Council, Municipal Code of Chicago (Cincinnati, OH: American Legal Publishing Corp., 1990), chaps 2–4, http://library.amlegal.com/nxt/gateway.dll/Illinois/chicago_il/municipalcodeofchicago?f=templates$fn=default.htm$3.0$vid=amlegal:chicago_il.
3. Office of Chief Financial Officer, District of Columbia, Tax Burdens Comparison, http://cfo.dc.gov/page/tax-burdens-comparison.
4. Claire Bushey, "Corporations Moving Their Headquarters to Chicago Arrive with Only a Handful of Employees and a Modest Economic Impact," *Crain's Chicago Business*, February 1, 2016, http://www.chicagobusiness.com/section/hq.
5. "The Chicago Way," Urban Dictionary, February 23, 2014, https://www.urban dictionary.com/define.php?term=The%20Chicago%20Way.

1. Cutting the Mayor Down to Size

1. Mary Wisniewski, "Chicago Drivers Pay More for On-Street Parking than Any Other City: Study," *Chicago Tribune*, July 12, 2017, http://www.chicagotribune.com/news/local/breaking/ct-parking-study-0712-20170711-story.html.
2. Ben Joravsky and Mick Dumke, "Fail, Part One: Chicago's Parking Meter Lease Deal," *Chicago Reader*, April 9, 2009, https://www.chicagoreader.com/chicago/features-cover-april-9-2009/Content?oid=1098561.
3. John Chase and Danny Ecker, "Pier Pressure: How City Power Players Diverted $55 Million in Blight-Fighting TIF Cash to Navy Pier," *Crain's Chicago Business*, July 21, 2017, http://www.chicagobusiness.com/article/20170721/ISSUE01/170729970/how-city-power-players-diverted-millions-in-blight-fighting-tif-cash-to-navy-pier.

4. Chicago Home Rule Commission, *Modernizing a City Government: A Report* (Chicago: University of Chicago Press, 1954), 320.

5. "Chicago's 'Menu' Program for Aldermen: 50 Ways to Waste Your Money," editorial, *Chicago Tribune*, April 20, 2017, http://www.chicagotribune.com/news /opinion/editorials/ct-menu-chicago-aldermen-cdot-infrastructure-city-council -0421-jm-20170420-story.html.

6. James R. Grossman, Ann Durkin Keating, and Janice L. Reiff, eds., *The Encyclopedia of Chicago* (Chicago: University of Chicago Press, 2004), 14.

7. Maya Dukmasova, "Aldermen's Absolute Veto Power over Ward Projects Gets Unlikely Court Challenge," *Chicago Reader*, April 16, 2018, https://www.chicago reader.com/Bleader/archives/2018/04/16/aldermens-absolute-veto-power -over-ward-projects-gets-unlikely-court-challenge; Gregory Pratt, "Aldermen Reject Northwest Side Affordable Housing Proposal after Heated Debate," *Chicago Tribune*, June 26, 2018, http://www.chicagotribune.com/news/local/politics /ct-met-chicago-affordable-housing-development-20180626-story.html.

8. Ryan Ori, "Lincoln Yards Plans Files, but Alderman Isn't Ready to Give a Thumbs-Up," *Chicago Tribune*, July 26, 2018, http://www.chicagotribune.com/business /columnists/ori/ct-biz-lincoln-yards-alderman-ryan-ori-20180725-story.html.

9. Douglas Muzzio and Tim Tompkins, "On the Size of the City Council: Finding the Mean," *Proceedings of the Academy of Political Science* 37, no. 3 (1989): 83–96, doi:10.2307/1173754.

10. Frank J. Mauro and Gerald Benjamin, eds., *Restructuring the New York City Government: The Reemergence of Municipal Reform* (New York: Academy of Political Science, 1989), 21.

11. Hal Dardick, "Emanuel Ally Ald. Burns Quits, Takes Airbnb Job," *Chicago Tribune*, February 1, 2016, http://www.chicagotribune.com/news/local/politics/ct -alderman-will-burns-resigns-20160201-story.html.

12. Fran Spielman, "Mayor Emanuel taps Mike Madigan ally Silvana Tabares for 23rd Ward seat," *Chicago Sun-Times*, June 15, 2018, https://chicago.suntimes .com/news/state-rep-silvana-tabares-appointed-23rd-ward-alderman/

13. Clayton Guse, "Chicago's Most Gerrymandered Wards," *Timeout Chicago*, April 1, 2015, https://www.timeout.com/chicago/blog/chicagos-most-gerrymandered -wards-040115.

14. Chris Lentino, "Chicago Aldermen Fail to Attend Committee Meetings Nearly Half the Time," Illinois Policy, August 22, 2017, https://www.illinoispolicy.org /chicago-aldermen-fail-to-attend-committee-meetings-nearly-half-the-time/.

15. "Editorial: Pull Back Curtain on Ald. Burke's Workers Comp Fiefdom," *Chicago Sun-Times*, February 29, 2016, https://chicago.suntimes.com/opinion/editorial -pull-back-curtain-on-ald-burkes-workers-comp-fiefdom/.

16. "The Need for This Ordinance Is Transparently Obvious," editorial, *Crain's Chicago Business*, December 1, 2017, http://www.chicagobusiness.com/article /20171201/ISSUE07/171139980/the-need-for-this-ordinance-is-transparently -obvious.

17. Chris Lentino, "Chicago City Council Records Reveal Severe Shortage of Serious Legislation," Illinois Policy, August 22, 2017, https://www.illinoispolicy.org /chicago-city-council-records-reveal-severe-shortage-of-serious-legislation/.

18. Frederick A. O. Schwartz Jr. and Eric Lane, "The Policy and Politics of Charter Making: The Story of New York City's 1989 Charter," *New York Law School Law Review* 42 (1998): 723–1015, http://scholarlycommons.law.hofstra.edu/cgi /viewcontent.cgi?article=1820&context=faculty_scholarship.

19. Ibid., 772.

20. Raphael J. Sonenshein, *The City at Stake: Secession, Reform, and the Battle for Los Angeles* (Princeton, NJ: Princeton University Press, 2004), 190 (emphasis in original).

21. Paul M. Green and Melvin G. Holli, eds., *The Mayors: The Chicago Political Tradition,* 4th ed. (Carbondale: Southern Illinois University Press, 2013), 111–60.

22. Chicago Home Rule Commission, *Modernizing a City Government,* 325.

23. Sonenshein, *The City at Stake,* 18.

24. Bill Ruthhart, "Amer Ahmad Was under Investigation 5 Months before Mayor Emanuel Hired Him," *Chicago Tribune,* August 24, 2013, http://articles .chicagotribune.com/2013-08-24/news/ct-met-city-comptroller-indicted -0825-20130825_1_federal-investigation-memo-subpoena.

25. Steven Erie, Vladimir Kogan, and Scott A. MacKenzie, *Paradise Plundered: Fiscal Crisis and Governance Failures in San Diego* (Stanford, CA: Stanford University Press, 2011), 282.

2. Discouraging Democracy

1. Milton L. Rakove, *Don't Make No Waves . . . Don't Back No Losers: An Insider's Analysis of the Daley Machine* (Bloomington: Indiana University Press, 1975), 179.

2. California SB-415 Voter participation, approved September 1, 2015, https:// leginfo.legislature.ca.gov/faces/billTextClient.xhtml?bill_id=201520160SB415.

3. "City of Los Angeles New City Election Dates and Schedules Charter Amendment, Measure 1 (March 2015)," Ballotpedia, https://ballotpedia.org/City_of _Los_Angeles_New_City_Election_Dates_and_Schedules_Charter_ Amendment,_Measure_1_(March_2015).

4. "Vote Yes on Charter Amendments 1 and 2," editorial, *Los Angeles Times,* February 9, 2015, http://www.latimes.com/opinion/endorsements/la-ed-end-charter -amendments-1-and-2-20150209-story.html.

5. Keith Williams, "The Odd Timing of City Elections in New York," *New York Times,* September 7, 2017, https://www.nytimes.com/2017/09/07/nyregion/city -elections-in-new-york-odd-numbered-years.html.

6. Amy McCaig, "Houston-Area Elections: Low Turnout, Underrepresentation and Incumbency Advantage," Rice University News and Media, October 4, 2017, http:// news.rice.edu/2017/10/04/houston-area-elections-low-turnout-underrepresentation -and-incumbency-advantage-2/.

7. Robert Rivard, "The Case for Local Election Reform," *Rivard Report*, April 23, 2017, https://therivardreport.com/the-case-for-reducing-frequency-and-timing -of-local-elections/

8. Zoltan L. Hajnal, *America's Uneven Democracy: Race, Turnout, and Representation in City Politics* (Cambridge: Cambridge University Press, 2010), 56.

9. Sarah F. Anzia, *Timing and Turnout: How Off-Cycle Elections Favor Organized Groups* (Chicago: University of Chicago Press, 2013), 88.

10. Vivekinan Ashok, Daniel Feder, Mary McGrath, and Eitan Hersh, "The Dynamic Election: Patterns of Early Voting across Time, State, Party, and Age," *Election Law Journal* 15, no. 2 (2016), https://doi.org/10.1089/elj.2015.0310.

11. Thomas Hardy, "City's Mayoral Election Likely to Become Nonpartisan," *Chicago Tribune*, May 24, 1995, http://articles.chicagotribune.com/1995-05-24/news /9505240221_1_harold-washington-party-mayoral-election-raymond-wardingley.

12. Green and Holli, *The Mayors*, 229.

13. Ibid., 230.

14. "Partisan vs. Nonpartisan Elections," National League of Cities, http://www.nlc .org/partisan-vs-nonpartisan-elections.

15. Brian F. Schaffner, Matthew Streb, and Gerald Wright, "Teams without Uniforms: The Nonpartisan Ballot in State and Local Elections," *Political Research Quarterly* 54, no. 1 (2001): 7, http://www.jstor.org/stable/449205.

3. Governing the Schools and the City

1. Fran Spielman, "Emanuel Takes Political Beating in Stride after Town Hall Meeting," *Chicago Sun-Times*, September 1, 2015, http://chicago.suntimes.com /chicago-politics/emanuel-takes-political-beating-in-stride-after-town-hall -meeting/.

2. Bill Ruthhart, "Vallas: Chicago 'in Big Trouble' under Emanuel's 'Politically Expedient' City Hall Approach," *Chicago Tribune*, May 1, 2018, http://www. chicagotribune.com/news/local/politics/ct-met-paul-vallas-chicago-mayor- 20180430-story.html.

3. Tim Novak, "The Watchdogs: Rahm's Tax Hike Will Slam 42nd Ward but Spare Most Wards," *Chicago Sun-Times*, June 24, 2016, http://chicago.suntimes.com /chicago-politics/the-watchdogs-rahms-tax-hike-will-slam-42nd-ward-but -spare-most-wards/.

4. Sean F. Reardon and Rebecca Hinze-Pifer, *Test Score Growth among Chicago Public School Students, 2009–2014* (Stanford, CA: Stanford Center for Education Policy Analysis, 2017), https://cepa.stanford.edu/content/test-score-growth -among-chicago-public-school-students-2009-2014.

5. Roger Biles, "Edward J. Kelly: New Deal Machine Builder," in Green and Holli, *The Mayors*, 112.

6. Jeffrey R. Henig and Wilbur C. Rich, eds., *Mayors in the Middle: Politics, Race, and Mayoral Control of Urban Schools* (Princeton, NJ: Princeton University Press, 2003), 69.

7. Amy Korte, "Chicago Teachers Highest Paid among Nation's 50 Largest School Districts," Illinois Policy Institute, February 5, 2016, https://www.illinoispolicy.org/cps-pays-the-highest-salaries-of-any-of-the-50-largest-school-districts/.

8. Archdiocese of Chicago, *Catholic Schools 2015/16 School Year Annual Report*, https://schools.archchicago.org/documents/80540/80677/Final+Annual+Report+2015-2016/dcc63c11-e67c-4325-bf3f-bd834a14ace7.

9. Ross Brenneman, "Understanding Teachers' Strikes: Where They Happen and How Often," *Teaching Now* (blog), *Education Week*, October 21, 2015, http://blogs.edweek.org/teachers/teaching_now/2015/10/where-do-teachers-strike-most-in-past-several-years.html.

10. Frederick M. Hess, "Looking for Leadership: Assessing the Case for Mayoral Control of Urban School Systems," *American Journal of Education* 114, no. 3 (May 2008): 220.

11. Ibid., 230–31.

12. Ibid., 235.

13. Henig and Rich, *Mayors in the Middle*, 229.

14. Thomas L. Alsbury, ed., *The Future of School Board Governance* (Lanham, MD: Rowman and Littlefield Education, 2008).

15. Alsbury, *The Future of School Board Governance*, 337.

16. Tony Favre, "US Mayors Are Divided about Merits of Controlling Schools," City Mayors, February 2, 2007, http://www.citymayors.com/education/usa_schoolboards.html.

17. "Bill Status of HB0557," Illinois General Assembly, http://www.ilga.gov/legislation/billstatus.asp?DocNum=557&GAID=13&GA=99&DocTypeID=HB&LegID=85009&SessionID=88.

18. Juan Perez Jr., "Federal Judge Rejects Lawsuit Demanding Elected School Board," *Chicago Tribune*, February 15, 2017, http://www.chicagotribune.com/news/local/breaking/ct-elected-school-board-lawsuit-met-20170215-story.html.

19. Andrew J. Rotherham, "Fenty's Loss in D.C.: A Blow to Education Reform?" *Time*, September 16, 2010, http://content.time.com/time/nation/article/0,8599,2019395,00.html.

20. Lisa Barrow and Lauren Sartain, "The Expansion of High School Choice in Chicago Public Schools," *Economic Perspectives* 41, no. 5 (2017): 2–29, https://www.chicagofed.org/publications/economic-perspectives/2017/5.

21. Consortium on School Research, "UChicago Consortium Studies Differences between CPS Charter, Non-charter Schools," *UChicago News*, https://news.uchicago.edu/article/2017/11/14/uchicago-consortium-studies-differences-between-cps-charter-non-charter-schools.

22. Juan Perez Jr., "Despite Leeway on Charter Caps, Teachers Union Adds Influence over District Policy," *Chicago Tribune*, November 4, 2016, http://www.chicagotribune.com/news/ct-chicago-school-contract-charter-policy-met-20161104-story.html.

23. Reardon and Hinze-Pifer, *Test Score Growth*.

24. EdBuild, *Fractured: The Breakdown of America's School Districts*, June 2017, https://edbuild.org/content/fractured/fractured-full-report.pdf.

25. Nikole Hannah-Jones, "The Resegregation of Jefferson County," *New York Times Magazine*, September 6, 2017.

26. Andy Smarick, *The Urban School System of the Future: Applying the Principles and Lessons of Chartering* (Lanham, MD: Rowman and Littlefield, 2012).

27. Gregory Pratt, "Interim CPS Chief Again Moves Up amid Turmoil," *Chicago Tribune*, December 8, 2017, http://www.chicagotribune.com/news/local/breaking/ct-met-chicago-schools-janice-jackson-20171208-story.html.

28. Smarick, *Urban School System of the Future*, 64.

29. Archdiocese of Chicago, *Catholic Schools 2015/16 School Year Annual Report*, 5. https://schools.archchicago.org/documents/80540/80677/Final+Annual+Report+2015-2016/dcc63c11-e67c-4325-bf3f-bd834a14ace7.

4. Chicago's Fiscal Ruin

1. Greg Hinz, "Mayor Reaches Labor Peace with Trade Unions," *Crain's Chicago Business*, August 7, 2007, http://www.chicagobusiness.com/article/20070807/NEWS02/200025947/mayor-reaches-labor-peace-with-tradeunions.

2. Greg Hinz, "Cash-Strapped Chicago Has a Window to Save Millions, Inspector Says," *Crain's Chicago Business*, May 31, 2017, http://www.chicagobusiness.com/article/20170531/BLOGS02/170539968/chicago-union-contract-renegotiations-could-save-city-millions-inspector-general.

3. City of Chicago, *Office of the Inspector General, Review of the City of Chicago's Expired and Expiring Collective Bargaining Agreements*, May 2017, https://igchicago.org/wp-content/uploads/2017/05/2017-CBA-Review-1.pdf.

4. Monica Eng, "First Responder: Why Do Fire Trucks Often Arrive before Ambulances for Medical Emergencies?" WBEZ, April 2, 2017, https://www.wbez.org/shows/curious-city/first-responder-why-do-fire-trucks-often-arrive-before-ambulances-for-medical-emergencies/75a435c4-2af3-4e75-b7c1-c9ccb3788ec9.

5. "Rahmbo's Toughest Mission: Can Rahm Emanuel Save Chicago from Financial Calamity?," *The Economist*, June 14, 2014, http://www.economist.com/news/united-states/21604165-can-rahm-emanuel-save-chicago-financial-calamity-rahmbos-toughest-mission.

6. "Annual Financial Analysis," City of Chicago, 2017, http://chicago.github.io/annual-financial-analysis/Long-term-asset-lease-and-reserve-funds/#asset-lease—concession-reserves.

7. Chicago Recovery Project, *The City of Chicago's ARRA Collaboration with the Chicago Philanthropic Community*, November 2010, https://www.cityofchicago.org/content/dam/city/progs/recovery_and_reinvestment/stimulusreports/RecoveryPartnershipFinalReportNov2010.pdf.

8. "How Chicago Racked Up a $662 Million Police Misconduct Bill," *Crain's Chicago Business*, March 20, 2016, http://www.chicagobusiness.com/article/20160320/NEWS07/160319758/how-chicago-racked-up-a-662-million-police-misconduct-bill.

9. Michael Hawthorne and Peter Matuszak, "Lead Water Pipes Funding," *Chicago Tribune*, September 21, 2016, http://www.chicagotribune.com/news/watchdog /ct-lead-water-pipes-funding-20160921-story.html; Andrea R. H. Putz and Alan E. Stark, *Lead Over Time in Chicago*, https://c.ymcdn.com/sites/www.isawwa .org/resource/resmgr/watercon2012-tuesday-pdf/tuewqpot130.pdf.

10. "Chicago Lead in Drinking Water Study," EPA in Illinois, https://www.epa.gov /il/chicago-lead-drinking-water-study.

11. "E-Books," Government Finance Officers Association, http://www.gfoa.org /products-and-services/resources/e-books.

12. Mark Glennon, "How Emanuel Is Misleading You on the City's Debt," *Crain's Chicago Business*, August 17, 2018, http://www.chicagobusiness.com/opinion /how-emanuel-misleading-you-citys-debt.

13. *City of Chicago 2015 Budget Overview*, https://www.cityofchicago.org/content /dam/city/depts/obm/supp_info/2015Budget/OV_book_2015_ver_11–24.pdf.

14. The Civic Federation, *City of Chicago FY2017 Proposed Budget: Analysis and Recommendations*, November 2, 2016, p. 19, https://www.civicfed.org/civic -federation/ChicagoFY2017.

15. City of Chicago Department of Finance, *Comprehensive Annual Financial Report for the Year Ended December 31, 2015*, 17, https://www.cityofchicago.org /content/dam/city/depts/fin/supp_info/CAFR/2015CAFR/2015CityCAFR.pdf.

16. D. Bradford Hunt and Jon B. DeVries, *Planning Chicago* (Chicago: American Planning Association, 2013; repr., New York: Routledge, 2017).

17. "Get the Numbers, Aldermen. Then Vote," editorial, *Chicago Tribune*, November 8, 2017, http://www.chicagotribune.com/news/opinion/editorials/ct-edit-cofa -fiscal-impact-chicago-aldermen-20171108-story.html.

18. Juan Perez Jr. and Peter Matuszak, "Chicago School Long Term Bond Cost Met," *Chicago Tribune*, July 31, 2017, http://www.chicagotribune.com/news/watchdog /ct-chicago-school-long-term-bond-cost-met-20170731-story.html.

19. Richard Ravitch, *So Much to Do: A Full Life of Business, Politics, and Confronting Fiscal Crises* (New York: Public Affairs Press, 2014), 219.

20. Schwartz and Lane, "Charter Making," 904.

21. From a letter to W. T. Barby, August 4, 1822, in *The Writings of James Madison*, ed. Gaillard Hunt (Charleston, SC: Nabu Press, 2010), 103; quoted in Schwartz and Lane, "Charter Making," 9.

22. Richard C. Kearney and Patrice M. Mareschal, *Labor Relations in the Public Sector*, 5th ed. (Boca Raton, FL: CRC Press, 2014), 202.

23. Ibid., 181.

24. Bill Ruthhart and Hal Dardick, "Rahm Emanuel Property Tax Rebate Spending Met," *Chicago Tribune*, January 19, 2017, http://www.chicagotribune.com /news/local/politics/ct-rahm-emanuel-property-tax-rebate-spending-met-0119 –20170118-story.html.

25. Tom Tresser, ed., *Chicago Is Not Broke: Funding the City We Deserve* (Chicago: Civic Lab, 2016).

5. Pension Apocalypse Now, Not Later

1. "Pension Database," State Data Lab, https://www.statedatalab.org/pension _database.
2. Society of Actuaries, *Report of the Blue Ribbon Panel on Public Pension Plan Funding* (Schaumburg, IL: Author, 2014), 16, https://www.soa.org/brpreport364/.
3. Heather Gillers, "Public Pensions Are Earning More Than 8%—That's Unlikely to Go On Much Longer," *Wall Street Journal*, July 22, 2018, https://www.wsj.com /articles/public-pensions-are-earning-more-than-8-thats-unlikely-to-go-on -much-longer-1532257201.
4. Society of Actuaries, *Report of the Blue Ribbon Panel*, 7.
5. Ibid., 6.
6. Municipal Employees' Annuity and Benefit Fund of Chicago, *Comprehensive Annual Financial Report* (Chicago: Author, 2000), 11, https://www.meabf.org /assets/pdfs/pubs/1999_MEABF_CAFR.pdf.
7. "2016 Comprehensive Annual Financial Report," Chicago Teachers' Pension Fund, p. 10, http://www.ctpf.org/general_info/Financial_lists.htm.
8. Society of Actuaries, *Report of the Blue Ribbon Panel*.
9. Article 13, section 5.
10. Consolidated actuarial report for 1981, Municipal Employees' Annuity and Benefit Fund of Chicago, https://www.meabf.org/assets/pdfs/pubs/1981_Consolidated _Actuarial_Report.pdf.
11. Lawrence J. McQuillan, "The Immorality of Pushing Pension Debt onto Millennials," *Forbes*, June 3, 2015, https://www.forbes.com/sites/realspin/2015/06/03 /the-immorality-of-pushing-pension-debt-onto-millennials/#51fedc2e7d81.
12. "Factsheet: 2015 Social Security Changes," Social Security Administration, https://www.ssa.gov/news/press/factsheets/colafacts2016.pdf.
13. Society of Actuaries, *Report of the Blue Ribbon Panel*, 33.
14. Adam Schuster, *Tax Hikes vs. Reform: Why Illinois Must Amend Its Constitution to Fix the Pension Crisis* (Chicago: Illinois Policy Institute, 2018), https://www. illinoispolicy.org/reports/tax-hikes-vs-reform-why-illinois-must-amend-its -constitution-to-fix-the-pension-crisis/.
15. "Ultimate Guide to Retirement," CNN Money, http://money.cnn.com/retirement /guide/pensions_basics.moneymag/index7.htm.
16. David N. Levine and Lars C. Golumbic, "Freezing Defined Benefit Plans," *Practical Law* (Thomson Reuters, 2014), https://www.groom.com/wp-content/uploads /2017/09/733_Freezing_Defined_Benefit_Plans_2014.pdf.
17. A.B.A.T.E. of Illinois, Inc. v. Quinn, 2011 IL 110611, p. 15, http://www.illinoiscourts .gov/Opinions/SupremeCourt/2011/October/110611.pdf.
18. Commission on Government Forecasting and Accountability, *Report on the Financial Condition of the Downstate Police and Downstate Fire Pension Funds in Illinois*, May 2015, p. 2, http://cgfa.ilga.gov/Upload/2015FinancialCondition DownstatePoliceFire.pdf.

19. Hal Dardick and John Byrne, "Court Strikes Down Chicago Park District Pension Plan," *Chicago Tribune*, April 2, 2018, http://www.chicagotribune.com /news/local/politics/ct-met-park-district-pension-court-ruling-20180402-story .html.

6. Overdue Oversight and the Reality of Corruption

1. Faisal Khan and Project Six Investigators, "Chicago Clout: How Campaign Finance Rules Are Used and Abused in the Windy City," Project Six, August 15, 2016, https://thesecretsix.com/investigation/chicago-clout-how-campaign-finance -rules-are-used-and-abused-in-the-windy-city/.

2. "City of Chicago Alderman Charged with Using Money from Charitable Fund to Pay Gambling Expenses and Daughter's Tuition," US Department of Justice, US Attorney's Office, Northern District of Illinois, news release, December 14, 2016.

3. Austin Berg, "Chicago City Council Passes Weakened Oversight Ordinance at Burke's Bidding," Illinois Policy Institute, February 11, 2016, www.illinoispolicy .org/bipartisan-majority-of-illinois-voters-support-criminal-justice-reform -study-shows/.

4. Dick W. Simpson, Thomas J. Gradel, Melissa Mouritsen, and John Johnson, *Chicago: Still the Capital of Corruption* (Chicago: University of Illinois at Chicago, Department of Political Science, 2015).

5. Adriana S. Cordis and Jeffrey Milyo, "Measuring Public Corruption in the United States: Evidence from Administrative Records of Federal Prosecutions," *Public Integrity* 18, no. 2 (2016): 127–148, doi:10.1080/10999922.2015.1111748; Oguzhan Dincer and Michael Johnston, "Measuring Illegal and Legal Corruption in American States Some Results from the Corruption in America Survey," Harvard University Edmond J. Safra Center for Ethics (blog), December 1, 2014, https://ethics.harvard.edu/blog/measuring-illegal-and-legal-corruption-american -states-some-results-safra.

6. Thomas Gradel and Dick Simpson, *Corrupt Illinois: Patronage, Cronyism, and Criminality* (Urbana, IL: University of Illinois Press, 2015).

7. "Report: CPS Tech Coordinator Stole More Than $400,000," CBS2, January 3, 2014, https://chicago.cbslocal.com/2014/01/03/report-cps-tech-coordinator-stole -more-than-400000/.

8. Committee for Economic Development, *Money in Chicago Politics Survey*, July 2016, https://www.ced.org/images/uploads/CED-Crains_Policy_and_Politics _Poll.pdf.

9. Gradel and Simpson, *Corrupt Illinois*, 88.

10. Shakman v. Democratic Organization of Cook County, 481 F. Supp. 1315 (N.D. Ill. 1979).

11. Andy Wright, "The Story Behind the Chicago Newspaper That Bought a Bar," *Topic*, no. 4 (October 2017), https://www.topic.com/the-story-behind-the-chicago -newspaper-that-bought-a-bar.

12. Gradel and Simpson, *Corrupt Illinois*, 66.
13. Chicago Municipal Code, §2–56–130.
14. Chicago Municipal Code, §2–56–030(h).
15. Ferguson v. Patton, 2013 IL 112488 (March 21, 2013).
16. Business and Professional People for the Public Interest, *Inspectors General and Government Corruption: A Guide to Best Practices and an Assessment of Five Illinois Offices*, May 2011, https://www.bpichicago.org/wp-content/uploads/2013/11/Inspectors-General-and-Public-Corruption.pdf.
17. Paris Schutz, "Ald. Ed Burke's Workers' Compensation Program Under Increased Scrutiny," *Chicago Tonight*, WTTW, February 25, 2016, https://news.wttw.com/2016/02/25/ald-ed-burke-s-workers-compensation-program-under-increased-scrutiny.
18. Rose Gill Hearn, "Integrity and the Department of Investigation," *Fordham Law Review* 72, no. 2 (2003): 415–420, https://ir.lawnet.fordham.edu/cgi/viewcontent.cgi?referer=https://search.yahoo.com/&httpsredir=1&article=3935&context=flr.
19. William K. Rashbaum, "Fight to Control Office That Roots Out Corruption in New York Schools," *New York Times*, March 16, 2018, https://www.nytimes.com/2018/03/16/nyregion/doi-schools-new-york-investigations.html.
20. NYC Conflicts of Interest Board, New York City Charter Chapter 68, https://www1.nyc.gov/site/coib/the-law/chapter-68-of-the-new-york-city-charter.page.
21. Lou Cannon, "One Bad Cop," *New York Times*, Oct. 1, 2000, https://www.nytimes.com/2000/10/01/magazine/one-bad-cop.html.
22. County of Los Angeles, Ord. 6.44.190—Office of Inspector General, https://oig.lacounty.gov/Portals/OIG/Reports/6.44.190___Office_of_Inspector_General.pdf?ver=2017–03–02–162755–183.
23. Ron Galperin, LA Controller, "About Our Office," http://www.lacontroller.org/about_our_office.
24. Ted Oberg and Trent Seibert, "City of Houston Keeps Secret Investigations into Own Employees," ABC 13, November 11, 2014, http://abc13.com/news/city-of-houston-keeps-secret-investigations-into-own-employees/391027/.
25. Russell Cooke, "New Office to Target City Waste," *Philadelphia Inquirer*, February 12, 1985, 13, https://www.newspapers.com/image/174034666/?terms=philadelphia%2Binspector%2Bgeneral.
26. Amy Kurland, "To Fight Corruption, Philly Needs a Permanent Office of the Inspector General," *Philadelphia Inquirer*, September 5, 2017, http://www.philly.com/philly/opinion/commentary/to-fight-corruption-philly-needs-permanent-office-of-the-inspector-general-20170905.html.
27. Phoenix City Code, article 2, sec. 2–49.
28. Phoenix City Charter, chapter 3, sec. 2-A.

7. Public Support for Private Enterprise at the Metropolitan Pier and Exposition Authority

1. Thomas Buck, "Blaze Branded as a 'Tragic Loss to the City,'" *Chicago Tribune*, January 17, 1967.

2. Joel Kaplan, "Board Named to Make Navy Pier Shipshape," *Chicago Tribune*, July 18, 1989.

3. Heywood T. Sanders, *Convention Center Follies: Politics, Power, and Public Investment in American Cities* (Philadelphia: University of Pennsylvania Press, 2014), 213.

4. Harvey Berkman, "To Scrub or Not to Scrub: The Deal to Save Illinois Coal," *Illinois Issues* 25 (August/September 1991), http://www.lib.niu.edu/1991/ii910823 .html.

5. Rick Pearson and Sue Ellen Christian, "Memo Tells How to Build Stadium with No New Taxes," *Chicago Tribune*, January 9, 1996.

6. State of Illinois, 87th General Assembly, Regular Session, Senate Transcript, July 18, 1991, http://www.ilga.gov/senate/transcripts/strans87/ST071891.pdf; State of Illinois, 87th General Assembly, House of Representatives, Transcription Debate, July 18, 1991, http://www.ilga.gov/house/transcripts/htrans87/HT071891 .pdf.

7. Gregory Meyer, "Report Criticizes McPier," *Crain's Chicago Business*, July 14, 2007, https://www.chicagobusiness.com/article/20070714/ISSUE01/100028097 /report-criticizes-mcpier; Metropolitan Pier and Exposition Authority, *Basic Financial Statements as of and for the Years Ended June 20, 2016 and 2015, Required Supplementary Information and Independent Auditors' Reports*, 17, http://www. mpea.com/wp-content/uploads/2017/03/MPEA-Audited-Financial-Statements -FY16.pdf.

8. Carri Jensen and Hil Anderson, "Big Changes at Nation's Biggest Convention Centers," *Trade Show Executive*, September 2013, 46–55.

9. Joe Cortright, "The Convention Center Business Turns Ugly," *City Observatory*, April 6, 2015, http://cityobservatory.org/the-convention-center-business-turns -ugly/.

10. Sanders, *Convention Center Follies*, 8.

11. Civic Federation, Selected Consumer Taxes in the City of Chicago, February 6, 2017, https://www.civicfed.org/sites/default/files/jan2017consumertaxesinchicago .pdf.

12. Metropolitan Pier and Exposition Authority, *Lake Michigan Area Boundaries Map*, http://www.revenue.state.il.us/TaxForms/Sales/MPEA/IDOR-535.pdf.

13. Metropolitan Pier and Exposition Authority, *Basic Financial Statements as of and for the Years Ended June 20, 2017 and 2016, Required Supplementary Information and Independent Auditors' Reports*, http://www.mpea.com/wp-content /uploads/2018/01/MPEA-Audited-Financial-Statements-FY17.pdf.

14. Ibid.

15. Sanders, *Convention Center Follies*, 231.

16. Ibid., 232.

17. See, for example, Metropolitan Pier and Exposition Authority (MPEA), *McCormick Square Economic Impact Study, February 2017*, https://www.scribd.com /document/338708862/MPEA-EconomicImpactStudy2017#from_embed, which

found the McCormick Place campus would generate $9.4 billion from operations, infrastructure improvements, and construction of the new Marriott Marquis Hotel and Wintrust Arena from 2014 through 2018. In this study, new hotel spending is assumed to have no substitution effects—in other words, it is assumed that the 1,200-room Marriot Marquis will not draw any visitors away from any other hotels. This is a fantasy. In March 2018, owners of the Hilton Chicago in the Loop reported their revenue per available room fell by 6.1 percent year over year, and they pointed to the Marquis as the culprit. As *Crain's Chicago Business* reported, "the sharp decline late in the year for the Hilton Chicago . . . is an early indication of what some major hoteliers have feared: that the publicly owned Marquis hotel might erode their group business" (Danny Ecker, "Hilton Chicago Takes Hit from New Marriott Marquis," *Crain's Chicago Business*, March 6, 2018, par. 4, http://www.chicagobusiness.com/article/20180306 /CRED03/180309925/hilton-chicago-takes-hit-from-new-marriott-marquis). The same faulty logic applies to analysis of Wintrust Arena. Wintrust is operating in direct competition not only with private event spaces, but also with another publicly funded arena on Chicago's near West Side, the UIC Pavilion. The Pavilion was already facing a downturn in event attendance before Wintrust opened its doors. "UIC will have a very difficult time competing," one local event mogul said in 2013. "For each [venue] to expect eight to 10 shows a year would be very difficult" (Danny Ecker, "That Empty Feeling," Crain's Chicago Business, November 16, 2013, par. 8, http://www.chicagobusiness.com/article/20131116 /ISSUE01/311169979/new-depaul-arena-threatens-uic-pavilion).

18. MPEA, *McCormick Square Economic Impact Study*.
19. Stacey E. Nadolny and Dana W. Floberg, *In Focus: Chicago, IL*, December 20, 2016, https://www.hvs.com/Print/In-Focus-Chicago-IL?id=7862.
20. Choose Chicago, "2016 Hotel Performance" factsheet, February 10, 2017, https:// res.cloudinary.com/simpleview/image/upload/v1/clients/choosechicago/Hotel _Performance_Annual_2016_5d45d402-014f-4e5f-a4f6-b51510461d75.pdf.
21. Airbnb, *Overview of the Airbnb Community in Chicago*, April 2017, https://www. airbnbcitizen.com/wp-content/uploads/sites/5/2017/05/Chicago-Economic -Impact-Report-.pdf.
22. Enterprise Holdings, "Chicago Group," https://go.enterpriseholdings.com/find -us/recruiters/chicago-group/.
23. Economists at credit-card company Mastercard have used public data to track international tourism among 132 "destination cities" worldwide, including Chicago, since 2010 (Yuwa Hedrick-Wong and Desmond Choong, *Global Destination Cities Index*, 2016, https://newsroom.mastercard.com/wp-content /uploads/2016/09/FINAL-Global-Destination-Cities-Index-Report.pdf).
24. 360 Chicago, "Ranking the Top Cities for International and Domestic Visitors," http://www.360chicago.com/top-us-cities-international-domestic-visitors/.
25. The US Travel Association calculates that there were 2.2 billion domestic person-trips nationally in 2016. Person-trips are defined as one person on a trip

away from home overnight in paid accommodations or on a day or overnight trip to places fifty miles or more away from home (one way) [US Travel Association, "U.S. Travel and Tourism Overview (2017)," factsheet, https://www.ustravel.org/system/files/media_root/document/Research_Fact-Sheet_US-Travel-and-Tourism-Overview.pdf].

26. "Timeline: How the Navy Pier TIF Shell Game Worked," *Crain's Chicago Business*, July 20, 2017, http://www.chicagobusiness.com/article/20170720/ISSUE01/170729983/timeline-how-the-navy-pier-tif-shell-game-worked.

27. John Chase, "Public Dollars to Keep Navy Pier Records from the Public: Nearly $670,000," Better Government Association, March 23, 2018, https://www.bettergov.org/news/public-dollars-to-keep-navy-pier-records-from-the-public-nearly-670000.

28. City of Chicago, Office of the Mayor, "Mayor Emanuel Announces Millennium Park Is Now the #1 Attraction in the Midwest and among the Top 10 Most-Visited Sites in the U.S.," press release, April 6, 2017, https://www.cityofchicago.org/city/en/depts/mayor/press_room/press_releases/2017/april/Millennium_Park_Tourism.html.

29. Navy Pier, Inc., *Financial Statements*, December 31, 2016 and 2015, https://navypier.org/wp-content/uploads/2017/10/2016-Navy-Pier-Inc-Financial-Statements.pdf.

30. Hunden Strategic Partners, *Downtown Milwaukee Entertainment and Hospitality Comparative Analysis*, May 9, 2015, chap. 2, p. 29, table 2.10, https://www.milwaukeedowntown.com/do-business/market-data.

31. MPEA, *Basic Financial Statements 2017 and 2016*.

32. William Gruber, "McCormick Center Hotel Checks Out," *Chicago Tribune*, August 4, 1993, http://articles.chicagotribune.com/1993–08–04/business/9308040009_1_new-hotel-ritz-carlton-hotel-management.

33. Steven Malanga, "The Convention Center Shell Game," *City Journal*, Spring 2004, https://www.city-journal.org/html/convention-center-shell-game-12511.html.

34. United States Congress, House Committee on Oversight and Government Reform, "Build It and They Will Come: Do Taxpayer-Financed Sports Stadiums, Convention Centers and Hotels Deliver as Promised for America's Cities?," 110 Cong., H. Doc. HRG-2007-CGR-0017, Proquest Congressional Web.

35. Terry Pristin, "A City Turns Innkeeper," *New York Times*, June 15, 2005, http://www.nytimes.com/2005/06/15/business/a-city-turns-innkeeper.html.

36. Fran Spielman, "TIF Flap Forgotten as Mayor Breaks Ground on DePaul Basketball Arena," *Chicago Sun-Times*, November 16, 2015, https://chicago.suntimes.com/news/tif-flap-forgotten-as-mayor-breaks-ground-on-depaul-basketball-arena/.

37. HVS Convention, Sports and Entertainment Facilities Consulting, *Neighborhood Impact Assessment: Hotel, Area, and Entertainment District Development Adjacent to McCormick Place*, May 13, 2013, https://assets.documentcloud.org/documents/2746543/McPierDePaulMarriott-HVSStudyDoc.pdf.

38. Eddie Damstra, "Taxpayer-Funded Wintrust Arena Falls Short of Attendance Projections," Illinois Policy Institute, June 23, 2018, https://www.illinoispolicy.org/taxpayer-funded-wintrust-arena-falls-short-of-attendance-projections/.

39. Michael Miner, "A Big To-Do over a Road That's Been Around since 2002," *Chicago Reader*, July 24, 2013, https://www.chicagoreader.com/Bleader/archives/2013/07/24/a-big-to-do-over-a-road-thats-been-around-since-2002.

40. Jon Hilkevitch, "Shortcut Clears Way to Events at McCormick," *Chicago Tribune*, January 14, 2002, http://articles.chicagotribune.com/2002-01-14/news/0201140186_1_busway-chicago-convention-convention-city.

41. Sanders, *Convention Center Follies*, ix.

42. Gabrielle Russon, "Orange County Convention Center Looks at Numbers behind Expansion," *Orlando Sentinel*, October 29, 2017, http://www.orlandosentinel.com/business/tourism/os-bz-county-convention-center-20171029-story.html.

43. Ibid.

44. Sanders, *Convention Center Follies*, 185.

45. Las Vegas Convention and Visitors Authority, "Mission and Purpose," http://www.lvcva.com/who-we-are/mission-and-purpose/.

46. Sanders, *Convention Center Follies*, 76.

47. Ibid., 77.

48. Ibid., 79.

49. Ibid., 154–55.

50. Ibid., 448.

51. Myles McGrane, "Decoding Convention Center Occupancy," Blog, Ungerboeck Software International, July 12, 2016, https://ungerboeck.com/blog/decoding-convention-center-occupancy.

52. Danny Ecker, "Lakeside Center: Obsolete but Critical," *Crain's Chicago Business*, April 22, 2017, http://www.chicagobusiness.com/article/20170422/ISSUE01/170429953/lakeside-center-obsolete-but-critical.

8. Policing in Chicago

1. Bill Ruthart, Stacy St. Clair, and John Chase, "New Emails Show Emanuel City Hall Scramble on Laquan McDonald Shooting," *Chicago Tribune*, January 1, 2015.

2. Ibid.

3. Jamie Kalven, "Sixteen Shots," *Slate*, February 10, 2015, accessed January 30, 2017, http://www.slate.com/news-and-politics/2018/02/house-republicans-try-to-squeeze-senate-democrats-on-spending-plan.html.

4. Ruthart, St. Clair, and Chase, "New Emails."

5. "$1 Million per Shot—How Laquan McDonald Settlement Unfolded after That Initial Demand," *Chicago Sun-Times*, June 24, 2018.

6. Ibid.

7. Patty Wetli, "Should City Council Have OK'd $5M for Laquan's Family without Seeing Video?" *DNAinfo Chicago*, December 2, 2015, https://www.dnainfo.com

/chicago/20151202/downtown/city-council-okd-5m-payout-laquans-family
-never-asked-see-video.

8. Ruthart, St. Clair, and Chase, "New Emails."

9. Dan Hinkel and Matthew Walberg, "Long Inquiry before Charges in Laquan
McDonald Shooting Prompts Scrutiny," *Chicago Tribune*, November 26, 2015.

10. Citizens Police Data Project, http://cpdb.co/findings.

11. Ibid.

12. Reade Levinson, "Across the U.S., Police Contracts Shield Officers from Scrutiny
and Discipline," Reuters, January 13, 2017, https://www.reuters.com/investigates
/special-report/usa-police-unions/.

13. John Chase and David Heinzmann, "Cops Traded away Pay for Protection in
Police Contracts," *Chicago Tribune*, May 20, 2016.

14. "Police Union Sues to Block Release of Decades of Officer Complaints," *Chicago
Tribune*, October 29, 2014, http://www.chicagotribune.com/news/ct-fop-police
-lawsuit-met-20141028-story.html.

15. Fraternal Order of Police, Chicago Lodge No. 7, Agreement between Fraternal
Order of Police Chicago Lodge No. 7 and the City of Chicago, July 1, 2012, to
June 30, 2017, https://cbschicago.files.wordpress.com/2015/11/a6149-chicago-fop
-contract.pdf.

16. Steve Mills, "Burge Reparations Deal a Product of Long Negotiations," *Chicago
Tribune*, May 6, 2015.

17. Jason Meisner, "City Agrees to Pay $9.3 Million for Wrongful Conviction Tied to
Burge Detectives," *Chicago Tribune*, January 11, 2018.

18. Fran Spielman, "Tab for Burge-Era Torture up Another $4 Million and Still
Rising," *Chicago Sun-Times*, January 25, 2017.

19. Steve Schmadeke, "Court Upholds Burge Pension," *Chicago Tribune*, July 4, 2014.

20. Jason Meisner, "Daley Medical Issue Raised in Federal Suit," *Chicago Tribune*,
March 26, 2017.

21. "Chicago's 762 Homicides in 2016 Is More than New York and Los Angeles Combined," *Daily News*, January 1, 2017, http://www.nydailynews.com/news/crime
/chicago-762-homicides-2016-nyc-la-article-1.2931020.

22. Julie Irwin Zimmerman, "The Problem with City Crime Rankings," CityLab,
December 9, 2011, https://www.citylab.com/equity/2011/12/problem-city-crime
-rankings/682/.

23. US Department of Justice Federal Bureau of Investigation, "Crime in the United
States 2010," https://ucr.fbi.gov/crime-in-the-u.s/2010/crime-in-the-u.s.-2010
/caution-against-ranking.

24. Paul Wormeli, "The Crime Reporting Dilemma," Wormeli Consulting LLC blog,
June 6, 2017, http://wormeliconsulting.com/the-crime-reporting-dilemma/.

25. Andy Grimm, "As Violence Persists, CPD Murder 'Clearance Rate' Continues
to Slide," *Chicago Sun-Times*, August 27, 2017, https://chicago.suntimes.com
/chicago-politics/as-violence-persists-cpd-murder-clearance-rate-continues
-to-slide/.

26. Murder Accountability Project, "Clearance Rates: Uniform Crime Report for Homicides, 1965–2016," http://www.murderdata.org/p/blog-page.html.

27. Brian Duignan, "McDonald v. City of Chicago: Law Case," *Encyclopaedia Britannica*, May 20, 2010, https://www.britannica.com/event/McDonald-v-City -of-Chicago.

28. US Department of Justice Civil Rights Division and US States Attorney's Office, Northern District of Illinois, *Investigation of the Chicago Police Department*, January 13, 2017, 1, https://www.justice.gov/opa/file/925846/download.

29. Eric Bradach, "City Council Gives Green Light to COPA," *Columbia Chronicle*, October 10, 2016, http://www.columbiachronicle.com/metro/article_81e0f754 -8ceb-11e6-ae0a-dbef6720d9b4.html.

30. Ibid.

31. Illinois Attorney General, "Attorney General Madigan Files Lawsuit Against City of Chicago to Obtain Consent Decree for Police Reform," press release, August 29, 2017, http://www.illinoisattorneygeneral.gov/pressroom/2017_08 /20170829.html.

32. Lise Olsen and James Pinkerton, "Grand Jury Never Told That Off-Duty Police Officer Was Drunk When He Shot Unarmed Brothers," *Houston Chronicle*, April 16, 2016, https://www.houstonchronicle.com/news/houston-texas/houston /article/Grand-jury-never-told-that-off-duty-police-7253246.php.

33. Christopher I. Haugh, "How the Dallas Police Department Reformed Itself," *Atlantic*, July 9, 2016, https://www.theatlantic.com/politics/archive/2016/07/dallas -police/490583/.

34. New York City Comptroller Scott M. Stringer, *Annual Claims Report: Fiscal Year 2017*, February 2018, https://comptroller.nyc.gov/reports/annual-claims-report/.

35. Mark Iris, "Your Tax Dollars at Work! Chicago Police Lawsuit Payments: How Much, and For What?," *Virginia Journal of Criminal Law* 2, no. 25 (2014): 38, http://virginiajournalofcriminallaw.com/wp-content/uploads/2014/08/2.1-Iris -SMW-3.31.14.pdf.

36. Jonah Newman, "Police Misconduct Payouts Continue to Break the Bank in Chicago," *Chicago Reporter*, June 8, 2017, http://www.chicagoreporter.com/police -misconduct-payouts-continue-to-break-the-bank-in-chicago/.

37. Jason Mesiner, "Chicago to Pay \$20 Million to Settle Code-of-Silence Lawsuit over Fatal Crash by Drunken Cop, Sources Say," *Chicago Tribune*, December 19, 2017, http://www.chicagotribune.com/news/local/breaking/ct-met-chicago-cop -fatal-dui-settlement-20171218-story.html.

38. Ibid.

39. Jason Meisner, "U.S. Judge Incensed at City's Law Team," *Chicago Tribune*, n.d., http://digitaledition.chicagotribune.com/tribune/article_popover.aspx?guid =6b48ef13-61ed-4c87-90f5-5d910cb462e3.

40. Jason Meisner and Stacy St. Clair, "Law Department Supervisor Loses Job after City's Latest Failure to Turn Over Evidence in Police Misconduct Cases,"

Chicago Tribune, February 6, 2018, http://www.chicagotribune.com/news/local
/breaking/ct-met-law-department-supervisor-resigned-20180206-story.html.

41. City of Chicago, *Comprehensive Annual Financial Report for the Year Ended December 31, 2016*, 121, https://www.cityofchicago.org/content/dam/city/depts /fin/supp_info/CAFR/2016/CAFR_2016.pdf.

42. Elizabeth Bart, "Product Liability: On Your Shelves but Not on Your Balance Sheet?," Milliman, March 22, 2012, http://www.milliman.com/insight/pc /Product-liability-On-your-shelves-but-not-on-your-balance-sheet/.

43. Grassroots Alliance for Police Accountability, *Leadership, Partnership, and Trust: A Community Plan for a Safer Chicago*, March 2018, http://chicagogapa .org/wp-content/uploads/2018/03/GAPA-Report-2018.pdf.

44. Annie Sweeney, "Chaos Rules at First Hearing on Civilian Oversight of CPD," *Chicago Tribune*, n.d., http://digitaledition.chicagotribune.com/tribune/article _popover.aspx?guid=9216fb6a-db3e-49fa-8f88-65065a51311e.

45. Bill Ruthhart, John Byrne, and Jeremy Gorner, "Chicago to Add Hundreds of Cops amid Wave of Rising Violence," *Chicago Tribune*, September 21, 2016, http://www.chicagotribune.com/news/local/breaking/ct-chicago-police-hiring -met-20160921-story.html.

46. City of Chicago, Office of the Inspector General, "OIG Audit Finds Widespread CPD Mismanagement of Overtime," press release, October 3, 2017, https:// igchicago.org/2017/10/03/oig-audit-finds-widespread-cpd-mismanagement-of -overtime/; City of Chicago, Office of the Inspector General, *CPD Overtime Control Audit*, October 3, 2017, https://igchicago.org/2017/10/03/cpd-overtime -controls-audit/.

47. Tracy Siska, "What Should Drive Chicago's Staffing Debate? How about Facts," *Crain's Chicago Business*, January 20, 2015, http://www.chicagobusiness.com /article/20150120/OPINION/150119863/what-should-drive-chicagos-police -staffing-debate-how-about-facts.

48. Fran Spielman, "City Council Confirms New Chief of Civilian Office of Police Accountability," *Chicago Sun-Times*, April 18, 2018, https://chicago.suntimes .com/news/city-council-confirms-new-chief-of-civilian-office-of-police -accountability/.

49. Iris, "Your Tax Dollars at Work!," 57.

9. Creations of the State

1. Schwartz and Lane, "Charter Making," 729.
2. Sonenshein, *The City at Stake*, xiii.
3. City of Chicago, Office of the City Clerk, "Journals of the Proceedings," http://www .chicityclerk.com/legislation-records/journals-and-reports/journals-proceedings.
4. Maureen A. Flanagan, "Charters, Municipal," in Grossman, Keating, and Reiff, *The Encyclopedia of Chicago*, 127, http://www.encyclopedia.chicagohistory.org /pages/231.html.

5. "New York Consolidated Laws, Municipal Home Rule Law—MHR," FindLaw, http://codes.findlaw.com/ny/municipal-home-rule-law/#!tid =N0E93A1FC19CD4C85B1FAD9DA079D7E24.

6. "Article XI, California Constitution," Ballotpedia, https://ballotpedia.org/Article _XI,_California_Constitution.

7. Kotte v. Normal Board of Fire and Police Commissioners, 269 Ill. App. 3d 517 (1995) 646 N.E.2d 292.

8. Dunne v. County of Cook, 108 Ill. 2d 161 (1985) 483 N.E.2d 13; Dunne v. County of Cook, 123 Ill. App. 3d 468 (1984) 462 N.E.2d 970.

9. National Civic League, *Guide for Charter Commissions*, 2011, https://www .nationalcivicleague.org/resources/guide-charter-commissions-2011/.

10. Ibid., 12–13.

11. Sonenshein, *The City at Stake*, 190.

12. Chicago Home Rule Commission, *Modernizing a City Government*, 325.

13. James H. Svara and Douglas J. Watson, eds., *More than Mayor or Manager: Campaigns to Change Form of Government in America's Largest Cities* (Washington, DC: Georgetown University Press, 2010), 312.

14. Chicago Home Rule Commission, *Modernizing a City Government*.

10. The Audacity of Hope?

1. James D. Nowlan and J. Thomas Johnson, *Fixing Illinois: Politics and Policy in the Prairie State* (Urbana: University of Illinois Press, 2014).

2. Greg Hinz, "Downtown Growth Leads Chicago to Highest Job Peak in Decades," *Crain's Chicago Business*, January 2, 2018, http://www.chicagobusiness.com/article /20180102/BLOGS02/180109998/chicago-job-growth-hits-highest-peak-in-decades.

3. Greg Hinz, "Chicago Job Growth Stalls," *Crain's Chicago Business*, April 27, 2018, http://www.chicagobusiness.com/article/20180427/BLOGS02/180429876/chicago -job-growth-stalls.

4. US Bureau of Labor Statistics, "Chicago Area Economic Summary," factsheet, August 29, 2018, https://www.bls.gov/regions/midwest/summary/blssummary _chicago.pdf.

5. Chicago Metropolitan Agency for Planning, *Demographic Shifts: Planning for a Diverse Region*, February 2017, http://www.cmap.illinois.gov/documents/10180 /514101/FY17–0054+Demographics+Snapshot/8a9caead-a16a-4cba-a57d -7ffcbf33a1c0.

6. Gail Marks Jarvis, "More Older Americans Becoming Renters," *Chicago Tribune*, April 2, 2016, http://www.chicagotribune.com/business/ct-boomer-renters -0403-biz-20160401-story.html.

7. Angie Stewart, "These Are Chicago's 25 Largest Employers," *Crain's Chicago Business*, January 12, 2018, http://www.chicagobusiness.com/article/20180112 /ISSUE01/180119954/these-are-chicagos-25-largest-employers.

8. Dick Simpson, Constance A. Mixon, and Melissa Mouritsen, *Twenty-First Century Chicago*, 2nd ed. (San Diego, CA: Cognella Academic Publishing, 2016), 61.

9. Aristotle, *Politics,* trans. Benjamin Jowett (New York: Modern Library, 1943), 272.

10. Ibid., 275.

11. Clarence Morris, ed., *The Great Legal Philosophers* (Philadelphia: University of Pennsylvania Press, 1959), 169.

12. Ibid., 255.

13. Ibid., 327.

14. "The Federalist Papers," Congress.gov, https://www.congress.gov/resources /display/content/The+Federalist+Papers#TheFederalistPapers-47.

15. Samuel P. Huntington, *Political Order in Changing Societies* (New Haven, CT: Yale University Press, 1968).

16. Ibid., 140.

17. Nassim Nicholas Taleb and Gregory F. Treverton, "The Calm before the Storm: Why Volatility Signals Stability, and Vice Versa," *Foreign Affairs* 94, no. 1 (January/ February 2015): 88, https://www.foreignaffairs.com/articles/africa/calm-storm.

18. The Trust for Public Land, "The Trust for Public Land Appoints Aaron Koch as Chicago Director," press release, November 6, 2017, https://www.tpl.org /media-room/trust-public-land-appoints-aaron-koch-chicago-director#sm .0000drfiv918pgcxbuivnxpbqmpvp.

19. Peter F. Drucker, *The Essential Drucker* (New York: HarperCollins, 2001), 254.

20. Ibid.

21. Quoted in Michael Lewis, "How Two Trailblazing Psychologists Turned the World of Decision Science Upside Down," *Vanity Fair,* December, 2016, par. 49, https://www.vanityfair.com/news/2016/11/decision-science-daniel-kahneman -amos-tversky.

22. Ibid.

23. Sonenshein, *The City at Stake,* 44.

24. Samuel P. Huntington, *American Politics: The Promise of Disharmony* (Cambridge, MA: Harvard University Press, 1981).

25. Dedre Gentner and Albert L. Stevens, eds., *Mental Models* (New York: Psychology Press, 1983).

26. Richard Devine, "Chicago Police Department Is Controlled by Civilians—in City Hall," *Crain's Chicago Business,* April 11, 2018, http://www.chicagobusiness .com/article/20180411/OPINION/180419978/chicago-police-department-already -is-controlled-by-civilians-in-city-hall.

27. Greg Trotter, "Riverwalk Rising: City Banking on Boom to Pay Off Cost of River Transformation," *Chicago Tribune,* April 14, 2018, http://www.chicagotribune .com/business/ct-biz-chicago-riverwalk-vendors-20180330-story.html.

Appendix B. Survey of Governance Characteristics of the Fifteen Largest US Cities by Population

1. Philadelphia Charter Commission, Philadelphia Home Rule Charter (Cincinnati, OH: American Legal Publishing Corp., December 11, 2013), http://www.coj.net/city -council/docs/consolidation-task-force/2014–01–09-philadelphiacharter.aspx.

2. Troy Graham, "Philadelphia Council Approves Redistricting Map," Philadelphia Inquirer, September 23, 2011, B01.

3. "FY2017–2021 Five Year Budget (Updated) Plan," City of Philadelphia Office of the Controller, August 26, 2016, http://www.philadelphiacontroller.org/audits -reports/fy2017–2021-five-year-budget-updated-plan.

4. "Phoenix City Code: A Codification of the General Ordinances of the City of Phoenix, Arizona," City of Phoenix (Seattle, WA: Code Publishing Co.), http:// www.codepublishing.com/AZ/Phoenix/.

5. "San Antonio: A Post-Recession Revenue Rebound Allowed Spending to Grow without Sacrificing Reserves," Pew Charitable Trusts, http://www.pewtrusts .org/~/media/assets/2013/11/11/san_antonio_profile.pdf?la=en; "The Fiscal Landscape of Large U.S. Cities: Local Governments Still Recovering Long after Great Recession's End," issue brief, Pew Charitable Trusts, December 13, 2016, http:// www.pewtrusts.org/en/research-and-analysis/issue-briefs/2016/12/the-fiscal -landscape-of-large-us-cities.

6. Charter Review Commission, City of San Antonio, http://www.sanantonio.gov /City-Attorney/Charter-Review-Commission.

7. Erie, Kogan, and MacKenzie, Paradise Plundered, 124–29.

8. City Charter, City of San Diego Office of the City Clerk, https://www.sandiego .gov/city-clerk/officialdocs/legisdocs/charter.

9. Erie, Kogan, and MacKenzie, Paradise Plundered.

10. Dennis Holder, "Dallas Is the Nation's Largest City Still Run by the Council-Manager Form of Government. Is It Time to Rewrite Our Charter?," D Magazine, January 1986, https://www.dmagazine.com/publications/d-magazine/1986 /january/dallas-is-the-nations-largest-city-still-run-by-the-council-manager -form-of-government-is-it-time-to-rewrite-our-charter/; Harvey J. Graff, The Dallas Myth: The Making and Unmaking of an American City (Minneapolis: University of Minnesota Press, 2008); Michael Ennis, "What's the Matter with Dallas?," Texas Monthly, July 2005, http://www.texasmonthly.com/articles /whats-the-matter-with-dallas/.

11. Charter, City of Dallas, February 2013, http://citysecretary2.dallascityhall.com /pdf/City_Charter.pdf.

12. City Charter, San Jose, CA, City Clerk, November 2016, https://www.sanjoseca .gov/index.aspx?nid=397.

13. City Code and Charter, Office of the City Clerk, Austin, Texas, http://www. austintexas.gov/department/city-code-and-charter.

14. Austin, TX, city website: http://www.austintexas.gov/department/2012-charter -revision.

15. Jacksonville, Florida, Code of Ordinances, Charter and Related Laws, https:// www.municode.com/library/fl/jacksonville/codes/code_of_ordinances?nodeId =CHRELA.

16. James Haas, "Evaluating the New City Charter: A Three-Year Report Card,"

Spur, October 1, 1999, http://www.spur.org/publications/urbanist-article/1999
-10-01/evaluating-new-city-charter.

17. City and County of San Francisco Municipal Code, 1996 Charter (Tallahassee,
FL: Municipal Code Corp., 2006), https://archive.org/details/gov.ca.sf.charter.

18. Greg Lindsey and Jamie Palmer, *Annexation in Indiana: Issues and Options* (Indianapolis, IN: Indiana Advisory Commission on Intergovernmental Relations,
Center for Urban Policy and the Environment, Indiana University School of
Public and Environmental Affairs, November 1998), http://www.iacir.spea.iupui
.edu/documents/Fullreport_fromWeb_wCover.pdf.

19. Yaël Ksander, "Unigov," Indiana Public Media, June 11, 2007, https://indianapublic
media.org/momentofindianahistory/unigov/.

20. Leonard Gilroy, "Looking Back at Indianapolis," Reason Foundation, June 27,
2012. http://reason.org/news/show/1012976.html.

21. Columbus, Ohio, Code of Ordinances, Charter of the City of Columbus, Ohio,
https://library.municode.com/oh/columbus/codes/code_of_ordinances?nodeId
=CHTR_THECICOOH.

Appendix C. Survey of the Fiscal History and Characteristics of the Fifteen Largest US Cities, Excluding Chicago

1. Ravitch, *So Much to Do*, 81.

2. Ibid., 75.

3. Sonenshein, *The City at Stake*, 115–16.

4. City of Houston, Charter, Article IV.—Power as to Bonds, Buffalo Bayou, Side-
walks, State Agency, Streetcar Equipment, Municode, https://library.municode
.com/tx/houston/codes/code_of_ordinances?nodeId=CH
_ARTIVPOBOBUBASISTAGSTEQ_S1AUISBO.

5. Mike DeBonis, "Phoenix CFO Tapped to Head Up D.C. Finances," *Washington
Post*, September 26, 2013, https://www.washingtonpost.com/local/dc-politics
/phoenix-cfo-tapped-to-head-up-dc-finances/2013/09/26/06899c76-2657-11e3
-b75d-5b7f66349852_story.html?utm_term=.45eb99ac6630.

6. City of San Antonio, Texas, Charter, Article II.—City Council, Municode,
https://www.municode.com/library/tx/san_antonio/codes/code_of_ordinances
?nodeId=PTICH_ARTIICICO_S4CRCOPO.

7. John M. Broder, "Five Officials in San Diego Are Indicted over Pensions," *New
York Times*, January 7, 2006, http://www.nytimes.com/2006/01/07/us/five-officials
-in-san-diego-are-indicted-over-pensions.html.

8. David Garrick, "San Diego Using Loophole to Hand Out Large Raises during
Pay Freeze," *San Diego Union-Tribune*, May 14, 2017, http://www.sandiegounion
tribune.com/news/politics/sd-me-raise-pension-20170511-story.html.

9. "State Supreme Court Rules against San Diego Pension Cuts," Fox 5 News, August 2, 2018, https://fox5sandiego.com/2018/08/02/state-supreme-court-rules
-against-san-diego-pension-reform/.

10. City of Dallas, Texas, *Comprehensive Annual Financial Report for the Fiscal Year Ended September 20, 2017*, p. 11, https://dallascityhall.com/departments/budget /financialtransparency/AuditedFinancials/CAFR_FY2017.pdf.

11. San Jose, CA, *Five-Year Economic Forecast and Revenue Projections, 2017–2021*, https://www.sanjoseca.gov/DocumentCenter/View/54737.

12. City of Austin, Texas, *Comprehensive Annual Financial Report for the Fiscal Year Ended September 30, 2017*, p. 14, https://assets.austintexas.gov/financeonline /downloads/cafr/cafr2017.pdf.

13. City of Austin, Texas, "Charter, Article II.—The Council," Municode, https:// library.municode.com/tx/austin/codes/code_of_ordinances?nodeId=CH _ARTIITHCO.

14. City of Jacksonville, *Comprehensive Annual Financial Report, Fiscal Year 2016*, http://www.coj.net/getattachment/Departments/Finance/Accounting /Comprehensive-Annual-Financial-Reports/City-of-Jacksonville-2016 -CAFR-SEC.pdf.aspx.

15. City and County of San Francisco, California, *Comprehensive Annual Financial Report, Year Ended June 30, 2016*, http://sfcontroller.org/sites/default/files /Documents/AOSD/11–29–16%20CCSF%20CAFR%20-%20Web%20Upload.pdf.

16. City and County of San Francisco, California, *Comprehensive Annual Financial Report Year Ended June 30, 2017*, p. 19, https://sfcontroller.org/sites/default/files /Documents/Accounting/CCSF%20CAFR%20FY2016–17%20no%20cover %20FINAL%20reduced.compressed.pdf.

17. City of Indianapolis, Indiana, *Comprehensive Annual Financial Report, Year Ended December 31, 2016*, http://www.indy.gov/eGov/City/OFM/SiteAssets/Pages /home/2016%20CAFR%20Final.pdf.

18. Rick Rouan, "Auditor Candidates Gather Support in Bids to Succeed Hugh Dorrian," *Columbus Dispatch*, December 23, 2016, http://www.dispatch.com/content /stories/local/2016/12/23/auditor-candidates-gather-support-in-bids-to-succeed -dorrian.html.

19. City of Columbus, Ohio, *Comprehensive Annual Financial Report for the Fiscal Year Ended December 31, 2015*, p. 12, https://www.columbus.gov/uploadedFiles /Columbus/Elected_Officials/City_Auditor/Reports/CAFR/2015_CAFR.pdf.

BIBLIOGRAPHY

Alsbury, Thomas L., ed. *The Future of School Board Governance*. Lanham, MD: Rowman and Littlefield Education, 2008.

Anzia, Sarah F. *Timing and Turnout: How Off-Cycle Elections Favor Organized Groups*. Chicago: University of Chicago Press, 2013.

Aristotle. *Politics*. Translated by Benjamin Jowett. New York: Modern Library, 1943.

Ashok, Vivekinan, Daniel Feder, Mary McGrath, and Eitan Hersh. "The Dynamic Election: Patterns of Early Voting across Time, State, Party, and Age." *Election Law Journal* 15, no. 2 (2016). https://doi.org/10.1089/elj.2015.0310.

Barrow, Lisa, and Lauren Sartain. "The Expansion of High School Choice in Chicago Public Schools." *Economic Perspectives* 41, no. 5 (2017): 2–29. https://www.chicagofed.org/publications/economic-perspectives/2017/5.

Chicago Home Rule Commission. *Modernizing a City Government: A Report*. Chicago: University of Chicago Press, 1954.

Chicago Metropolitan Agency for Planning. *Demographic Shifts: Planning for a Diverse Region*. February 2017. http://www.cmap.illinois.gov/documents/10180/514101/FY17–0054+Demographics+Snapshot/8a9caead-a16a-4cba-a57d-7ffcbf33a1c0.

Chicago Recovery Project. *The City of Chicago's ARRA Collaboration with the Chicago Philanthropic Community*. November 2010. https://www.cityofchicago.org/content/dam/city/progs/recovery_and_reinvestment/stimulusreports/RecoveryPartnershipFinalReportNov2010.pdf.

Committee for Economic Development. *Money in Chicago Politics Survey*. July 2016. https://www.ced.org/images/uploads/CED-Crains_Policy_and_Politics_Poll.pdf.

Cordis, Adriana S., and Jeffrey Milyo. "Measuring Public Corruption in the United States: Evidence from Administrative Records of Federal Prosecutions." *Public Integrity* 18, no. 2 (2016): 127–148. doi:10.1080/10999922.2015.1111748.

Drucker, Peter F. *The Essential Drucker.* New York: HarperCollins, 2001.

EdBuild. *Fractured: The Breakdown of America's School Districts.* June 2017. https://edbuild.org/content/fractured/fractured-full-report.pdf.

Erie, Steven, Vladimir Kogan, and Scott A. MacKenzie. *Paradise Plundered: Fiscal Crisis and Governance Failures in San Diego.* Stanford, CA: Stanford University Press, 2011.

Gentner, Dedre, and Albert L. Stevens, eds. *Mental Models.* New York: Psychology Press, 1983.

Gradel, Thomas, and Dick Simpson. *Corrupt Illinois: Patronage, Cronyism, and Criminality.* Urbana, IL: University of Illinois Press, 2015.

Graff, Harvey J. *The Dallas Myth: The Making and Unmaking of an American City.* Minneapolis: University of Minnesota Press, 2008.

Grassroots Alliance for Police Accountability. *Leadership, Partnership, and Trust: A Community Plan for a Safer Chicago.* March 2018. http://chicagogapa.org/wp -content/uploads/2018/03/GAPA-Report-2018.pdf.

Green, Paul M., and Melvin G. Holli, eds. *The Mayors: The Chicago Political Tradition,* 4th ed. Carbondale: Southern Illinois University Press, 2013.

Grossman, James R., Ann Durkin Keating, and Janice L. Reiff, eds. *The Encyclopedia of Chicago.* Chicago: University of Chicago Press, 2004.

Hajnal, Zoltan L. *America's Uneven Democracy: Race, Turnout, and Representation in City Politics.* Cambridge: Cambridge University Press, 2010.

Hearn, Rose Gill. "Integrity and the Department of Investigation." *Fordham Law Review* 72, no. 2 (2003): 415–420. https://ir.lawnet.fordham.edu/cgi/viewcontent.cgi ?referer=https://search.yahoo.com/&httpsredir=1&article=3935&context=flr.

Henig, Jeffrey R., and Wilbur C. Rich, eds. *Mayors in the Middle: Politics, Race, and Mayoral Control of Urban Schools.* Princeton, NJ: Princeton University Press, 2003.

Hess, Frederick M. "Looking for Leadership: Assessing the Case for Mayoral Control of Urban School Systems." *American Journal of Education* 114, no. 3 (May 2008): 219–245.

Hunt, D. Bradford, and Jon B. DeVries. *Planning Chicago.* New York: Routledge, 2017. Originally published by the American Planning Association, 2013.

Huntington, Samuel P. *Political Order in Changing Societies.* New Haven, CT: Yale University, 1968.

———. *American Politics: The Promise of Disharmony.* Cambridge, MA: Harvard University Press, 1981.

Iris, Mark. "Your Tax Dollars at Work! Chicago Police Lawsuit Payments: How Much, and for What?" *Virginia Journal of Criminal Law* 2, no. 25 (2014): 25–61.

http://virginiajournalofcriminallaw.com/wp-content/uploads/2014/08/2.1-Iris
-SMW-3.31.14.pdf.

Kearney, Richard C., and Patrice M. Mareschal. *Labor Relations in the Public
Sector*, 5th edition. Boca Raton, FL: CRC Press, 2014.

Lindsey, Greg, and Jamie Palmer. *Annexation in Indiana: Issues and Options*. Indianapolis, IN: Indiana Advisory Commission on Intergovernmental Relations,
Center for Urban Policy and the Environment, Indiana University School of
Public and Environmental Affairs, November 1998. http://www.iacir.spea.iupui
.edu/documents/Fullreport_fromWeb_wCover.pdf.

Madison, James. *The Writings of James Madison*. Edited by Gaillard Hunt.
Charleston, SC: Nabu Press, 2010.

Mauro, Frank J., and Gerald Benjamin, eds. *Restructuring the New York City
Government: The Reemergence of Municipal Reform*. New York: Academy of
Political Science, 1989.

Morris, Clarence, ed. *The Great Legal Philosophers*. Philadelphia: University of
Pennsylvania Press, 1959.

Muzzio, Douglas, and Tim Tompkins. "On the Size of the City Council: Finding
the Mean." *Proceedings of the Academy of Political Science* 37, no. 3 (1989): 83–96.
doi:10.2307/1173754.

National Civic League. *Guide for Charter Commissions*. 2011. https://www.
nationalcivicleague.org/resources/guide-charter-commissions-2011/.

Nowlan, James D., and J. Thomas Johnson. *Fixing Illinois: Politics and Policy in the
Prairie State*. Urbana: University of Illinois Press, 2014.

Rakove, Milton L. *Don't Make No Waves . . . Don't Back No Losers: An Insider's
Analysis of the Daley Machine*. Bloomington: Indiana University Press, 1975.

Ravitch, Richard. *So Much to Do: A Full Life of Business, Politics, and Confronting
Fiscal Crises*. New York: Public Affairs Press, 2014.

Reardon, Sean F., and Rebecca Hinze-Pifer. *Test Score Growth among Chicago
Public School Students, 2009–2014*. Stanford, CA: Stanford Center for Education
Policy Analysis, 2017. https://cepa.stanford.edu/content/test-score-growth
-among-chicago-public-school-students-2009–2014.

Sanders, Heywood T. *Convention Center Follies: Politics, Power, and Public Investment in American Cities*. Philadelphia: University of Pennsylvania Press, 2014.

Schaffner, Brian F., Matthew Streb, and Gerald Wright. "Teams without Uniforms:
The Nonpartisan Ballot in State and Local Elections." *Political Research Quarterly* 54, no. 1 (2001): 7–30.

Schuster, Adam. *Tax Hikes vs. Reform: Why Illinois Must Amend Its Constitution
to Fix the Pension Crisis*. Chicago: Illinois Policy Institute, 2018. https://www.

illinoispolicy.org/reports/tax-hikes-vs-reform-why-illinois-must-amend-its -constitution-to-fix-the-pension-crisis/.

Schwartz, Frederick A. O., Jr., and Eric Lane. "The Policy and Politics of Charter Making: The Story of New York City's 1989 Charter," *New York Law School Law Review* 42 (1998): 723–1015. http://scholarlycommons.law.hofstra.edu/cgi /viewcontent.cgi?article=1820&context=faculty_scholarship.

Simpson, Dick W., Thomas J. Gradel, Melissa Mouritsen, and John Johnson. *Chicago: Still the Capital of Corruption.* Chicago: University of Illinois at Chicago, Department of Political Science, 2015.

Simpson, Dick W., Constance A. Mixon, and Melissa Mouritsen. *Twenty-First Century Chicago,* 2nd edition. San Diego, CA: Cognella Academic Publishing, 2016.

Smarick, Andy. *The Urban School System of the Future: Applying the Principles and Lessons of Chartering.* Lanham, MD: Rowman and Littlefield, 2012.

Society of Actuaries. *Report of the Blue Ribbon Panel on Public Pension Plan Funding.* Schaumberg, IL: Author, 2014. https://www.soa.org/brpreport364/.

Sonenshein, Raphael J. *The City at Stake: Secession, Reform, and the Battle for Los Angeles.* Princeton, NJ: Princeton University Press, 2004.

Svara, James H., and Douglas J. Watson, eds. *More than Mayor or Manager: Campaigns to Change Form of Government in America's Largest Cities.* Washington, DC: Georgetown University Press, 2010.

Taleb, Nassim Nicholas, and Gregory F. Treverton. "The Calm before the Storm: Why Volatility Signals Stability, and Vice Versa." *Foreign Affairs* 94, no. 1 (January/February 2015): 86–95.

Tresser, Tom, ed. *Chicago Is Not Broke: Funding the City We Deserve.* Chicago: Civic Lab, 2016.

US Department of Justice Civil Rights Division and US States Attorney's Office, Northern District of Illinois. *Investigation of the Chicago Police Department.* January 13, 2017. https://www.justice.gov/opa/file/925846/download.

INDEX

Page number in italics indicates a figure; page number in bold indicates a table.

accountability, 9, 31, **32**, 41, 210–11
Aircraft Owners and Pilots Association, 2
aldermanic ward system, 20–21, 31, 35, 180, 205, 217
aldermen, 4, 20–22, **23**, 30; discretionary funds, 127, 141, 217, 219; misconduct, 127–28
Allen, Tom, 12
Alsbury, Thomas L., 64
American Recovery and Reinvestment Act, 84
American Society of Criminologists, 167
amortization, of pension debt (the ramp), 111–15, 119–20, 124–25
Anzia, Sarah, 41, 45
Archdiocese of Chicago Catholic Schools, 55, 72, 75
Arena, John, 134
Aristotle, 206
Austin, 224–25, 233. *See also* US cities, comparisons

back loading, of pension debt, 114
Ballard, Greg, 227
bankruptcy, 97, 99, 124–25, 213
Banks, Patricia, 183
Berrios, Joseph, 44
Better Government Association, 82
Bills, John, 129, 131
Bloomberg, Michael, 43
bonds, 87–88, 97
borrowing, municipal, 82, 90, 93–94. *See also* debt
Broad, Eli, 62
Brown, David O., 176
Brown, Michael, 41
budget, for City of Chicago, 5, 84, 86, 88
Burge, Jon, 18, 164, 184
Burke, Ed, 14–15, 24–25, 89, 133
Burnham, Daniel, 211
Burns, Will, 22
busway, 153
Byrd-Bennett, Barbara, 128, 131
Byrne, Jane, 42

Cardenas, George, 16
Carothers, Ike, 15–16
casinos, 159, 219
Center for Tax and Budget Account-
ability, 82
charter schools, 51, 65, 69, 74, 76, 218
Chicago, a divided city, 204. *See also*
US cities, comparisons
Chicago Alliance Against Racist and
Political Repression, 182
Chicago City Council, 18, 22, 21;
committees, 25–26; Finance Com-
mittee, 25, 133; revision of the city
code, 186, 191, 196
Chicago City Council Office of Fi-
nancial Analysis, 25, 89, 91, 93
Chicago City Department of Fi-
nance, 89–90, 93
Chicago City Office of Budget and
Management, 89
Chicago Department of Aviation, 4,
19
Chicago Department of Transporta-
tion, corruption, 129
Chicago Grassroots Alliance for Po-
lice Accountability (GAPA), 182
Chicago Home Rule Commission,
20–21, 29–30, 195, 197. *See also*
home rule
Chicago Housing Authority, 134
Chicago Infrastructure Trust, 8, 19,
90
Chicago law department, 26, 32, 131,
133, 140, 161–63, 178–80, 184, 217
Chicago Park District, 2, 4, 82, 112,
123, 134, 200
Chicago Parking Meters LLC, 10,
14–16
Chicago Police Board, 170–71, 181

Chicago Public Schools, 4–8,
47–48, 82, 134, 205, 218; and charter
schools, 48, 50–52, 54, 57, 70, 73;
corruption, 128, 131; demographic
problems, 48, 50–51; and digital
technology, 71; enrollment, 47, 50,
50, **53**, 54–55, 57, 69, 72, 76; fiscal
problems and debt, 48, **49**, 52–58,
53; general obligation debt and revenue, 48, **49**, 52, 54–57, 70, 76–77;
mayoral control, 47–49, 55–56,
65–67; pensions and pension debt,
48, **50**, 52–54, 56, 67, 76, 102, 204;
school choice, 50–52; sociopolitical
problems, 48–52; special education,
49, 73; teacher salaries, 52, **53**, 55;
testing and test scores, 52, 71
Chicago Riverwalk, 160, 211
Chicago School Finance Authority,
66
Chicago Teachers' Pension Fund, 48,
56, 77, 107, 109, 111–12, 196
Chicago Teachers Union, 36, 47, 51,
57–58, 70, 75, 77
Chicago Transit Authority, 4, 112, 134
Chicago Way, 3, 7–9, 37
chief financial officer, 26, 31–33, 93,
95, 218–19
Churchill, Winston, 1
city attorney, 32–33, **32**, 141, 180–81, 183
city charter, 192–94; for Chicago, 31,
33, 93, 186, 189, 197–98, 217, 220
city clerk, in Chicago, 14, 26, 33
City Colleges of Chicago, 4, 82, 134
city controller, 31, **32**
city councils, 93; size, 21, **23**, 30, 33;
term limits, 30, 33
city manager form of municipal
government, 31–32

city treasurer, in Chicago, 26, 33, 89
Civic Federation, 82, 89, 200
civic leadership, 34, 63, 67, 96, 212
Civilian Office of Police Accountability (COPA), 170, 183
Cochran, Willie, 127
collective bargaining, 79, 94–97, 110, 219; with police unions, 96, 163–65, 180–82, 220; with teachers, 47, 58, 70. *See also* labor relations, in Chicago
Colon, Rey, 15
Columbus, 227–28, 234. *See also* US cities, comparisons
contracting and procurement, with City of Chicago, 134
convention centers, 6, 145, **146**, 154–57, **155**. *See also* McCormick Place
convention industry, 145–47, 152, 157–58, 160
Cook County, 82, 200
Cook County Forest Preserve District, 82
corruption, 8, 21, 100, 127–28, **130**, 142; role of political institutions, 131
cost of living adjustment (COLA), 107, 110, 117, 119
council wars, 9, 18, 209
Counts, George S., 46
credit rating: for Chicago, 82, 101; for Chicago Public Schools, 82; of municipal bonds, 84, 85
crime, 5, 165–69
crisis, 199–200, 213
cronyism, 131

Daffenberg, Mike, 1
Daley, Richard J., 44, 143

Daley, Richard M., 1–2, 11–14, 16, 36, 42, 44, 46, 52, 79, 153, 164
Daley machine, 37–39
Dallas, 176–77, 223–24, 232. *See also* US cities, comparisons
Dean, Howard, 36
debt, 82, **83**, 84, 86, 89, 98, 204; general obligation, 82–83, 90, 98–100, 218. *See also* pension debt
decision making, by government officials, 3, 5, 8, 31, 58, 68, 75, 93, 95, 185, 201, 206–8, 213
decision scoring, independent, 94
defeasance, 56–57
defined-contribution plan, 117, 121–23, 125, 219
democracy, 3, 36–37, 41–42, 44–45
DePaul University, 153
Detroit, 99
Devine, Richard, 210
DeVries, Jon B., 91
DeWitt, Jeffrey S., 231
Dillon's Rule, 187
disaggregation, of school districts, 72–73, 76
Dixon, Lorraine, 186
Dogium, Bob, 139
Dorrian, Hugh, 234
Drucker, Peter F., 207
Dumke, Mick, 11
Duncan, Arne, 172
Durbin, Dick, 36

education: governance structure, 48, 52, 62, 68; as a right vs. a good, 51; school systems of the future, 73–76
Einstein, Albert, 102
elections: county, 37; municipal, in Chicago, 7–8, 25, 33, 35–39, **38**,

elections (*continued*)
217–18; municipal, in fifteen largest
US cities, 39, **40**; nonpartisan,
42–44
Emanuel, Rahm, 35–36, 42, 46,
99–100, 150–51, 153, 161–63, 179–80;
and Chicago Public Schools, 47–48
Employee Retirement Income Security Act of 1974 (ERISA), 109–10,
116, 121
Eng, Monica, 80
Epton, Bernard, 42
ethics, in city government, 137, 141,
212, 219

Fairbanks, Frank, 223, 231
Fairley, Sharon, 183
FBI, crime statistics, 166–67, **166, 167**
Ferguson, Joe, 21
Ferguson, Missouri, 41, 161
financial information, accessible, 94
financial management, 8, 81, 86–88,
92–95, **92**. *See also* budget, for City
of Chicago
financial officer, elected. *See* chief
financial officer
financial planning, long-term, 95
Finn, Chester E., Jr., 63
Fioretti, Robert, 15, 17–18, 24–25, 35
Fraternal Order of Police, 161, 163, 172
Friedman, Milton, 199
funding ratio, for pension funds,
109–10

GAAP (generally accepted accounting principles), 88–89, 94
gainsharing, 96
García, Jesús "Chuy," 35–36, 42, 162

Georgia World Congress Center
(Atlanta), 156–57
gerrymandering, of aldermanic
wards, 37
Giuliani, Rudolph, 174
Glass, Thomas E., 64
Goode, Wilson, 139, 222, 231
Gore, Al, 96
governance structures, municipal,
20, 201, 206
Government Accounting Standards
Board, 88
Government Finance Officers Asso-
ciation, 88
Great Recession, 18
gun control, 169

Haider, Donald, 26, 82
Hairston, Leslie, 15
Hajnal, Zoltan, 40–41
Hegel, Georg Wilhelm Friedrich, 206
Henig, Jeffrey R., 63
Hess, Frederick M., 62–63
Hilkevitch, Jon, 16
Hinz, Greg, 79
home rule, 8, 30, 187–89, 191, 194,
196–97. *See also* Chicago Home
Rule Commission
Homeland Security, 2
homeschooling, 69
homicide rates, 165–70, **165**, *168*, 172,
173, 176, 180, 205
hotels, and hotel rooms, in Chicago,
149–52

Houston, 138–39, 176, 221–22, 230. *See
also* US cities, comparisons
Hudnut, William, 227

Hunt, D. Bradford, 91
Huntington, Samuel, 4, 206–7, 209, 212
Hyatt, 151–52

Illinois Constitution, 188–91, 194–95, 197, 201, 220
Illinois Municipal Code, 22, 187, 189, 191, 195
Illinois Municipal Retirement Fund, 122
Illinois Pension Code, 110, 123
Illinois Police Benevolent and Protective Association, 163
Illinois Policy Institute, 82
Indianapolis, 226–27, 234. *See also* US cities, comparisons
infrastructure, and capital expenditure, 86–87
inspectors general, 131–41, 219
interest groups, 90–91
intergenerational equity, 109
Iris, Mark, 177, 183–84

Jackson, Janice, 74–75
Jackson, Sandi, 16
Jacksonville, 225–27, 233. *See also* US cities, comparisons
jobs, in Chicago, 3, 149–50, 157–58, 169, 202–4
Johnson, Eddie, 180
Joravsky, Ben, 11

Kahneman, Daniel, 208
Kalven, Jamie, 162
Kant, Immanuel, 206
Kearney, Richard, 96
Kelly, Edward, 29

Kennedy, John F., 110
Kennedy, Robert, 161
Kennelly, Martin, 29
Kerner Commission, 204
Khan, Faisal, 126–27, 133
King, Rodney, 28, 138, 171, 175
Koch, Ed, 27, 135
Kurland, Amy, 139

La Guardia, Fiorello, 27
labor relations, in Chicago, 79, 95–97, 110, 219–20
Lane, Eric, 30
Las Vegas Convention Center, 155–56
LAZ Parking, 16–17
legacy costs, 84, 97–101, 204–5, 208, 220
Lewis, Karen, 36
Lewis, Michael, 208
Lincoln, Abraham, 185
local school councils, in Chicago, 66, 73
Los Angeles, 28–29, 230; charter revision, 29, 186, 188, 193–94, 209; corruption, 137–38; municipal costs, 80–81, 95; policing, 138, 174–75, 181–82; schools, 65, 72; secession, 185–86; and voting, 39. *See also* US cities, comparisons
Lugar, Richard, 227

machine politics, 8, 62, 127. *See also* Daley machine
Madigan, Michael, 22, 44
Madison, James, 10, 94, 206
Mareschal, Patrice, 96
Marin, Carol, 16
Marriot Marquis, 151–53, 246n17

Marti, Jose, 35
mayor, control over city finances, 89,
    92–93, 100–101; election of, 36, 44;
    role, 6, 211
mayoral power, 3–4, 9, 20, 26, 31
McCarron, John, 2
McCarthy, Garry, 171, 180–81
McCormick Inn, 152
McCormick Place, 7, 19, 143–50, 158,
    219; expansion, 145–46, 149; impact
    studies and performance projec-
    tions, 149; repurposing, 159, 219
McDonald, Jim, 15
McDonald, Laquan, 18–19, 26, 161–63,
    169–71, 180, 183
McGrath, Mary, 41
McQuillan, Lawrence, 117
Meier, Kenneth J., 63–64
Meigs Field, 1–3
Mell, Richard (Dick), 15, 24
mental models, 209–12, **210**
menu money. *See* aldermen: discre-
    tionary funds
Metropolitan Pier and Exposition
    Authority (MPEA), 4, 83, 143–53,
    158–60, 219–20; debt, 148–49, 160,
    204
Metropolitan Water Reclamation
    District, 82, 200
Midway Airport, privatization, 11–13,
    16–17
Milk, Harvey, 226
Millennium Park, 151, 160
Montesquieu, 206
Moscone, George, 226
multiplier framework, 102, 110
Municipal Acceptance Corporation
    (NYC), 56, 58, 76

Municipal Code of Chicago, 23–24,
    189
municipal costs (cost of public
    services), Chicago vs. Los Angeles,
    80–81, **81**
Municipal Employees' Annuity and
    Benefit Fund of Chicago, 103, 109,
    119
municipal law, legal environment for,
    187–91

National Civic League, 192
National Partnership for Reinventing
    Government, 96
Navy Pier, 7, 19, 144, 150–51, 158, 160,
    220
new public management, 96
New York City, 21, 229–30; charter
    revision, 27–28, 30, 93–94, 185–86,
    188, 193–94; elections, 39, 43–44;
    legacy debt, 56, 58, 82, 99; over-
    sight, 135–37, 141; policing, 173–74,
    177. *See also* US cities, comparisons
Northerly Island, 2, 199

Obama, Barack, 36, 213
Ocasio, Billy, 13, 15, 17–18
Office of the Inspector General
    (OIG), 127, 132–34, 141
Office of the Legislative Inspector
    General (OLIG), 126–27
O'Hare International Airport, 19
Olympic bid, by Chicago for 2016,
    19, 79
Orange County Convention Center
    (Orlando), 154–55
oversight: in Chicago, 132–34, 140; in
    other cities, 135–40, **136**

parking meter concession, 7, 10–17, 25, 84, 86
party leadership, by elected officials, 44
Patton, Stephen, 161–62
Pedrelli, Dennis, 16
Pennsylvania Intergovernmental Cooperation Authority (PICA), 222, 231
pension debt (pension liability), 103–9, **106**, 111–12, *112*, **113**, 115–16, 118–20, *120*, 115, 219. *See also* debt
pension funds, for Chicago employees, 5–6, 8, 96, 102, **104**, **105**. *See also* Municipal Employees' Annuity and Benefit Fund of Chicago
pension holidays, 47–48, 53–54, 84, 102–3, 115, 118–19, 123
pension plans: constitutional guarantee, 110, 118–19, 121–23; freezing or discontinuing, 121–23; individual case, 106–7, **108**; life expectancy and retirement periods, 110, 112; maturity ratio, 105; in the private sector, 109, 116
performance audits, 95, 100
person-trips, as a measure of tourism, 150, 246n25
Philadelphia, 139–40, 176, 222, 231. *See also* US cities, comparisons
Phoenix, 140, 222–23, 231. *See also* US cities, comparisons
policing, 165, 167, **173**, 205, 220; accountability and oversight, 169–72, 175, 180–81, 183; discipline, 163, 171; staffing, 182–83
police misconduct (police abuse), 26, 84, 90, 100, 131, 165, 177; settlements

and reparations, 162–64, 177–80, **178**, **179**, 183–84, 220
Policemen's Annuity and Benefit Fund of Chicago, 117
political systems (culture), 4, 34, 131, 207–8, 211
population, of Chicago, 6, 21, 110, 203
Preckwinkle, Toni, 15
private and faith-based schools, 74–75
public corruption convictions, 127–28, **129**, 137–40
public good, 51, 81–82, 88, 158, 184, 200
public safety, 165, 167, 172, 180, 182, 184
public schools, and mayoral control, 62–65. *See also* Chicago Public Schools: mayoral control

Quinn, Pat, 43

Rakove, Milton, 37
Rampart scandal (Los Angeles), 28, 138, 175
Rauner, Bruce, 43
Ravitch, Diane, 36
Ravitch, Dick, 229
Reagan, Ronald, 79
Reboyras, Ariel, 16
redistricting, 23–25, 30, 36, 222, 224, 228
red-light (traffic) cameras, 90, 127, 129
referendum process, 195
Renaissance 2010, 48, 70
Republican Party, in Chicago, 43–45

resilience plan, 207
revenue, for City of Chicago, 86–87,
    90, 100
Rich, Wilbur, 63
ridesharing companies, settlement
    with, 90
Ridge, Tom, 2
Riordan, Richard, 43
Rohn, Jim, 208

San Antonio, 223, 231–32. *See also* US
    cities, comparisons
San Diego, 33, 223, 232. *See also* US
    cities, comparisons
San Francisco, 226, 233–34. *See also*
    US cities, comparisons
San Jose, 224, 232–33. *See also* US
    cities, comparisons
Sanders, Bernie, 36
Sanders, Heywood, 146, 157
school boards, appointed vs. elected,
    62–68, 77
school choice, 50–52, 57, 69
school closings, in Chicago, 46–48,
    75–76
school districts, comparative data,
    58–62, **59**, **60–61**, 72
School Finance Authority, 52, 56
Schrader, Lisa, 14
Schwartz, Frederick A. O., 30
Second Ward, Chicago, 24–25, *24*
Serpico, Frank, 141
Sessions, Jeff, 171
Shakman, Michael, 132
Shen, Francis X., 64–65
Shiller, Helen, 13, 16
Simpson, Dick, 18, 21
sister units of government, in Chi-
    cago (seven sisters), 82–83, 196. *See*

also individual units of govern-
    ment
Skyway, 11–12, 14
Sloan, Alfred P., 207–8
Smarick, Andy, 74–75
Smith, Brandon, 162
Smith, Wanda, 186
Sneed, Michael, 11
Social Security, 110, 117–18, 121
Society of Actuaries, 109, 119
Sonenshein, Raphael, xiv, 209, 230
Spielman, Fran, 36
Stone, Berny, 14–15
structural deficit, 84, 90, 93, 95, 97,
    101, 114
Svara, James H., 195, 223

Taleb, Nassim Nicholas, 143, 207
tax increment financing, 19, 151
taxes, 82, 87–88, 93, 99, 200; local, 6,
    111, 114, 121, 125, 144; property, 5,
    12, 55, 70, 82, 98, 111, 121, 156, 200;
    in support of the MPEA, 144–45,
    147–48, **147**, **148**, 158–59
teacher strikes, 57, 67, 70, 77
Teachers' Retirement System, State of
    Illinois, 122
Tefank, Richard, 175
Terkel, Studs, 126, 132
terrorism, 174
testing, in public schools, 69, 71
Thompson, William H., 42
Tkac, David, 3
tourism, 7, 144, 149–51, 158, 220
town hall meetings, 46–47
Tresser, Tom, 100
Troutman, Arenda, 186
Trump, Donald, 171
trust, in government, 57–58

Unigov, 227
union contracts, 79, 84
US cities, comparisons, **23**, **32**, **40**,
   59, **83**, **92**, **106**, **129**, **136**, **166**, **167**,
   173, **178**
US Constitution, 187, 206
US Department of Justice (DOJ),
   127–28, **129**; investigation of the
   Chicago Police Department,
   169–72
US Travel Association, 150, 246n25

Van Dyke, Jason, 161–64
Volpe, Paul, 12–15, 17
voter approval, for bonds, taxes,
   municipal borrowing, and changes
   to governance structure, 56–57,
   60–61, 87, 89, 93, 143, 159, 191, 218,
   220, 225, 230–34
voter disenfranchisement, 36
voter identification, 36–37, 45
voter turnout, 37–41, **38**, 44

voting, early and absentee, 41
Voting Rights Act of 1965, 36
vouchers. *See* school choice

Waguespack, Scott, 15, 17, 25
Walls, William Dock, 35
wards. *See* aldermanic ward system
Washington, Harold, 18, 42
water and sewer system, 86
Watson, Douglas J., 195
White, Dan, 226
Wigrizer, Leon, 139
Wilson, Darren, 41
Wilson, Willie, 35
Wintrust Arena, 153, 219, 246n17
Wong, Kenneth K., 64–65
workers' compensation program, in
   Chicago, 25, 89, 133, 141, 219
Wormeli, Paul, 167–68

Zalewski, Michael, 22
Zimmerman, Don, 225, 233

ED BACHRACH is the retired CEO of Bachrach Clothing and founder and president of the Center for Pension Integrity in Chicago. His op-eds have been published in the *Wall Street Journal,* the *Chicago Tribune,* and the *Chicago Sun Times,* among other media outlets, and he has been a commentator on Chicago-area television. He is also the founder and chairman of Build Cambodia.

⌣

AUSTIN BERG is an award-winning writer and director of content strategy at the Illinois Policy Institute. His work centers on the stories of individuals affected by public policy, and has been featured by CBS, the *Washington Post,* and the *Chicago Tribune.* He wrote the 2016 documentary film *Madigan: Power. Privilege. Politics.*